Customized Editions

FOOD&WINE
MAGAZINE'S

OFFICIAL
WINE
GUIDE
2 0 0 0

ADD
YOUR COMPANY
LOGO
—OR—
DESIGN A NEW
4 COLOR
CUSTOM COVER

Ideal as a:

- Corporate gift
- Sales tool
- Gift with purchase
- Holiday thank-you or remembrance for employees or clients
- Sales-call leave behind

Join these innovative marketers...

- Hilton
- Lincoln-Mercury
- Marriott
- McKessonHBOC
- Mova Labs

- Neiman Marcus
- Ortho McNeil
- Salomon Smith Barney
- Wyeth-Ayerst Laboratories

For more information, call
1-800-779-0084

EDITOR IN CHIEF **Judith Hill**

ART DIRECTOR **Perri DeFino**

MANAGING EDITOR **Terri Mauro**

PROJECT DIRECTOR **Barbara A. Mateer**

DESIGNER **Leslie Andersen**

ASSISTANT EDITOR **Dana Speers**

EDITORIAL ASSISTANT **Colleen McKinney**

CONTRIBUTING EDITORS **Kim Ginsburg, Linda Lawry, Candela Pro**

RESEARCH ASSISTANTS **Sharon Kapnick, Lixandra Urresta**

PRODUCTION COORDINATOR **Lawrence Kennedy**

SENIOR VICE PRESIDENT, PUBLISHER **Mark V. Stanich**

MARKETING DIRECTOR **David Geller**

RETAIL SALES DIRECTOR **Marshall Corey**

BRAND DEVELOPMENT MANAGER **Sara Braun**

BUSINESS MANAGER **Keith Strohmeier**

COVER PHOTOGRAPH **Elizabeth Watt**

FOOD&WINE

MAGAZINE'S

WOFFICIAL WINE GUIDE 2000

BY **Steven Miller**

FOOD&**WINE**
BOOKS

American Express Publishing Corporation
New York

contents

USING THIS GUIDE   6

GRAPE VARIETIES   7

SHORTCUT TO FINDING VARIETALS   10

WINE-STYLE FINDER   11

PAIRING WINE WITH FOOD   15

WINE LABELS: THE TWO BASIC TYPES   16

FRANCE   18
  Alsace   20
  Bordeaux   26
  Burgundy   33
  Languedoc-Roussillon   47
  Loire Valley   54
  Provence   62
  Rhône Valley   66
  Southwest France   76

ITALY   80
  Northwest Italy   82
  Northeast Italy   90
  Tuscany   94
  Other Central Italian
    Wine Regions   102
  Southern Italy & the Islands   105

IBERIAN PENINSULA   110
  SPAIN   110
    Rioja   112
    Ribera del Duero   115
    Other Spanish Red Wines   117
    Other Spanish White Wines   119
    Spanish Rosé Wines   121
  PORTUGAL   122
    Portuguese Red Wines   123
    Portuguese White Wines   125

GERMANY   128
  Mosel-Saar-Ruwer   131
  Pfalz   134
  Rheingau   136
  Rheinhessen   138
  Other German Wine Regions   140

AUSTRIA   142
  Lower Austria   144
  Burgenland   146
  Other Austrian Regions   147

CALIFORNIA   148
  Chardonnay   150
  Sauvignon Blanc   154
  Viognier   156
  Other California White Wines   157
  Cabernet Sauvignon   157
  Merlot   161
  Pinot Noir   162
  Syrah   164
  Zinfandel   166
  California Wines from
    Italian Grapes   168
  Other California Red Wines   169

PACIFIC NORTHWEST   172
  OREGON   172
    Pinot Gris   173
    Other Oregon White Wines   175
    Pinot Noir   175
  WASHINGTON STATE   177
    Chardonnay   178
    Sémillon &
      Sauvignon Blanc   179
    Other Washington State
      White Wines   181
    Merlot &
      Cabernet Sauvignon   182
    Other Washington State
      Red Wines   184

NEW YORK STATE   186
Chardonnay   186
Other New York State
   White Wines   188
New York State Red Wines   190

SOUTH AFRICA   192
South African White Wines   193
South African Red Wines   194

AUSTRALIA   196
Chardonnay   196
Other Australian White Wines   199
Cabernet Sauvignon   201
Shiraz   202
Other Australian Red Wines   204

NEW ZEALAND   206
Sauvignon Blanc   206
Chardonnay   209
Riesling   210
Pinot Noir   210

SOUTH AMERICA   212
ARGENTINA   212
Argentinian White Wines   214
Argentinian Red Wines   215

CHILE   216
Chilean White Wines   217
Chilean Red Wines   218

**CHAMPAGNE & OTHER
SPARKLING WINES**   222
Champagne   223
Cava   227
From Italy   228
From the United States.   229
Other Sparkling Wines   231

FORTIFIED WINES   234
Sherry   234
Port   239
Australian Muscats & Ports   243
Madeira   244
Vin Doux Naturel   247

DESSERT WINES   250
From France   252
From Germany   257
From Other Countries   259

VINTAGE CHART   264

NAMES YOU CAN TRUST   266

FOOD & WINE AMERICAN WINE AWARDS   268

TOP WINE SHOPS   269

BEST STORES FOR BOOKS ON WINE   278

50 HOTTEST WINE WEB SITES   280

MOST EXCITING WINE TOURS   282

TERMS USED IN THIS GUIDE   284

LIST OF LISTS

10 MOST OVERLOOKED WINES   78

THE WORLD'S MOST VERSATILE WINES   141

MERITORIOUS MERITAGES   150

10 OUTSTANDING CABERNET SAUVIGNONS   159

TOMORROW'S LEGENDS TO BUY TODAY   170

WINES OF THE CENTURY — THE LEGENDS   233

USING tHIS gUIDE

FOOD & WINE Magazine's Official Wine Guide 2000 is different from most wine books: It's up to date. Our recommendations are for the exact wines being released for sale this year. In addition, our recommendations emphasize inexpensive and moderately priced wines that offer great value. You simply won't find a wine in this highly selective guide unless it is very good indeed—no matter how many or few stars we have given it. So don't be starstruck. EVERY WINE IN THIS BOOK IS A GOOD WINE.

key to symboLs
Each wine recommendation includes symbols that represent a quality rating and a price range.

QUALITY	★ ★ ★ ★	OUTSTANDING worth a search
	★ ★ ★	EXCELLENT top-notch example of its type
	★ ★	VERY GOOD distinctive
	★	GOOD delicious everyday wine

PRICE	$$$$	$50 and up
	$$$	$25 to $50
	$$	$12 to $25
	$	$12 or less
	$–$$$$	Red = exceptional quality for the price

features

GRAPES AND STYLES tells which grape varieties are grown in the geographic area and the styles of wines produced.

ON THE LABEL notes whether the region's wines are labeled geographically or varietally, explains any special terms, and details any significant departures from or additions to the norm.

AT THE TABLE offers no-nonsense recommendations for food that will be complemented by the wines.

THE BOTTOM LINE gives you the inside word on how much you should expect to pay and how the wines under discussion stack up against others in terms of value for money.

WHAT TO BUY provides ratings, for those wines that have aging potential, of the vintages now generally available in shops. **NOTE** See Vintage Chart (page 264) for key to What to Buy.

Grape Varieties

Just as a person is the product of both nature and nurture, so is wine. Many factors, among them climate, soil, and winemaking techniques, make up a particular wine's nurture, and all of them affect flavor and style. But none has as big an impact on the wine as the characteristics of the grape variety or varieties from which it is made. The grapes are the wine's nature.

Over 1,000 grape varieties are used around the world to produce wine, but luckily for those of us trying to make sense of it all, only 40 to 50 varieties go into the wines we commonly drink. Of these, just nine result in such good wine in so many places or such great wine in one long-established region that we call them the noble (or classic) grapes.

The noble grapes give us the great European (or Old World) wines of Bordeaux, Burgundy, Champagne, the Rhône, and Germany, as well as a whole generation of new and distinctive wine styles from such New World areas as the Napa Valley, New Zealand, Australia, and Chile. Insight into all of these wines begins with understanding the typical characteristics that come from the variety (in varietal wines) or varieties (in blends) that comprise them.

NOBLE WHITE VARIETIES

CHARDONNAY

Winemakers all over the world grow Chardonnay, from the Burgundy region in France to California, Australia, New Zealand, and Italy. The aromas of wines made from this grape range from lemon to apple to tropical fruit; sometimes they are smoky, buttery, or steely. Chardonnay has an affinity for oak, which imparts spice, mocha, and vanilla scents. Wine made from this grape is usually full-bodied and rather low in acid. Chardonnay is often high in alcohol, making it problematic with many foods. It ages moderately well.

CHENIN BLANC

Startling acidity is Chenin Blanc's signature, combined with high alcohol and a full-bodied, almost oily texture. Though Chenin is most often seen in simple, off-dry quaffing wines, in the Loire Valley it makes great wines in a variety of styles. These have exciting aromas and flavors that include quince, lanolin, linden, apricots, flowers, wet stones, and honey. Serious Chenin Blancs can age seemingly forever.

RIESLING

The world's greatest white grape, Riesling, produces wines of amazing delicacy, complexity, and longevity. The wine's aromas and flavors include peaches and apricots, flowers, minerals, wet slate, and petrol. Riesling wines range from steely, bone dry to supersweet and luscious, but should always have high acidity, which makes them refreshing regardless of their sweetness. Well-made examples often require aging and continue to develop for decades.

SAUVIGNON BLANC

Frequently described as grassy because its aroma can be assertively herbal, Sauvignon Blanc can also smell like melons or figs, especially when grown in a warm climate. The Sauvignon Blanc grape's high acidity yields brisk, light-bodied wines with citrus, herb, and melon flavors. The overall taste of the wine reminds many people of gooseberries. Sauvignon Blanc–based wines are rarely made for aging.

SÉMILLON

The rather elusive aromas of Sémillon most often hint at beeswax, lemon, and orange marmalade. Sémillon is full-bodied, high in alcohol, and low in acidity. In both dry and sweet versions, it's commonly blended with Sauvignon Blanc to increase aroma and acidity. The Sémillon grape's susceptibility to botrytis (see page 251) makes it ideal for dessert wines. Sémillons age surprisingly well, developing nutty notes and vanilla flavors that mimic those of oak.

NOBLE RED VARIETIES

CABERNET SAUVIGNON

A thick-skinned grape variety, Cabernet Sauvignon therefore produces tannic, deep-colored wines. They can be powerful and worthy of cellaring, although lesser examples are usually fresh and fruity. Cabernet Sauvignon has aromas of black currants and cedarwood; sometimes it can be herbaceous, plummy, or vegetal. With age, Cabernets can develop intriguing nuances of tobacco, underbrush, and leather. Cabernet has a good affinity for oak.

MERLOT

Aromas and flavors found in Merlot include berries, hay, jam, and, especially, plums and chocolate. Wines made from Merlot are deep in color and medium-to-full bodied. They have less tannin, lower acidity, and a higher alcohol content than Cabernet Sauvignons, giving them a smooth texture. Merlot ages well but matures sooner than Cabernet Sauvignon.

PINOT NOIR

Fragrance and finesse, rather than power, characterizes Pinot Noir. Aromas of red fruits (such as raspberries, strawberries, and plums) abound, although there can also be jam (cooked fruit), smoke, or what are called barnyard aromas. Fruity when young, Pinot Noirs become complex and seductive with age. They are moderately tannic yet mellow and smooth. They often have good acidity and a core of concentrated fruit. They are medium bodied, with a relatively high alcohol level.

SYRAH

Deeply colored, highly tannic Syrah grapes produce full-bodied wines with an excellent balance between alcohol and acidity. They have intense, spicy-berry flavors, particularly suggestive of cassis, with distinct black-pepper and smoky notes. Seriously made Syrah-based wines can age beautifully for many years, while simpler, fruity styles offer early drinking pleasure.

OTHER POPULAR GRAPES

GEWÜRZTRAMINER A flamboyant white grape with exotic apricot, litchi, rose, and spice aromas. Full body. High alcohol.

MUSCAT Family of white grapes with similar floral, musk, peach, and orange aromas and flavors. Makes excellent dry and sweet wines.

PINOT BLANC Makes medium-bodied, mildly flavored white wines.

PINOT GRIS Full body, nutty flavor. In Italy, where it's called Pinot Grigio, it's made into light, brisk white wines.

VIOGNIER Peach and floral scented white grape. Lived in obscurity in the northern Rhône until it recently became the rage in California.

CABERNET FRANC Important red grape of Bordeaux and the Loire. Like Cabernet Sauvignon but lighter and more perfumed.

ZINFANDEL Red wine grape with bold blackberry and spice flavors; lots of tannin. Has found its zenith in California.

shortcut to finding varietals

CABERNET FRANC
California, 169
Loire Valley, 61
New York State, 190
Washington State, 184

CABERNET SAUVIGNON
Argentina, 215
Australia, 201
Bordeaux, 27
California, 157
Chile, 218
New York State, 190
South Africa, 195
Spain, 117
Washington State, 182

CHARDONNAY
Argentina, 214
Australia, 196
Burgundy, 33
California, 150
Chile, 217
New York State, 186
New Zealand, 209
Oregon, 175
South Africa, 193
Washington State, 178

CHENIN BLANC
California, 157
Loire Valley, 55
South Africa, 194
Washington State, 181

GEWÜRZTRAMINER
Alsace, 21
California, 157
Germany, 128
Italy, 90
New York State, 188
Oregon, 175
Washington State, 181

MERLOT
Argentina, 215
Australia, 204
Bordeaux, 27
California, 161
Chile, 218
Italy, 90
New York State, 190
South Africa, 195
Spain, 117
Washington State, 182

MUSCAT
Alsace, 23
Austria, 142
Italy (Moscato), 106

PINOT BLANC
Alsace, 22
Austria, 142
California, 157
New York State, 186
Oregon, 175

PINOT GRIS
Alsace, 22
California, 157
Germany, 128
Italy (Pinot Grigio), 90
Oregon, 173

PINOT NOIR
Argentina, 215
Australia, 204
Austria, 142
Burgundy, 33
California, 162
Germany, 128
New Zealand, 210
Oregon, 175
Washington State, 184

RIESLING
Alsace, 23
Australia, 199
Austria, 142
Germany, 128
New York State, 188
New Zealand, 210
Oregon, 175
South Africa, 193
Washington State, 181

SAUVIGNON BLANC
Argentina, 214
Australia, 199
Austria, 142
Bordeaux, 31
California, 154
Chile, 217
Italy, 90
Loire Valley, 58
New Zealand, 206
South Africa, 193
Southwest France, 76
Washington State, 179

SÉMILLON
Australia, 199
Bordeaux, 31
Washington State, 179

SYRAH
Argentina, 214
Australia (Shiraz), 202
California, 164
Rhône Valley, 66
South Africa (Shiraz), 195
Washington State, 184

VIOGNIER
California, 156
Rhône Valley, 74

ZINFANDEL
California, 166

10

wine - style finder

COUNTRY	REGION	WINES

LIGHT-BODIED, DRY WHITE WINES

COUNTRY	REGION	WINES
ARGENTINA		Sauvignon Blanc, 214; Torrontés, 214
CALIFORNIA		Chenin Blanc, 157; Gewürztraminer, 157
CHILE		Sauvignon Blanc, 217
FRANCE	Alsace	Chasselas, 23; Muscat, 23; Sylvaner, 23
	Bordeaux	Bordeaux Blanc, 32; Entre-Deux-Mers, 32
	Loire Valley	Menetou-Salon, 58; Montlouis Sec, 55; Muscadet, 57; Quincy, 58; Sancerre, 58
	Southwest	Côtes de Duras, 76
ITALY	Central	Frascati, 102; Orvieto, 103; Trebbiano d'Abruzzi, 102; Verdicchio, 103
	Northeast	Müller-Thurgau, 90; Pinot Bianco, 90; Pinot Grigio, 90; Riesling, 90; Sauvignon Blanc, 90; Soave, 90
	Northwest	Gavi, 89
NEW YORK STATE		Chardonnay, 186; Riesling, 188
NEW ZEALAND		Riesling, 210; Sauvignon Blanc, 206
OREGON		Pinot Blanc, 175; Riesling, 175
PORTUGAL	Vinho Verde	Vinho Verde, 125
SOUTH AFRICA		Riesling, 193; Sauvignon Blanc, 193; Steen, 193
WASHINGTON STATE		Sauvignon Blanc, 179

MEDIUM-BODIED, DRY WHITE WINES

COUNTRY	REGION	WINES
ARGENTINA		Chardonnay, 214
AUSTRALIA		Riesling, 199; Sauvignon Blanc, 199
CALIFORNIA		Marsanne, 157; Pinot Blanc, 157; Pinot Gris, 157; Sauvignon Blanc, 154; Unoaked Chardonnay, 150;
CHILE		Chardonnay, 217
FRANCE	Alsace	Pinot Blanc, 22; Riesling, 23
	Bordeaux	Graves, 31
	Burgundy	Burgundy, 33
	Loire Valley	Pouilly-Fumé, 58; Savennières, 55; Touraine, 55; Touraine-Azay-le-Rideau, 55; Vouvray Sec, 55
	Rhône Valley	Côtes-du-Rhône, 74
	Southwest	Jurançon, 76
GERMANY		Silvaner, 140
ITALY	Central	Albana di Romagna, 102
	Northeast	Gewürztraminer, 90; Tocai Friulano, 90
	Northwest	Roero Arneis, 89
	Southern	Fiano di Avellino, 106; Moscato, 106; Vermentino, 106

COUNTRY	REGION	WINES
NEW YORK STATE		Gewürztraminer, 189
NEW ZEALAND		Chardonnay, 209
OREGON		Chardonnay, 175; Gewürztraminer, 175; Pinot Gris, 173
PORTUGAL		Arinto, 125; Bairrada, 125; Bucelas, 125; Dão, 125
SOUTH AFRICA		Chardonnay, 193
SPAIN		Albariño, 119; Penedès, 119; Rioja, 112; Rueda, 119
WASHINGTON STATE		Chardonnay, 178; Sémillon, 179

FULL-BODIED, DRY WHITE WINES

COUNTRY	REGION	WINES
AUSTRALIA		Chardonnay, 196; Sémillon, 199; Sémillon/Chardonnay blends, 199
CALIFORNIA		Oaked Chardonnay, 150; Viognier, 156
FRANCE	Alsace	Gewürztraminer, 21; Pinot Gris, 22
	Bordeaux	Graves, 31
	Burgundy	Premier and Grand Cru, 34
	Rhône Valley	Condrieu, 74; Châteauneuf-du-Pape, 74; Hermitage, 74
ITALY	Southern	Greco di Tufo, 106

LIGHTLY SWEET TO MODERATELY SWEET WHITE WINES

COUNTRY	REGION	WINES
GERMANY	Mosel-Saar-Ruwer	Riesling, 131
	Pfalz	Gewürztraminer, 134; Kerner, 134; Müller-Thurgau, 134; Pinot Gris, 134; Rieslaner, 134; Riesling, 134; Scheurebe, 134
	Rheingau	Riesling, 136
	Rheinhessen	Kerner, 138; Müller-Thurgau, 138; Riesling, 139; Silvaner, 138;
NEW YORK STATE		Seyval Blanc, 189; Vidal, 189; Vignoles, 189
SOUTH AFRICA		Steen, 193
WASHINGTON STATE		Chenin Blanc, 181; Gewürztraminer, 181; Johannisberg Riesling, 181

LIGHT-BODIED RED WINES

COUNTRY	REGION	WINES
FRANCE	Bordeaux	Bordeaux, 26
	Burgundy	Beaujolais, 44
	Southwest	Bergerac, 76
GERMANY	Rheingau	Spätburgunder, 137
ITALY	Central	Lambrusco, 102
	Northeast	Bardolino, 90; Merlot, 90; Pinot Nero, 90; Schiava, 90; Valpolicella, 90
	Northwest	Barbera, 86
SOUTH AFRICA		Pinotage, 194

COUNTRY   REGION   WINES

MEDIUM-BODIED RED WINES

COUNTRY	REGION	WINES
ARGENTINA		Cabernet Sauvignon, 215; Merlot, 215; Pinot Noir, 215; Syrah, 214
AUSTRALIA		Cabernet Sauvignon, 201; Grenache, 204; Mourvèdre, 204; Pinot Noir, 204
CALIFORNIA		Barbera, 168; Cabernet Franc, 169; Pinot Noir, 162; Sangiovese, 168
CHILE		Cabernet Sauvignon, 218; Merlot, 218
FRANCE	Bordeaux	Bordeaux Supérieur, 26
	Burgundy	Burgundy, 33
	Languedoc-Roussillon	Corbières and Minervois, 50; Coteaux du Languedoc, 48; Côtes du Roussillon and Côtes du Roussillon-Villages, 51; Costières de Nîmes, 51; Fitou, 51
	Loire Valley	Bourgueil, 61; Chinon, 61; Saumur-Champigny, 61; St-Nicholas-de-Bourgueil, 61
	Provence	Coteaux d'Aix-en-Provence, 64; Coteaux d'Aix-en-Provence-les-Baux, 64; Côtes de Provence, 64
	Rhône Valley	Coteaux du Tricastin, 71; Côtes du Lubéron, 71; Côtes-du-Rhône and Côtes-du-Rhône Villages, 70; Côtes du Ventoux, 71; Crozes-Hermitage, 67; Lirac, 71; St-Joseph, 67
ITALY	Central	Montepulciano d'Abruzzi, 102; Rosso Conero, 103; Rosso Piceno, 103
	Northeast	Cabernet Sauvignon, 90; Refosco, 90; Teroldego, 90
	Northwest	Barbaresco, 82; Dolcetto, 86; Gattinara, 85; Nebbiolo d'Alba, 85; Nebbiolo delle Langhe, 85; Valtellina, 85
	Southern	Gaglioppo, 105; Salice Salentino, 105
	Tuscany	Carmignano, 100; Chianti, 95; Other Sangiovese-based wines, 99; Rosso di Montalcino, 100; Vino Nobile, 100
NEW YORK STATE		Cabernet Franc, 190; Cabernet Sauvignon, 190; Merlot, 190
NEW ZEALAND		Pinot Noir, 210
OREGON		Pinot Noir, 175
SOUTH AFRICA		Cabernet Sauvignon, 195; Merlot, 195; Pinotage, 194; Shiraz, 195
SPAIN		Jumilla, 117; Navarra, 117; Penedès, 117; Rioja, 112; Somontano, 117
WASHINGTON STATE		Cabernet Franc, 184; Cabernet Sauvignon, 182; Lemberger, 184; Merlot, 182; Syrah, 184

COUNTRY	REGION	WINES

FULL-BODIED RED WINES

COUNTRY	REGION	WINES
ARGENTINA		Malbec, 212
AUSTRALIA		Shiraz, 202; Shiraz/Cabernet Sauvignon blends, 204
CALIFORNIA		Cabernet Sauvignon, 157; Carignan, 169; Grenache, 169; Merlot, 161; Mourvèdre, 169; Petite Sirah, 169; Syrah, 164; Zinfandel, 166
FRANCE	Bordeaux	Top Classified Growths, 26
	Burgundy	Grand Cru, 34
	Languedoc-Roussillon	Collioure, 51; La Clape, 48; La Méjanelle, 48; Montpeyroux, 48; Pic-St-Loup, 48
	Provence	Bandol, 63
	Rhône Valley	Châteauneuf-du-Pape, 70; Côte-Rôtie, 67; Cornas, 67; Gigondas, 70; Hermitage, 67; Vacqueyras, 70
	Southwest	Cahors, 76; Madiran, 76
ITALY	Northeast	Amarone, 90
	Northwest	Barolo, 82
	Southern	Aglianico del Vulture, 105; Cannonau, 106; Taurasi, 106
	Tuscany	Brunello, 99; Super Tuscans, 98
SPAIN		Priorato, 117; Ribera del Duero, 115

pairing wine with food

In the At the Table sections throughout this book, we suggest dishes that go with each wine type particularly well. But these are by no means the only options. Today's vast world of wine and food offers almost limitless possibilities. Let the half-dozen underlying principles that we've followed in our selections point you toward other good matches.

1. THE TWO MAIN PRINCIPLES OF PAIRING CAN BE SUMMED UP AS MATCH AND CONTRAST. These two possibilities apply to both body and flavor. We can match a rich dish such as chicken in cream sauce with a similarly full, buttery California Chardonnay. Or, we can enjoy dynamic contrast by serving a lighter white wine with high acidity. In this case, matching or contrasting will result in equally good pairings. Sometimes, one or the other basic rule works better: For instance, the smoky tang of barbecue pairs especially well with Syrah's smoky flavors; whereas complex earthy ingredients, such as mushrooms or root vegetables, often taste best when contrasted with a simple, refreshing, fruity wine.

2. ALWAYS MATCH THE INTENSITY. A delicate wine, whether contrasting or matching, will be steamrolled by a hearty dish, just as a powerful wine will obliterate subtle flavors.

3. ACIDIC FOODS REQUIRE HIGH-ACID WINES. Italians, with their cuisine's generous use of tomatoes, lemon, and vinegar, understand this well, thus their wines' typically high acidity .

4. TANNIC WINES NEED HIGH-PROTEIN FOOD. Protein blunts the puckering effect of tannin, making robust red wines seem smoother. Hence, tannic Bordeaux with red meat.

5. SWEETNESS MUTES THE FIRE OF CHILIES. A wine like German Spätlese (see page 130) makes a great choice for spicy foods.

6. PAY ATTENTION TO THE SAUCE. It is often the dominant flavor in the dish. When this is the case, pair the wine with the sauce, not with the food it enhances.

WINE LABELS: THE TWO BASIC TYPES

Wine labels fall into two categories: geographic and varietal. For the most part, the label on a bottle of European wine indicates only where that wine comes from, while a bottle from anywhere else in the world indicates, in addition, the grape from which the wine was made.

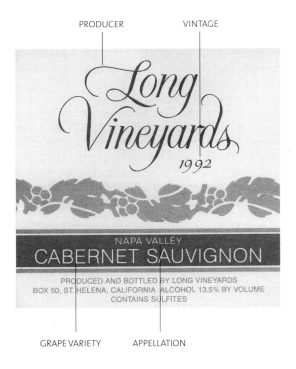

PRODUCER VINTAGE

Long Vineyards

1992

NAPA VALLEY
CABERNET SAUVIGNON

PRODUCED AND BOTTLED BY LONG VINEYARDS
BOX 50, ST. HELENA, CALIFORNIA ALCOHOL 13.5% BY VOLUME
CONTAINS SULFITES

GRAPE VARIETY APPELLATION

VARIETAL labels feature the relevant grape name. Depending on the laws of the country and region of origin, a wine must contain a minimum of 75 percent to 85 percent of the variety named. As you would expect, wines so labeled tend to emphasize the character of the grape from which the wine is made over the influence of the place where it was grown. The label includes an indication of origin as well, but in New World countries that is often a poor indicator of style.

PRODUCER

TENUTA DEL PORTALE

AGLIANICO DEL VULTURE
DENOMINAZIONE DI ORIGINE CONTROLLATA
1993

PRODOTTO ED IMBOTTIGLIATO DA
CA.VI.DA. RIONERO IN VULTURE - ITALIA

ITALIA

0,750 l ℮   NON DISPERDERE IL VETRO NELL'AMBIENTE   13% vol

VINTAGE   APPELLATION

GEOGRAPHIC labels are based on the idea of *terroir*, that a particular region's soil, climate, and winemaking traditions imbue a wine with a unique and recognizable character. Old World regions have had centuries to figure out which grapes grow best in which locations and how to work with those grapes. The results of that experience have been codified into laws dictating not only what grape varieties can be used but how ripe they must be and a host of other factors that influence the final product. Therefore, when you read a geographic label, the grape variety (or more often blend of varieties) is implied. In theory, so too, is the style. For example if the wine is a red from Burgundy, it must be made from Pinot Noir, and you can expect it to have restrained fruitiness and distinct earth or mineral characteristics.

FRANCE

Each year, France produces about 55 million hectoliters of wine, challenged only by Italy for the number one spot in terms of sheer volume. By other measures, France is not to be toppled from the premier position. Her classic wines, such as Bordeaux, Burgundy, and Sancerre, are global benchmarks for quality and style, spawning imitators from California to South Africa to Australia. Competition is now stiff, but France is still not only the most prolific, but the most varied and important source of exciting wines, in all price categories, anywhere in the world.

grapes and styles

France produces almost every type and style of wine. Red, white, rosé; bone-dry table wines to lusciously sweet dessert sippers; still wines and sparkling wines; inexpensive, easy-drinking charmers as well as some of the most complex, age-worthy, and costly wines available. Some growers remain staunchly traditional while others push the envelope with trendy, fruit-driven, oak-influenced, international-style wines. The list of grapes grown in France includes every noble variety and most of the other significant ones. In general, France, as do other European countries, emphasizes subtlety and complexity in her wines, in contrast to the New World's focus on fruit flavor.

on the label

In response to widespread wine fraud in the early 20th century, France evolved a series of regulations and oversight organizations that culminated in its system of Appellation d'Origine Contrôlée (AOC or AC). Instituted in 1935, it became the model

CHAMPAGNE

Paris •

Strasbourg •
ALSACE

LOIRE VALLEY

Loire R.

BURGUNDY

Bordeaux

BORDEAUX

Lyon

RHÔNE
VALLEY

Rhône R.

SOUTHWEST
FRANCE

PROVENCE

LANGUEDOC-
ROUSSILLON

Marseille

Wine growing
regions

for similar systems throughout wine-producing Europe. Its purpose was to stabilize the industry by protecting the names and traditional styles of France's famous wines. It was never intended to be, as is widely misperceived, a guarantee of wine quality for the consumer.

Appellation d'Origine Contrôlée literally means *controlled name of origin*, and it is based on the concept that the wine from every area has a particular character resulting from *terroir* (see page 17) and tradition. The more specific the area, the more specific the character. Because the place of origin of a wine is so important in France, the majority of its bottles are labeled geographically. There are four categories of classification, of which AOC is the highest.

● **Appellation d'Origine Contrôlée** About one third of French wines carry the classification Appellation d'Origine Contrôlée (AOC). To be an AOC wine, the wine must conform to strict rules governing prescribed geography, permitted grape varieties, maximum yields, methods of viticulture and vinification, and minimum alcohol content. Most of France's mainstream wines fall into this category.

● **Vin Délimité de Qualité Supérieure** Only about 1 percent of French wines are categorized as Vin Délimité de Qualité Supérieure (VDQS; superior-quality wine from a defined area), a stepping stone to AOC. In recent years, many VDQS wines, such as the Loire's Cheverny in 1993, have been elevated to AOC.

● **Vin de Pays** In 1973, the category Vin de Pays (VdP; country wine) was created to address persistent overproduction and abysmal quality in areas such as the Languedoc-Roussillon. The areas specified as Vin de Pays are usually entire regions or departments. This less-stringent designation allows varietal labeling and encourages the use of nontraditional grapes, while at the same time tightening quality standards. The concept has been extremely successful, resulting in some of France's most exciting experimental wines of recent years in addition to countless tasty, well-priced quaffers.

● **Vin de Table** The lowest category, Vin de Table (table wine), is basically jug wine, although occasionally high-quality wines that don't meet the rules of AOC, VDQS, or VdP end up in this catch-all category.

aLsace

Why more Alsace wine isn't drunk in the United States is beyond us. Is everybody leery of the unfamiliar? Is it the Germanic labels? Do you think Alsace wines are sweet? Well, get over it. Wine from Alsace is refreshing and full-bodied and almost always unoaked to let its vibrant, fruit-driven character take center stage. Except for two rare sweet styles, it is generally dry. And it's as food-friendly as wine gets.

ON tHe LabeL

Alsace is one of France's few exceptions to the geographic labeling rule; the region chooses instead to label by grape variety. You may see a vineyard indicated and possibly the term

Grand Cru (great growth). Since 1983, 50 Alsace vineyards have been awarded Grand Cru status, but politics has played a big part in the process and some Grands Crus are not worthy of the name. Also, a number of established houses such as Léon Beyer, Hugel, and Trimbach refuse to employ Grand Cru names even though their grapes come from Grand Cru vineyards. They prefer to market their wines using their own brand names rather than the vineyard names. Whether the Grand Cru designation is meaningful or not, you will pay more for these wines, so if you're not terribly familiar with Alsace producers, either follow our recommendations below or ask your wine merchant for advice.

wHat to Buy ALSACE WINES

1993	1994	1995	1996	1997	1998
★ ★ ★	★ ★ ★ ★	★ ★ ★	★ ★ ★	★ ★ ★	★ ★

varietaLs

GEWÜRZTRAMINER

Gewürztraminer is the love-it-or-hate-it wine of Alsace. It's powerful, exotic, and voluptuous, with an enthralling perfume of rose petals, apricots, spices, and litchis. Some drinkers find Gewürztraminers a bit overwhelming. We don't.

at tHe taBle

Gewürztraminer's high alcohol content, low acidity, and assertive flavors require food with equal oomph. In Alsace, traditional partners are pungent Munster cheese and rich foie gras. Gewürztraminer's floral flavors, however, allow it to venture far from the classic pairings. It works well, for instance, with squash soup, pumpkin ravioli, and vegetarian lasagna with sweet potatoes. Gewürztraminer makes a good match for mildly spiced Indian dishes, but not incendiary ones, because hot peppers make the alcohol in the wine taste unpleasantly bitter.

tHe BottoM LiNe You'll find plenty of good Gewürztraminers available starting at about $15. The wines of this variety that have the best quality for money ratio tend to be in the $20 to $30 range.

PINOT BLANC

When confronted with a wine list on which we don't recognize a single wine, we'll always pick the Alsace Pinot Blanc. These well-balanced, nutty, subtly fruity whites are among the most reliable and versatile anywhere.

at tHe taBLe

Pinot Blanc's moderate acidity and subtle flavors make it an excellent choice for a wide array of dishes. Mildly spiced fish and chicken are both good pairings as are shellfish and simple pork and veal preparations. Some Pinot Blancs have ripe-fruit flavors that can stand up to fruit sauces and salsas. Avoid strongly flavored dishes, especially those with a lot of lemon as its tartness will overwhelm all but the most bracing of Pinot Blancs.

tHe BottoM LINe Pinot Blanc offers consistent quality and ready availability in the $10 to $15 range—a superb value.

PINOT GRIS

Known locally as Tokay–Pinot Gris, Pinot Gris produces full-bodied wines with broad smoky, nut, peach, apricot, and banana flavors. This varietal can be even more powerful than Gewürztraminer, but it is more adaptable at the table and is also a better candidate for aging. Some of Alsace's greatest wines are her sweet Vendanges Tardives and Sélections de Grains Nobles made from Pinot Gris (see page 256). Confusingly, neither the grape nor the wine, is in any way related to the Tokay of Hungary (see page 260).

at tHe taBLe

The unique combination of good acidity and lush, almost decadent texture in Pinot Gris allows it to stand up to a range of foods unexpectedly wide for a white wine. Light meats, such as pork and veal, are naturals, as are hearty fish steaks, like tuna, salmon, and swordfish. In Alsace, however, Pinot Gris traditionally accompanies choucroute garnie, the extremely hearty mélange of sauerkraut and pork, goose, or duck. Pinot Gris will amaze you, too, with its affinity for Indian dishes that are spiced with cinnamon, cardamom, clove, and coriander.

ᴛʜᴇ ʙᴏᴛᴛᴏᴍ ʟɪɴᴇ Pinot Gris tends to be expensive since there isn't much to go around. Basic bottles run $15 to $20. For Grand Cru, expect to pay $25 to $45 and up.

RIESLING

Alsace produces some of the world's great Rieslings, especially true to the character of the grape. These wines are dry, powerful, and refreshing, with aromas and flavors of citrus zest, flowers, peaches, and minerals. With age, they develop the classic petrol aroma prized by lovers of this grape.

at the table

High acidity, a strong mineral undertow, and absence of oak make Alsace Rieslings extremely versatile with food. They complement a wide array of fish and shellfish and are particularly suited to sushi. They can easily cut through the richness of butter and cream sauces to refresh the palate, and they stand up to full-flavored oily fish. Pork and poultry are traditional matches in Alsace. Try them also with salads and mildly spiced Asian cuisines.

ᴛʜᴇ ʙᴏᴛᴛᴏᴍ ʟɪɴᴇ Many basic Rieslings are priced between $12 and $15. The majority of Grand Cru wines generally cost $25 to $35; some rare and highly rated wines can run a good deal more.

OTHER VARIETALS

Muscat is one of Alsace's noble grapes, but there is very little of the variety. Its wines abound in heady floral and fresh grapey aromas combined with musky notes for a haunting perfume and delightful, delicate flavor. Sylvaner (Silvaner in Germany) and Chasselas are made into some simple wines on their own but are most often used in the once popular regional blends called Edelzwicker. Now marketed in the U.S. under such names as Hugel's Gentil and Beyer's La Cuvée, these easy-drinking picnic wines are some of Alsace's best values. Auxerrois, thought to be a clone of Pinot Blanc, is blended into both Edelzwickers and Pinot Blanc to add body. Some is bottled unblended. A surprising amount of occasionally good Pinot Noir is produced as well.

producers and their wines

TRIMBACH
★★★★ $$$–$$$$

Dry, steely wines with laserlike acidity and strong mineral underpinnings. The basic *cuvées* are solid, but the four stars are for Trimbach's Réserve wines. These wines need time. LOOK FOR Gewürztraminer Seigneurs de Ribeaupierre, Riesling Cuvée Frédéric Émile, and especially Clos Ste-Hune, which, in our opinion, is the finest Riesling in the world.

DOMAINE ZIND-HUMBRECHT
★★★★ $$$–$$$$

Full-bodied, intensely concentrated, aromatic, beautifully balanced wines that rank among the world's greatest. They often show considerable sweetness when first bottled and need a few years' aging to really come together. Stunning and priced accordingly. LOOK FOR Go for anything you can afford; life is too short not to try Zind-Humbrecht.

DOMAINE WEINBACH
★★★★ $$–$$$$

The once thick, fruity, sweet, exotic style has been reined in a bit in recent years, but the wines are still superb. LOOK FOR If you like the style, everything is good here, but the Riesling Ste-Cathérine and the Cuvées Théo and Laurence excel.

DOMAINE MARCEL DEISS
★★★ $$–$$$$

A devoted exponent of *terroir*, Jean-Michel Deiss produces powerful, concentrated wines that embody the character of their sites. Deiss's wines require age to develop fully. LOOK FOR basic *cuvées* labeled Bergheim; Riesling Grand Crus Altenberg, Grasberg, and Schoenenbourg; and the Gewürztraminers St-Hippolyte and Altenberg.

MARK KREYDENWEISS
★★★ $$–$$$$

Organic farming and stubbornly traditional, hands-on techniques combine with avant-garde labels and unique blends to produce wines that are among the most iconoclastic Alsace wines, some of which are truly great. LOOK FOR the honeyed, spicy Klevner Kritt (Pinot Blanc) and the tart and fruity Riesling Kastelberg.

ALBERT BOXLER
★★★ $$$

Excellent producer of classic steely Rieslings and smoky, creamy, hazelnut-scented Pinot Gris. Can sometimes miss, but when Boxler's on, the wines are superb. LOOK FOR Rieslings Sommerberg and Brand; Pinot Gris Brand.

JOSMEYER
★★★ $$$

Josmeyer is a devoted champion of Alsace's lesser grapes, such as Chasselas, which the house grows in Grand Cru vineyards.

The grapes may be lowly, but the wines fashioned from them are special. LOOK FOR Auxerrois H Vieilles Vignes and Riesling Hengst.

DOMAINE PAUL BLANCK ★ ★ ★ $$–$$$

Beautifully made, silky smooth, well-balanced wines. The basic wines focus on varietal character, but Phillippe and Frédéric Blanck's mission is to manifest unique *terroir* (see page 17) characteristics of the Grand Cru Furstentum. LOOK FOR anything you can find—Domaine Blank's wines offer amazing consistency across the entire line.

LÉON BEYER ★ ★ ★ $–$$$

Marc Beyer believes his wines must have 14 percent alcohol for proper balance. He must be right because these very dry, very powerful wines age beautifully. LOOK FOR the blend La Cuvée and Pinot Blanc (one of Alsace's best) for early drinking; the Riesling called Les Ecaillers, Pinot Gris Réserve, and the Comte d'Eguisheim Riesling, Gewürztraminer, and Pinot Gris for serious cellaring.

HUGEL ET FILS ★ ★ ★ $–$$$

One of the oldest merchant houses in Alsace, Hugel et Fils turns out consistent, textbook wines in a dry, high-alcohol style. True greatness shows in the firm's late-harvest wines. LOOK FOR Tradition and Jubilee wines, Vendages Tardives, and Sélections de Grains Nobles. Their blended Gentil is a delicious value.

ADDITIONAL TOP-NOTCH PRODUCERS

J. B. Adam (*Pinot Blanc, Riesling Kaefferkopf and Jean Baptiste bottlings*), Lucien Albrecht (*Tokay–Pinot Gris Pfingstberg, Riesling Pfingstberg*), Ernest Burn (*Gewürztraminer, Tokay–Pinot Gris and Muscat, all from their wholly owned Clos St-Imer within the Goldert Grand Cru*), Jean-Pierre Dirler (*Grand Cru Rieslings Kessler, Saering and Spiegel*), André Kientzler (*Auxerrois K— Alsace's finest, Grand Cru Rieslings Geisberg and Osterberg*), Albert Mann (*Riesling Schlossberg and Gewürztraminer Hengst*), Mittnacht-Klack (*Riesling Schoenenbourg, Gewürztraminer Rosacker, both Grand Cru*), Muré (*Clos St-Landelin Riesling and Gewürztraminer*), André Ostertag (*Sylvaner Vieilles Vignes, Tokay–Pinot Gris Muenchberg, Riesling Muenchberg*), Rolly-Gassmann (*Muscat Moenchreben, Auxerrois Moenchreben*), Charles Schleret (*Tokay–Pinot Gris, Muscat*), Schlumberger (*Grand Cru Gewürztraminers Kessler and Kitterlé, and Tokay–Pinot Gris Réserve Spéciale*), Bernard Schoffit (*Chasselas, Gewürztraminer Harth and Tokay–Pinot Gris Clos St-Théobald*), Pierre Sparr (*Pinot Gris Prestige, Gewürztraminer Mambourg Grand Cru and Riesling Schlossberg*)

BORDEAUX

Wine collectors around the world prize Bordeaux's long-lived red, dry white, and luscious dessert wines (see page 252). Annually, Bordeaux produces more wine, more consistently, and at a higher quality level than any other area. It is quite simply the world's leading wine region. While many of its top wines are now within reach only of kings and Microsoft millionaires, Bordeaux also provides an ocean of affordable, delicious, everyday wines in all styles.

ON THE LABEL

Bordeaux wines are labeled geographically. The region is a large one, and its appellations include both Bordeaux in its entirety and smaller units within it. Bottles marked simply Bordeaux or with the names of the largest appellations in the overall region, Bordeaux Supérieur and Entre-Deux-Mers, offer relatively simple, easy-drinking reds and whites. In good years, they are some of Bordeaux's best values.

Look to the somewhat smaller district appellations for red wines with a bit more complexity and concentration. Among these districts are the Médoc, the Haut-Médoc, and the Côtes, including the Côtes de Bourg, the Côtes de Blaye, and the Côtes de Castillon.

Bordeaux's best reds come from the famous appellations Graves, St-Émilion, and Pomerol and the small *communes*, or villages, within the Médoc—St-Estèphe, Pauillac, St-Julien, and Margaux. A few great whites and the best reds from the Graves are produced in Pessac-Léognan, a subdistrict of the northern Graves. Sauternes (see page 252) is nestled in the southern end of the Graves.

Even smaller than the subdistrict, of course is the individual château, and the greatest ones produce the supposedly very finest red wines in all Bordeaux. They are certainly the most expensive.

RED WINES OF BORDEAUX

Bordeaux is practically synonymous with its red wines, which make up more than four fifths of its production. At their best, these aristocratic, complex, harmonious treasures offer a gustatory and intellectual experience unmatched by any other wines. They set the standard for Cabernet Sauvignon– and Merlot-based wines everywhere.

Grapes and Styles

The vast majority of Bordeaux are blended wines, with Cabernet Sauvignon and Merlot making up the bulk of the blend. The fragrant Cabernet Franc plays a large supporting role on the right bank (see below), while Malbec and Petit Verdot are used in small amounts for added aroma and body throughout Bordeaux. Malbec is dwindling, but Petit Verdot, with its powerful violet and blueberry scents, is once again on the rise.

Bordeaux's lesser wines, made for immediate drinking, contain high percentages of Merlot: some even contain 100 percent. High-end wines, especially those based on Cabernet Sauvignon, can be unpleasantly tannic in their youth, requiring 10 to 20 years of cellaring to reach their peak. Many growers of these top wines are responding to the current demand for earlier drinkability by, among other things, upping the proportion of Merlot. They insist that, given improvements in vinification and viticulture, ultimate longevity won't be affected. We'll see.

LEFT BANK, RIGHT BANK

The Gironde Estuary divides Bordeaux in two. The Médoc, Haut-Médoc, and Graves to its west and south are known collectively as the left bank. Areas to the east, including St-Émilion, Pomerol, Fronsac, Canon-Fronsac, Bourg, Blaye, and the Côtes de Castillon make up the right bank. The well-drained, gravelly soil on the left bank fosters Cabernet Sauvignon while the moister clay soil of the right bank benefits Merlot. Therefore, you can expect left-bank wines, with their higher percentage of Cabernet Sauvignon, to be tannic, complex, and long lived, with flavors of cassis, herbs, and cedar. Those of the Graves also include notes of tobacco and smoke, along with a slightly dry, earthy finish. The Merlot-based wines of the right bank tend to be less tannic and therefore smoother, with flavors of plum, tobacco, and chocolate. They mature a bit more quickly.

at the table

Young red Bordeaux requires fat and protein to offset its tannin and bring out its fruitiness. Lamb is a traditional partner since its herbal gamy flavors mirror similar notes in the wine. Beef is also superb. Try filet mignon with a béarnaise sauce. An older, mature wine should be served with simply prepared meats in order not to overwhelm the wine's delicate complexity. Steak or rib roast and lamb rack or chops are best. Bordeaux is also a classic accompaniment to the cheese course. Pair younger wines with sharp, hard cheeses. Select mature wines for milder, creamier cheeses. Lighter, Merlot-based Bordeaux is also at home with white meats and roast chicken.

the bottom Line Prices for wines from the most famous châteaux have surged well beyond the reach of all but the most wealthy. The top names are $200 a bottle, wines from some second-tier châteaux well over $100. Wines of lesser pedigree furnish ample pleasure at sane prices. Excellent basic Bordeaux, Bordeaux Supérieur, and wines from the Côtes run $10 to $15. Fronsac and Canon-Fronsac offer good value at $18 to $25. And $25 to $35 buys less known, very good St-Émilions.

what to Buy BORDEAUX RIGHT BANK

1988	1989	1990	1991	1992	1993
★★★	★★★★	★★★★	O	★	★★

1994	1995	1996	1997	1998
★★★	★★★	★★★★	★★	★★★★

what to Buy BORDEAUX LEFT BANK, EXCLUDING GRAVES

1988	1989	1990	1991	1992	1993
★★★	★	★★★★	★	★	★★

1994	1995	1996	1997	1998
★★★	★★★★	★★★★	★★	★★★

what to Buy RED GRAVES

1988	1989	1990	1991	1992	1993
★★★	★★★★	★★★★	★	★	★★★

1994	1995	1996	1997	1998
★★★	★★★	★★★	★★★	★★

1996 Château Duhart-Milon-Rothschild, Pauillac ★★★★ $$$

After the initial sulfur clears off, there are aromas of black currants, smoky oak, and cloves. Big and concentrated, with gentle tannin, succulent plum and cassis flavors, and a pleasing leathery note. Long finish.

1996 Château Carbonnieux, Pessac-Léognan ★★★ $$$

Lots of charred oak and classic Graves aromas of tobacco and earth. This very elegant, medium-bodied wine is one of the best reds from Carbonnieux in years.

1996 Château de Fieuzal, Pessac-Léognan ★★★ $$$

Dense black color. Cassis, cherry, tobacco, and iodine nose—classic Graves. Well integrated oak. Right now the succulent core of ripe fruit is bound up in acidity and dry tannin. Give it 5 to 10 years.

1996 La Réserve de Léoville Barton, St-Julien ★★★ $$$

Deep, bright ruby color—impressive! The nose is gorgeous, too: Cassis, violets, toast, and vanilla. This youthful wine shows beautifully ripe and concentrated cassis and vanilla flavors and a very long, spicy cassis finish. There is ample depth and fullness allied with classic St-Julien elegance. One of Bordeaux's best second labels.

1996 Château Coufran, Haut-Médoc ★★★ $$

Quite attractive, full cassis, plum, and spice nose. Well-balanced, with excellent acidity playing off concentrated flavors and just the right amount of oak. Give this another two years.

1996 Château Faugères, St-Émilion ★★★ $$

The deep chocolaty nose shows lots of berry and plum fruit. Excellent fruit and spice flavors, a velvety texture, and a long, satisfying finish all show why Faugères is a rising star in Bordeaux.

1996 Château Fontenil, Fronsac ★★★ $$

Beautiful nose of wild cherries, raspberries, and fresh herbs. This harmonious, medium-bodied wine has exquisite balance between oak and penetrating red-fruit flavors. Will develop nicely over 5 to 10 years.

1996 Château Haut-Bergey, Pessac-Léognan ★★★ $$

Huge fruit and spice aromas mingled with some sweaty animal scents that clear off after a few minutes. Concentrated and elegant red-fruit, smoky-meat, and tobacco flavors. Nice tannin in the long finish. Good balance of flavor, tannin, acidity, and alcohol content.

1996 Château Poujeaux, Moulis ★★★ $$

This wine has a beautiful dense ruby color and a gorgeous nose of black currants, cassis, chocolate, plums, and cloves. It's velvety textured, with concentrated cassis flavors flecked with herbs and chocolate on the snappy finish. Complete from start to finish.

1996 Château Terre de Turenne, Côtes de Castillon ★ ★ ★ $$
Lively cherry and plum aromas indicate a lot of Merlot in this blend. Full flavored with vibrant acidity, and good tannin on the finish. Nice.

1996 Château Haut de Carles Cuvée Spéciale, Fronsac★ ★ $$$
This voluptuous and very oaky wine is dominated by its smoky, toasty vanilla aromas and flavors. Still, there are lots of sweet black-plum flavors lurking under the oak and tannin.

1996 Château St-Georges, St-Georges St-Émilion ★ ★ $$$
Lots of spicy, leathery aromas mingle with scents of ripe plums and chocolate. Ripe, earthy plum and saddle leather flavors are supported by mouthwatering acidity and a strong, tannic finish.

1996 Château Côte Montpezat, Côtes de Castillon ★ ★ $$
Lovely, full cassis, plum, cherry, and vanilla aromas. Big for a Côtes de Castillon, with spicy cherry flavors and a long, fruity finish. An attractive, full-bodied style.

1996 Château de La Dauphine, Fronsac ★ ★ $$
Clear plum aromas with notes of cocoa, tobacco, and damp forest. Slightly too tannic now, this nonetheless has a concentrated core of cherry and chocolate flavors. It will be delicious in two to three years.

1996 Château Fombrauge, St-Émilion ★ ★ $$
The understated, but complex, nose evokes ripe damson plums, baker's chocolate, warm leather, and gamy nuances. It's fairly acidic now, but has an excellent core of concentrated, ripe fruit that carries through well on the long finish.

1996 Château Grand Lys, Bordeaux ★ ★ $$
Cassis, plums, lots of herbs, and generous oak aromas in the nose. This is a very oaky wine, but concentrated fruit flavors and gentle tannin manage to keep it in balance

1996 Château Lanessan, Haut-Médoc ★ ★ $$
This excellent wine plays it right down the middle with slightly reserved, balanced cassis and herb flavors that have good concentration and length of finish.

1996 Château La Louvière, Pessac-Léognan ★ ★ $$
Very smoky, toasty oak driven aromas. Black-cherry fruit flavors and earthy Graves nuances take over. Lively fruit is still firmly gripped by acid and slightly astringent tannin. Needs five years to mellow.

1996 Château de Pez, St-Estèphe ★★ $$

Boysenberry and blueberry nose. Only modest concentration, but excellent balance of flavor, tannin, acidity, and alcohol. Medium weight, and a fruity finish tinged with hints of newly turned earth.

1996 Château Roc de Calon, Montagne St-Émilion ★★ $$

Aromas of plums, shoe leather, spice, and a whiff of barnyard. Plum flavors and velvety tannin make this easy to drink. The finish serves up a nice hint of baker's chocolate.

1996 Vieux Château St-André, Montagne St-Émilion ★★ $$

The plum nose shows some sophisticated hints of mineral and woodsmoke. Medium bodied with generous oak but the flavor concentration to match. Lovely notes of woodsmoke on the finish.

1996 Château Pascaud, Bordeaux Supérieur ★★ $

The nose, with its plum aromas, suggests lots of Merlot. Made in a St-Émilion style: smooth and mellow with earthy, leathery, plummy flavors. Perfectly ready for drinking now.

1996 Château Fourcas-Hosten, Listrac ★ $$

The nose features cassis, cherry, and iron aromas. Initially dry and not very flavorful on the palate, there is some fruit flavor that emerges as the wine is exposed to air in the glass.

1996 Château Jonqueyres, Bordeaux Supérieur ★ $$

Snappy fresh cranberry and plum fruit aromas mixed with those of fennel and smoked meat. This light-bodied charmer has spicy red-fruit flavors leading to an equally spicy, lightly tannic finish.

DRY WHITE WINES OF BORDEAUX

Bordeaux's dry whites used to be highly respected, but in the seventies and eighties, fruity New World challengers exposed them as often tired, thin, and oxidized. The Bordelais took notice and made improvements. Today's white Bordeaux are fresher, fruitier, and more enjoyable than ever.

gRapes and styLes

Classic white Bordeaux is a blend of Sauvignon Blanc, which contributes zippy acidity and citrusy, grassy flavors, and Sémillon, which provides body and a honeyed, nutty nuance. Serious white Graves, powerful and meant for aging, are predominantly Sémillon and are aged in new oak barrels for complexity, texture, and additional body. The Graves intended for immediate imbibing are mostly Sauvignon Blanc. They are fermented in temperature-controlled, stainless-steel tanks to preserve their tart, fresh-fruit flavors.

at tHe taBle

Treat the light, refreshing Sauvignon Blanc–based styles as you might a Loire wine, serving them with river fish, simple chicken dishes, and salads. These wines have an earthy note that suits raw shellfish particularly well. Full, serious Graves, on the other hand, have the weight and power of white Burgundies, and so you have to take care not to overmatch the food. They make delicious partners to chicken in cream sauces, oily fish steaks, and, most especially, lobster and scallops.

tHe Bottom LIne The few top-end white Graves are priced more as collectibles than beverages. For much better value, stick to the many fine Entre-Deux-Mers, Bordeaux Blancs, and lesser Graves that are easy on the wallet at $9 to $15.

1996 Château de Fieuzal Blanc, Pessac-Léognan ★ ★ ★ $$$$
Lovely acidity, full melony fruit flavors. Full-bodied and harmonious, partly from unusually restrained use of oak. Long finish. Elegant.

1996 Château Haut-Bergey Blanc, Pessac-Léognan ★ ★ ★ $$$
Toasty vanilla, spice, vibrant citrus, melon, and herb aromas. Fine balance of succulent fruit, full-throttle acidity, and spicy oak. A lovely wine.

1998 Château Graville-Lacoste, Graves ★ ★ ★ $$
Typical Sauvignon nose of celery seed and fresh-cut grass. Lots of earthy *terroir* to balance the full, almost peachy, flavors. Has substantial body and a long concentrated finish. Excellent quality.

1998 Château Rahoul, Graves ★ ★ ★ $$
First up is the spicy vanilla aroma of oak, but the fruitiness still comes through. Vanilla, plum, mineral, and peach flavors. This wine's for fans of full-bodied, complex, and oaky white Bordeaux.

1998 Château de Cugat, Bordeaux ★ ★ $$
Full flavored and concentrated, with nuts, malt, and asparagus on the palate. Very good Sauvignon Blanc.

1998 Château Bonnet, Entre-Deux-Mers ★ ★ $
An inviting nose exudes herbs, flowers, citrus, and earth. Medium bodied and lively with pretty floral, herbal, and melon flavors leading to a refreshing finish. This year's version is another winner.

1998 Château Haut-Rian, Bordeaux ★ ★ $

Classic cut-grass, hay, and lemon Sauvignon nose. A straightforward wine made and aged in stainless steel, with grassy flavors and a moderately long, herbal finish.

1997 Château Ducla, Bordeaux Sec ★ $

Smoky banana and apple nose. Simple, light pear and apple flavors and a medium-length finish. Low acidity makes it go down easy.

1997 Château Fongrave, Entre-Deux-Mers Haut-Benauge ★ $

This is a typical, basic 100 percent Sauvignon Blanc, stainless-steel-fermented white Bordeaux. A good, simple everyday wine.

BURGUNDY

The most exhilarating wines we have ever drunk were Burgundies. We have also had more disappoint-ments with Burgundies than with wines from any other region. Yes, the Burgundy region can be mad-deningly frustrating. With its huge variety and its emphasis on the many, many producers and *domaines* and the very, very small individual vineyards, there's a great deal to know and to keep

up on. Yet the memory of those silky smooth, complex, per-fumed Pinot Noirs and the luscious, sophisticated Chardonnays will always keep us coming back for more.

GRApes AND StyLes

Burgundies (with very rare exceptions) are made from a single grape variety. Pinot Noir and Chardonnay are the bases for its greatest reds and whites respectively. These are the magical wines that have launched thousands of imitators everywhere in the world. Nowhere else are these varietals as elegant and satisfying as here. Gamay is the grape of the charming and fruity Beaujolais, and a tiny bit of tart, peach-pit flavored white is made from Aligoté.

Five districts make up Burgundy. From north to south they are Chablis, the Côte d'Or (with its subdistricts, Côte de Nuits and Côte de Beaune), Côte Chalonnaise, the Mâconnais, and Beaujolais. White styles range from refreshing, steely Chablis in the north to full-bodied, creamy, higher alcohol wines in the Mâconnais. Reds are fuller bodied in the Côte de Nuits, more elegant in the Côte de Beaune, and simpler in the Mâconnais. Both reds and whites reach their zenith in the Côte d'Or.

ON THE LABEL

No other wine region celebrates the cult of *terroir* (see page 17) like Burgundy. Its wines are classified into appellations of increasingly smaller divisions of the land. In theory, as the source becomes more specific, so too do the characteristics of the wine. Progressively more stringent production rules should, but don't always, result in stepped up quality as well.

● **Regional** The majority of these Burgundies can come from anywhere within the entire region and are often blends from many sites. The name Bourgogne appears on the label either alone or with further descriptors, such as Bourgogne-Aligoté for wines made with that grape variety.

● **District** The district wines, Chablis, Côte Chalonnaise, Côte d'Or, Beaujolais, and Mâcon, carry their own name and offer a bit more complexity, concentration, and character.

● **Village** These wines must come from within a specific village, or *commune*, such as Gevrey-Chambertin, the name of which will appear on the label. The specific *terroir* characteristics (see page 17) of the place are evident in well-made examples of the wine.

● **Premier Cru** Of the roughly 4,000 vineyards in Burgundy that bottle their own wine, 561 consistently produce more concentrated, focused, and complex wines than their neighbors. Often they have signature flavors as well. These vineyards are recognized by Premier Cru (1er Cru) status. On the label, you will see the name of the vineyard after the village name, as in Beaune-Grèves. If the village name is followed by Premier Cru but no vineyard name, it means that the wine is a blend from more than one Premier Cru vineyard within the village.

● **Grand Cru** At the very pinnacle of the Burgundy hierarchy stand the 38 Grand Cru vineyards, hallowed sites that have the potential to yield Burgundy's most spectacular, ageworthy wines. On the label, the name of the vineyard appears without the village name. Beware of look-alike village wines: In the early part of this century, a few villages appended the names of their famous Grand Cru vineyards to their original names. Thus the village of Gevrey was renamed Gevrey-Chambertin and Chambolle, Chambolle-Musigny. On the label, Le Chambertin and Le Musigny signify Grand Crus, but Gevrey-Chambertin and Chambolle-Musigny merely mean village wines.

Despite the guarantees that this detailed hierarchical system seems to imply, it is far more important to rely upon good producers than vineyards or vintage charts. Search out the advice of a trusted merchant for selections other than those listed in this book.

at the table

Red Burgundy is all about delicacy and perfume, not power. So pair it with medium-weight dishes, rather than big, beefy or gamy flavors. It's great with fish steaks, such as grilled salmon; excellent alongside pork, chicken, and veal; perfect for duck with fruit sauces like cherry or blackberry. To match specific flavors, remember that Burgundy has an earthy note; try it with mushrooms or anything topped with truffle oil. When you want to drink the same wine throughout a multicourse meal, Burgundy, like most Pinot Noirs, is your answer, since it will complement both fish and meat courses. Serve this versatile wine also with mild cow's-milk cheeses like Morbier, Lancashire, or Gouda.

The whole spectrum of Burgundy whites matches beautifully with chicken and fish steaks. Bourgogne Blanc, Chablis, and the simpler of the Mâconnais wines prove easier to pair with food due to their lighter, less oaky flavors. The full, creamy Mâconnais wines find their place with lobster and scallops and with butter-based sauces such as *beurre blanc*. These whites also suit all-American sautéed soft-shell crabs to a T.

the côte d'or

Literally, the *slope of gold,* the Côte d'Or is named for the burnished blaze of its yellow-leafed vines in the autumn, but the region might as well be so called because it is arguably the world's most revered and expensive viticultural neighborhood. The Côte d'Or produces Burgundy's greatest, most coveted, and costliest Chardonnays and Pinot Noirs.

tHe Bottom Line There never has been enough Burgundy to go around, and, as the worldwide boom in wine consumption continues, demand for top-quality, limited-production gems from the Côte d'Or is unprecedented. Grand Cru reds begin around $60 but soar to well over $100. Premier Crus are $35 to $65. Expect village bottlings to cost $25 to $50. Regional and district wines from good producers in good vintages are often the best values; you'll pay $15 to $35. Côte d'Or whites tend to be a bit more dear, as their production averages only one quarter that of the reds.

wHat to Buy RED WINES

1995	1996	1997	1998
★★★★	★★★	★★★	★★★

PRODUCERS AND tHeIR ReD WINeS

DUJAC ★★★★ $$$–$$$$

One of Burgundy's most forward thinkers and revered winemakers, Jacques Seysses produces sensuous wines, perfumed and spicy with silky texture and succulent red-fruit flavors. They age magnificently. LOOK FOR wines from the village of Morey-St-Denis, from its Grand Cru vineyards Clos de la Roche and Clos St-Denis, and from the village of Gevrey-Chambertin's Premier Cru vineyard Aux Combottes.

GEORGES ROUMIER ★★★★ $$$–$$$$

Textbook, top-end Côte de Nuits: full and spicy with deep red-berry flavors. Roumier's wines can be astringent when young; with time they develop smoothness and complexity. LOOK FOR wines from the village of Chambolle-Musigny, from its Grand Cru vineyard Bonnes Mares, and for Morey-St-Denis Clos de la Bussière.

ARMAND ROUSSEAU ★★★ $$$$

Traditional-style wines with spicy complexity. Like Comte de Vogüé, Rousseau is on the upswing after a brief decline. Since 1985, these wines have once again been in Burgundy's top echelon. LOOK FOR Chambertin Clos de Bèze, Clos St-Jacques, and Clos des Ruchottes.

COMTE GEORGES DE VOGÜÉ ★★★ $$$$

After a bad patch in the 1970s and 80s, this estate came roaring back with great wines in the 1990 vintage: intense yet seductive and brimming with red- and black-fruit flavors. LOOK FOR wines simply from the village of Chambolle-Musigny and from its Grand Cru vineyards, Bonnes Mares and Musigny, especially Musigny Cuvée Vieilles Vignes.

DOMAINE DE L'ARLOT
★ ★ ★ $$$-$$$$

Inspired by Dujac's Jacques Seysses, Jean-Pierre de Smet eschews the characteristic gamy rusticity of wines from Nuit-St-Georges in favor of a more fruity and polished style. LOOK FOR Nuits-St-Georges Clos des Forêts and Clos de L'Arlot and for Vosne-Romanée Les Suchots.

LOUIS JADOT
★ ★ ★ $$$–$$$$

Burgundy's best *négociant* house offers a wide array of wines that admirably reflect their *terroir*. The full-bodied, full-flavored style can occasionally lack a bit of subtlety. LOOK FOR Vosne-Romanée Les Suchots, Gevrey-Chambertin Le Clos St-Jacques, Chambertin Clos de Bèze, and Beaune Clos des Ursules.

MARQUIS D'ANGERVILLE
★ ★ ★ $$$

Low yields and minimalist winemaking result in gossamer wines with astonishingly clear and succulent flavors. These are elegant wines. LOOK FOR wines from the Champans, Taillepieds, or Clos des Ducs vineyards in Volnay and for simple Bourgogne Rouge.

TOLLOT-BEAUT & FILS
★ ★ ★ $$–$$$

Extremely reliable producer of delicate, red-fruit-scented wines with noticeable vanilla flavor from new oak. Very good values from minor appellations. LOOK FOR plain Bourgogne Rouge and, from the Côte de Beaune, Savigny-lès-Beaune Les Lavières and Chorey-lès-Beaune.

ADDITIONAL TOP-NOTCH PRODUCERS—EXPENSIVE

Robert Chevillon, Claude Dugat, René Engel, Domaine Anne-François Gros, Michel Lafarge, Dominique Laurent, Domaine Leroy, Domaine Hubert Lignier, Domaine Mongeard-Mugneret, Hubert de Montille, Denis Mortet, Domaine de la Romanée-Conti, Joseph Roty, Serafin Père et Fils

GOOD VALUES

Burgundy is expensive, but even on the Côte d'Or values exist. In good vintages, such as the 1996 and 1997 that are now in stores, look for such regional wines as Bourgogne-Hautes Côtes de Nuits, Bourgogne-Hautes Côtes de Beaune, Côte de Nuits-Villages, and Côte de Beaune-Villages from top producers. Some routinely declassify portions of their village and Cru wines to Bourgogne AC. In addition, choose among the following:

Philippe Charlopin-Parizot, Michel Gaunoux *(Pommard Grands Epenots and Pommard Rugiens)*, Louis Jadot *(Fixin)*, Labouré-Roi *(Bourgogne Rouge and Chambolle-Musign*y*)*, Olivier Leflaive *(Pommard and Volnay)*, Domaine Leroy *(Bourgogne Rouge)*, Henri Perrot-Minot *(Chambolle-Musigny)*, Domaine Michel Pont *(Pommard)*, Domaine Sirugue *(Côte de Nuits-Village Belle Marguerite)*

what to buy WHITE WINES

1995	1996	1997	1998
★★★★	★★★★	★★★	★★★

producers and their white wines

DOMAINE LEFLAIVE ★★★★ $$$$
Seek out Leflaive for quintessential Puligny-Montrachets: steely, densely concentrated whites with citrusy pineapple and smoky, spicy oak flavors. These are for the cellar. LOOK FOR Puligny-Montrachet Les Pucelles, Puligny-Montrachet Clavoillon, Puligny-Montrachet Folatières, and Chevalier-Montrachet.

DOMAINE RAMONET ★★★★ $$$$
Tough to find, and some are very expensive, but no one does white Burgundy better. These powerful, concentrated, complex, and harmonious wines are utterly ravishing. They are worth the splurge. LOOK FOR anything you can find, especially Chassagne-Montrachet Morgeot, Bâtard-Montrachet, and Le Montrachet.

DOMAINE MICHEL COLIN-DELÉGER ★★★★ $$$–$$$$
Michel Colin and his wife, Mme. Colin-Deléger, produce mouthwatering Puligny-Montrachets, Chassagne-Montrachets, and St-Aubins, all from a hall of fame list of top vineyards. LOOK FOR anything you can find, but especially Puligny-Montrachet Les Demoiselles and the rare La Truffière, a vineyard in Puligny-Montrachet.

JEAN-MARC BOILLOT ★★★ $$$$
Flamboyant, tropical-fruit-filled wines that taste magnificent when young but age surprisingly well. These can almost be mistaken for Californians. LOOK FOR Puligny-Montrachets from the vineyards Referts, Champ Canet, and La Truffière.

MARC COLIN ★★★ $$$–$$$$
Fine, well-priced whites from Chassagne-Montrachet and St-Aubin. The Chassagnes are peachy and full; the St-Aubins, light, but concentrated with limestone and almond flavors. LOOK FOR St-Aubin La Chatenière, St-Aubin Les Combes, and St-Aubin En Remilly; Chassagne-Montrachet Les Caillerets and Chassagne-Montrachet Les Champs-Gains.

LOUIS JADOT ★★★ $$$–$$$$
In contrast to its bold reds, Jadot's whites are light-to-medium bodied and citric. They are unusual in that some of the malolactic fer-

mentations have been partially blocked, giving the wines the acidity to age gracefully. LOOK FOR The village whites from Meursault, Chassagne-Montrachet, and Puligny-Montrachet are very good. Meursault-Perrières, Puligny-Montrachet Perrières, and Corton-Charlemagne are often excellent.

OLIVIER LEFLAIVE ★★★ $$–$$$$

The wines from this *négociant* have improved dramatically over the last few years, and the further good news is that there is a lot to go around. Judicious use of oak aging, faithfulness to *terroir*, and straightforward flavors are Olivier Leflaive hallmarks. LOOK FOR Puligny-Montrachet Les Folatières; St-Aubin, St-Aubin En Remilly, and Rully are terrific values.

VERGET ★★★ $$–$$$$

Verget brings an international approach to the production of his Burgundies. They have explosive fruitiness and a smooth, full texture that make them arresting, but *terroir* characteristics are sometimes sacrificed. LOOK FOR Anything you can find. The lower-end wines represent excellent values.

ADDITIONAL TOP-NOTCH PRODUCERS

Guy Bocard, Bonneau du Martray *(Corton-Charlemagne)*, Louis Carillon et Fils, Fontaine-Gagnard, Gagnard-Delagrange, François Jobard, Domaine Comtes Lafon, Domaine Leroy, Domaine Maroslavac-Leger, Marc Morey, Michel Niellon, Paul Pernot, Étienne Sauzet

côte chalonnaise

The Côte Chalonnaise, sometimes known as the Région de Mercurey, is divided into five appellations occupying separate hilltops south of the Côte d'Or. The newest, Bouzeron, gained appellation status for its tart, white Aligotés in 1979. The four other appellations are Montagny, known primarily for its whites; Mercurey and Givry, specializing in reds; and Rully, which offers both reds and whites. Though one still encounters rustic examples, wines from the Chalonnaise have improved dramatically in the last decade.

THE BOTTOM LINE This is an excellent source of bargain-priced red and white Burgundies. Prices generally run from $15 to $25. Don't overlook the lemony Aligotés from Bouzeron starting at about $10.

PRODUCERS AND THEIR WINES

DOMAINE JEAN-MARC JOBLOT ★ ★ ★ $$$
Jean-Marc says he loves the smell of wood, so expect a lot of new oak aromas in his dense, fruity, spicy Givrys. The oak doesn't upset the balance of the wines, and they're by far the best reds of the appellation. LOOK FOR Givry Clos du Cellier aux Moines, Givry Clos de la Servoisine.

FAIVELEY ★ ★ ★ $$–$$$
This well known *négociant* house bottles excellent red wines from all over Burgundy, but its Mercureys have always struck us as especially outstanding among their peers. LOOK FOR the Mercureys Clos des Myglands, Les Mauvarennes, and Clos du Roy.

MICHEL JUILLOT ★ ★ ★ $$–$$$
What Joblot is to Givry, Juillot is to Mercurey: the best and most dynamic estate in the appellation. Both reds and whites are superb and represent some of the most consistent values in all of Burgundy. LOOK FOR Mercurey Blanc and the red Mercureys Clos des Barraults and Les Champs Martin.

ANTONIN RODET ★ ★ $$
One of the largest producers in the Chalonnaise, Rodet's widely distributed Château de Chamirey and Château de Rully wines are going from strength to strength. LOOK FOR Château de Rully Blanc and the red Château de Chamirey Mercureys Le Clos du Roi, Le Clos L'Evêque, and La Mission.

A & P DE VILLAINE ★ ★ $$
Aubert de Villaine makes the wildly expensive wines at the legendary Domaine de la Romanée-Conti. Here, he and his wife, Pamela, produce modest, but beautiful wines at down to earth prices. His Aligoté transcends the category. LOOK FOR Bouzeron Aligoté, Rully Blanc, and Bourgogne Côte Chalonnaise Blanc and Rouge.

OTHER TOP-NOTCH PRODUCERS
Domaine Michel Briday, Paul de Launay, André Delorme, Louis Latour, Protheau et Fils, Domaine de Rully St-Michael

mâconnais

Burgundy's best source for bargain-priced everyday white wines is the Mâconnais, hands down. Good, medium-bodied wines for early, uncritical quaffing are the rule, but choice wines from the district can rival California's for ripe tropical fruitiness and alcoholic clout. The top Mâcons have mineral flavors so similar to those of Chablis that the wines can sometimes be confused.

ON THE LABEL

Mâcon's classification system has levels:

● **Mâcon** The basic district appellation indicates the simplest, lightest wines.

● **Mâcon-Villages** Must be from one of the highly rated villages whose wines offer more concentration and character than a simple Mâcon. The wine may be labeled either Mâcon-Villages or Mâcon followed by the name of the village itself. The best known villages are Lugny, Viré, Prissé, and Clessé.

● **Pouilly-Fuissé** and **Saint-Véran** The top appellations of the Mâconnais. At its best, Pouilly-Fuissé delivers more than any other Mâcon wine; it's honeyed, tropical, and famously full-bodied. St-Véran is lighter, about halfway between Mâcon-Villages and Pouilly-Fuissé in style.

THE BOTTOM LINE Some of Burgundy's best values in white wines. Mâcon-Villages, particularly those with village names, and the St-Véran can be excellent buys in good years. All of these wines routinely sell for $12 to $18. Be skeptical about Pouilly-Fuissé; it is often vastly overpriced.

WHAT TO BUY MÂCONNAIS

1995	1996	1997	1998
★★★	★★★★	★★★	★★★

PRODUCERS AND THEIR WINES

J. A. FERRET ★★★ $$$
Madame Jeanne Ferret passed away in 1993, but daughter Colette continues to make Mâcons of the highest order. Lavishly honeyed, with superb fruit flavors, these hedonistic wines are irresistible young but also age remarkably well. LOOK FOR anything you can find.

JEAN THÉVENET DOMAINE DE LA BONGRAN
AND DOMAINE EMILIAN GILLET ★★★ $$$
Low yields, no chemicals, old vines, late harvesting, and botrytis add up to spectacularly opulent and exuberantly exotic wines. Outstanding. LOOK FOR Bongran Mâcon-Clessé, Emilian Gillet Mâcon-Clessé, and Tradition.

J. J. VINCENT ★ ★ ★ $$–$$$
Impeccable winemaking here yields correct and occasionally unex-
citing wines, but the bottlings from the Château Fuissé are special.
Refreshing, concentrated, and long on the finish, these are some of
the best of the Mâconnais. LOOK FOR Pouilly-Fuissé Vieilles Vignes,
Les Brûlées, and Le Clos. St-Véran is very good, too.

DOMAINE ANDRÉ BONHOMME ★ ★ ★ $$
An elder statesman in the Mâcon and one of the first to domaine
bottle. His Mâcon-Viré is a superb, vividly fruity wine with silky texture and an almost endless finish. Use of 25 percent new oak adds
creamy texture and spicy complexity. LOOK FOR Mâcon-Viré.

VERGET ★ ★ ★ $$
This excellent *négociant* does some of his best work in the
Mâconnais, where the earthy *terroir* character seems to play into
Verget's full-flavored, full-bodied, fruity style. LOOK FOR St-Véran,
Pouilly-Fuissé, and Mâcon-Villages Tête de Cuvée.

ADDITIONAL TOP-NOTCH PRODUCERS
Domaine des Chazelles, Guffens-Heynen, Domaine Guillemot-
Michel, Domaine Manciat-Poncet, Domaine de Roally *(Henri
Goyard)*, Domaine du Vieux Saint-Sorlin *(Olivier Merlin)*

CHABLIS

The cool climate and chalky limestone soil of Chablis produces
our favorite Chardonnays, bar none. They are medium bodied
and citric with a prominent mineral signature and forceful
acidity. The best made Chablis develop slowly into wines of complexity, subtlety, and sophistication. The insipid California jug
wines of the same name in no way resemble their namesake.

grapes and styles
Chablis is made from the Chardonnay grape, but there are two
distinct styles, unoaked and oaked. For years, producers have
debated which is the true Chablis. Young unoaked versions
emphasize tart pear and apple flavors and often, since it's not
obscured by the wood, more Chablis *terroir* character (see page
17). Before aging, oaked wines tend to be smoother, fuller bodied, more complex, and spicier. Both can be excellent young,
and both age well. With time, they seem to meet in the middle
stylistically.

Of greater concern is the continued expansion of the Chablis district into questionable land at the fringes of the appellation. Advocates point to the fact that the soil is quite similar to the Kimmeridgean clay of Chablis proper, but opponents cry foul. The proof will be in the wines over time.

at tHe taBLe

Raw oysters and Chablis are perhaps the best known classic pairing. Is it because the soil of Chablis is literally composed of ancient, decomposed oyster shells? Choose the best Chablis you can afford, either young or aged, for oysters, and other shellfish, as well. In France, basic Chablis often accompanies mild fish and chicken dishes, its acidity easily handling any creamy sauces. You'll need Premier Cru and Grand Cru Chablis with any fried fish, shellfish, or calamari (skip the clichéd red sauce, which would overwhelm the wine). Cru wines also match more robust poultry and stronger, oilier fish, like salmon and tuna. Mature Chablis develops earthy tones that perfectly complement wild mushrooms.

tHe BottoM LiNe If all the bottles sold each year that are called "Chablis" actually came from Chablis, they would represent more than 30 years' production. Real Chablis are relatively rare, and prices reflect it. Yet they're bargains compared to wines of the Côte d'Or. Appellation Contrôlée Chablis run $15 to $30, Premier Crus $18 to $45, and Grand Crus $35 to $70. Buy at the higher end where concentration and character justify the prices; only occasionally do we find basic Chablis to be good value.

wHat to BuY CHABLIS

1994	1995	1996	1997	1998
★★	★★★	★★★★	★★★	★★★

pRoDuceRs aND tHeIR wiNes

RENÉ ET VINCENT DAUVISSAT   ★★★★ $$$–$$$$
The house of Dauvissat is one of the titans of Chablis. Their totally traditional wines are among the most enchanting you will encounter anywhere. They capture *terroir* characteristics with amazing precision. LOOK FOR Chablis Les Clos Grand Cru, Les Preuses Grand Cru, Vaillons Premier Cru, and Les Fôrets Premier Cru.

LOUIS MICHEL ET FILS ★★★ $$$–$$$$

Oak is avoided here. These modern wines are made entirely with stainless-steel equipment, which allows the character of the grape and the vineyards to take center stage. The wines age extremely well. LOOK FOR Chablis Les Clos Grand Cru, Grenouilles Grand Cru, Vaudésir Grand Cru, and Montée de Tonnerre Premier Cru.

J. M. MOREAU ET FILS ★★★ $$–$$$$

Clear yet subtle flavors mark these Chablis produced in a modern style by this firm, using all stainless-steel fermentation and no oak. The wines often seem disappointing when young but just need a bit of time to develop. LOOK FOR Chablis Valmur, Les Clos, and Vaillons.

JEAN-MARC BROCARD ★★★ $$–$$$

This producer is a sleeper. Young Brocard's nicely acidic wines have a delicious lemon-cream flavor and strong sense of minerally *terroir*. His Chardonnay Bourgogne sur Kimmeridgien, from a plot 15 meters outside the Chablis boundary, is an awesome bargain. LOOK FOR Chablis Les Clos and Bougros (Grand Crus), Montmains and Fourchaume (Premier Crus), and the aforementioned Chardonnay Kimmeridgien.

LA CHABLISIENNE ★★★ $$–$$$

Cooperative is not necessarily a dirty word. Many cooperatives maintain high standards for their members and produce admirable wine. Founded in 1923, La Chablisienne co-op is responsible for about a third of all the Chablis produced, and most of their wines are remarkably good. LOOK FOR Grand Crus are best, but all wines are at least good.

ADDITIONAL TOP-NOTCH PRODUCERS

Domaine Jean Dauvissat, Jean Defaix, Jean-Paul Droin, Domaine Laroche, Domaine de la Maladière *(William Fèvre)*, Château de Maligny, Albert Pic & Fils, Domaine François and Jean-Marie Raveneau *(very hard to find)*, Verget

BEAUJOLAIS

Vivacious Gamay-based Beaujolais is familiar to everyone as a light, grapey red for picnics and bistro fare. Its fresh cherry and raspberry flavors, refreshing tartness, and mild tannin make it ideal as both an introduction to wine and an everyday sipper. Most Beaujolais is made by the process of carbonic maceration, an anaerobic fermentation that accounts for its fruitiness and gentle tannin. More serious Beaujolais, including many Cru wines, are made by traditional methods, giving them greater body and stronger tannin.

ON THE LABEL

You'll find Beaujolais in four categories:

● **Beaujolais Nouveau** Always released on the third Thursday of November with much marketing hoopla, Nouveau is a pale, delicate version of the better wines to follow. A huge chunk of the output of Beaujolais is sold this way. The wine should be drunk within six months of that November release date. Only the best are worth the price.

● **Beaujolais** Basic Beaujolais that may, by law, come from anywhere within the appellation. In fact, these are mostly very light wines from the sandy soils in the southern part of Beaujolais.

● **Beaujolais-Villages** These wines come from a number of well-regarded villages situated in and around the granite hills in the northern part of the district.

● **Cru Beaujolais** Ten of the best hillside villages have the right to put their names on the label. These are many of best and most individual Beaujolais. The Crus are: Brouilly, Chénas, Chiroubles, Côte de Brouilly, Fleurie, Juliénas, Morgon, Moulin-à-Vent, Régnié, St-Amour.

at the table

When in doubt, order a Beaujolais. It's one of the best food wines anywhere. Beaujolais is good with vegetables (especially bitter greens), with fish steaks, chicken, all but the heartiest meats, practically whatever you name. Though roast chicken and pork are the traditional pairings with Beaujolais, nothing works better with a simple ham sandwich or burger. This fruity red is also a lifesaver with difficult foods, such as hot, spicy dishes or main-dish salads with lots of components. Keep it in mind for the times when she has chicken and he has meat: Beaujolais will bridge the gap.

THE BOTTOM LINE Basic Beaujolais and Beaujolais-Villages range from $7 to $12. Pay the extra dollar for the villages wines. Cru wines from *négociant* houses are rarely distinguishable from their basic bottlings, but those from better growers and small estates offer intriguing values in the $15 to $20 range. Gulp Nouveau just for the sheer fun of it.

PRODUCERS AND THEIR WINES

DOMAINE BERROD   ★★★ $–$$
The fine, deeply colored wines made here can easily be mistaken for top-notch Burgundy. The vines are 40 years old on average, and that shows in the bottle. The wines are made in clean, modern cellars, but the most traditional of techniques are employed. These wines are astonishingly good. LOOK FOR Beaujolais-Villages, Fleurie, and Moulin-à-Vent.

TRENEL FILS   ★★★ $–$$
A small, but very fine producer offering fruity Beaujolais with an extra degree of elegance and harmony. Their Nouveau is definitely one of the best on the market. LOOK FOR Beaujolais-Villages, Chiroubles, Morgon Côte de Py, and Moulin-à-Vent Domaine de la Tour du Bief.

GEORGES DUBOEUF   ★★ $–$$
Duboeuf is the 800-pound gorilla of Beaujolais production, and it is a chest-thumping achievement that this firm makes so much wine so well. The flower-label wines are reliably charming; those bottled under individual estate names are even better, offering a bit more complexity. LOOK FOR Beaujolais-Villages and all other flower-label wines; Fleurie Château des Déduits; Morgons Jean Descombes and Domaine des Versauds; and Moulin-à-Vent Domaine des Rosiers.

LOUIS JADOT   ★★ $–$$
A good, reliable source for sturdy, somewhat dense Beaujolais. Louis Jadot also markets some white Beaujolais made from Chardonnay, and it's quite good. LOOK FOR Beaujolais-Villages, Fleurie, Morgon, Moulin-à-Vent.

ADDITIONAL TOP-NOTCH PRODUCERS
Guy Bréton *(Morgon)*, Château de la Chaize *(Brouilly)*, Louis-Claude Desvignes *(Morgon Côte de Py and Javernières)*, Durdilly *(Beaujolais Nouveau and Beaujolais Les Grandes Coasses)*, Paul Janin *(Moulin-à-Vent)*, Jacky Janodet *(Moulin-à-Vent)*, Château de Juliénas *(Juliénas)*, GAEC René et Christian Miolane *(Beaujolais-Villages)*, Château de Raousset *(Chiroubles, Fleurie, and Morgon)*, Joël Rochette *(Brouilly and Régnié)*, Clos de la Roilette *(Fleurie)*, Michele Tête *(Beaujolais-Villages, Juliénas, and Juliénas Cuvée Prestige)*, Jean-Paul Thévenet *(Morgon Vieilles Vignes)*

LANGUEDOC-ROUSSILLON

Consumers who are shell-shocked by rocketing wine prices, take heart. The sun-baked Languedoc-Roussillon (lahn-guh-doc roo-see-yohn) in the south of France provides a staggering array of good, flavorful wines at almost giddy bargain prices. But it wasn't always so. For centuries, this region was content to produce prodigious amounts of thin, acidic swill that barely qualified as wine. Most of it was destined for distilleries to be turned into industrial alcohol. In 1973, France responded to a national decrease in wine consumption, the demand for better quality, and intense international competition by passing the Vin de Pays reforms. In the Languedoc-Roussillon, these resulted in new financial support that encouraged growers to replant with better varieties and reduce yields. Wineries invested in modern equipment and new oak barrels. Improvements came swiftly, and the region has become one of France's most exciting.

grapes and styles

The red grape Carignan, once the mainstay of the Languedoc, used to go into huge quantities of overly tannic wines that were often totally devoid of charm. Thankfully, this grape is fading in favor of increased plantings of Mourvèdre and particularly Syrah, which is responsible for many of the Languedoc's finest new wines. Carignan is still successful where yields are kept very low or where, as in Corbières, it is made fruity and less tannic by carbonic maceration. Grenache and Cinsaut play minor roles in the Languedoc. Styles of red wines range from easy-drinking, simple blends to powerful, rough-hewn, Syrah- and Mourvèdre-based blockbusters and modern *barrique*-influenced, international-style wines based on Cabernet Sauvignon and Merlot. Best of all, because of the consistently hot climate, vintages matter little; you can buy with confidence most every year.

47

Whites have a tough time in the Languedoc heat. Only recently have new plantings of Sauvignon Blanc, Viognier, and Chardonnay and investments in temperature-controlled, stainless-steel fermentation tanks resulted in worthwhile white wines. A specialty of the Languedoc-Roussillon is its Vins Doux Naturels, heady, sweet, fortified wines from Grenache or Muscat (see page 247). Some tasty rosés are produced, as well.

COTEAUX DU LANGUEDOC

Behind Montpellier and Béziers, and their vast, searing, *vin ordinaire* vineyards, is a line of cool, rocky hills harboring a treasure trove of flavor-packed red wines. This is the Coteaux du Languedoc, and scattered throughout it are 12 Crus whose favorable microclimates have earned them the right to put their own names on their labels. Look especially for Pic-St-Loup, Montpeyroux, La Clape, and La Méjanelle. These wines are typically robust and full-bodied, but finer and with less roasted flavor than many of their peers.

at the table

The modern reds based on Cabernet Sauvignon and Syrah have good tannin, balancing acidity, and a depth of flavor requiring hearty fare. They work well with grilled meats or with vegetables marinated in olive oil, garlic, and Mediterranean herbs. Pair more traditional styles with foods echoing the local dishes of the south of France. Stews of lamb, duck, sausages, and pork, cassoulet, and braised root vegetables all come to mind.

the bottom line You'll feel like the proverbial kid in a candy store when you realize just how many of these excellent wines cost less than $12. Some of them *much* less. The few more expensive wines are generally worth the stretch.

what to buy COTEAUX DU LANGUEDOC

1994	1995	1996	1997	1998
★★★	★★★★	★★★	★★★	★★★★

1996 Mas Mortiès, Pic-St-Loup   ★★★★ $$
What a nose. The essence of garigue—thyme, rosemary, lavender—and spices. This is a big wine, full in alcohol and excitingly wild in flavor.

Spice, garigue, and intense cassis and game flavors evolve into a long, gamy finish with powerful yet velvety tannin. The wine has had just enough bottle age to tame it a bit. A fabulous buy.

1996 Domaine l'Aiguelière, Montpeyroux ★★★ $$

Strong garigue aromas of spices and herbs, especially lavender. Medium bodied with brisk balancing acidity and strong tannin, this wine has wonderful flavors of leather, super-ripe, roasted red fruits, cinnamon, nutmeg, cumin, fennel, and herbs, and a long, spicy finish. Perfectly developed for drinking now.

1997 Domaine Grès St-Paul Cuvée Antonin, Coteaux du Languedoc ★★★ $$

The nose is a beautiful rendition of Syrah's gamy, cassis character. On the palate, the wine is full and has the classic Syrah flavors, which repeat the aromas. Full tannin on the finish.

1997 Mas Champart, St-Chinian ★★★ $$

Dense black color. Aromas of damp earth, crushed blackberries, and damson plums mingle with a gamy Syrah nuance. This beautifully balanced wine has deliciously restrained blackberry, leather, herb and spice flavors. The finish is long and elegant.

1996 Canet Valette, St-Chinian ★★ $$

Nose of oak spice, garigue, and cherries. This wine is full-bodied with flavors of smoky coffee, herbs, and cooked plums. It's concentrated and has an admirably long finish.

1996 Domaine Deshenrys, Coteaux du Languedoc ★★ $$

This has a huge nose of fresh black cherries, lavender, fennel, herbs, and vanilla. It's a very modern-style wine with gobs of fresh cherry fruit, polished tannin, and a generous helping of vanillin oak.

1996 Mas des Chimères, Coteaux du Languedoc ★★ $

This fairly big wine still seems quite young. Its nose of mulberries, vanilla, and forest smells is difficult to discern at this point. The flavors are hidden at first, too, but exposure to air reveals chocolate and plum on the palate, a lush texture, and the balance of flavor, tannin, and alcohol to age well. Give this wine another year, or three.

1998 Château Sainte-Croix le Quatourze, Coteaux du Languedoc ★★ $

Blueberry and blackberry aromas explode in this fruit bomb of a wine, and a rush of blueberry flavor hits the palate. Good tannin on the lengthy finish. This medium-to-full bodied wine is almost too fruity for its own good.

corbières & minervois

Recognition that the Carignan grape benefits from carbonic maceration has led to vast improvement in the wines of Corbières (cor-b'yair) in the last decade. Minervois (mee-nair-v'wah) is the Languedoc's best source for fruity reds. Increasing use of Mourvèdre, Syrah, and new oak has had a positive effect on both wines.

at the table

In general, these are the fruitiest and least tannic wines of the Languedoc, and their fresh-fruit flavors pair well with roasted, rather than grilled, duck, pork, or beef. Their spiciness also complements pâté, ham, and sausage. These same spice notes recall North African preparations of exotically spicy eggplant, zucchini, and tomatoes. Lamb dishes with couscous and Asian curries are inspired matches.

the bottom line Values like Corbières and Minervois won't last forever, but while they do, buy by the case! At $7 to $11 per bottle, maybe you should buy two.

what to buy CORBIÈRES & MINERVOIS

1994	1995	1996	1997	1998
★★★	★★★	★★★	★★	★★★★

1996 Château la Voulte Gasparet, Corbières ★★★ $$
A brawny, leathery, traditionally styled Corbières that sports a nose redolent of spicy garigue and roasted red fruits. Lots of tobacco, cigar-box, vanilla, and spice flavors season the predominant cherry and raspberry, and there's a blast of vanilla on the finish.

1998 Les Deux Rives, Corbières ★★★ $
The attractive nose includes pepper, raspberry, mineral, garigue, and cinnamon. This medium-bodied wine offers understated spice, pepper, berry, and herb flavors. More like a Bordeaux in style than a southern wine. Strong tannin and a long, fruity finish.

1997 Domaine de la Combe Hautes, Minervois ★★ $
An inviting spicy nose. Cherry and prune flavors are accented by those of spices and earth. The wine has a long, fruity finish.

1997 Château d'Oupia, Minervois ★ ★ $
Lovely spice aromas: nutmeg, cinnamon, clove, pepper. Medium bodied with light tannin. Its spicy red-berry and game flavors are delicious.

1998 Château Prat de Cest, Corbières ★ ★ $
This brash and blatantly youthful charmer gushes aromas and flavors of berries and violets. The finish is luscious and spicy.

1997 Château la Baronne Montagne d'Alaric, Corbières ★ $
Has a wonderful, spicy garrigue nose but comes off overwhelmingly tannic on the palate. Still, it has attractive plum, herb, and spice flavors that may develop nicely with another year or two in the bottle.

1997 Domaine Borie de Maurel Syrah, Minervois ★ $
Black-cherry, plum, and vanilla nose, with more of the same following on the palate. This medium-bodied charmer has a good, spicy finish.

1997 Château Pasquier, Corbières ★ $
Cooked cherry on the nose, with smoky coffee, cumin, and faintly sweaty notes lurking beneath. Raspberry flavor leads to a fruity finish.

OTHER WINES OF THE LANGUEDOC-ROUSSILLON

Don't overlook the many other fine wine values from the Languedoc-Roussillon. Fitou was first in the region to gain appellation status (in 1948), but failed to live up to expectations for almost four decades. Since the mid-eighties, it has been a rising star, producing wines similar to those of Corbières. Côtes du Roussillon and Côtes du Roussillon-Villages are excellent sources for full, traditional reds. The obscure Collioure is a powerful, Grenache-based dry red made a stone's throw from the Spanish border. At the eastern end of the Languedoc, the high-quality reds and whites of the Costières de Nîmes put many more prestigious appellations to shame.

Though there are Vins de Pays (VdP) throughout France, the vast majority of VdP wines come from the Languedoc-Roussillon. Varietal labeling; modern, fruity style; good supply; excellent value; and aggressive marketing of large brands have made these hugely popular in the U.S. and elsewhere. At their best, they are the perfect everyday wines. Vin de Pays d'Oc (van duh peh-yee doc) is the designation you'll see most; it covers the entire Languedoc-Roussillon. Others, such as VdP du Gard and VdP de l'Hérault are restricted to smaller areas. A few of the Languedoc's finest wines, Mas de Daumas Gassac for one, are Vin de Pays.

WHITE WINES

1998 Domaine de Coussergues Sauvignon,
Vin de Pays d'Oc ★★ $
The incredible nose exudes aromas of gooseberry, malt, fresh-cut hay, and citrus fruits. It's the best part of this very full-flavored, full-bodied wine in which high alcohol adds a bitter note in the finish. Still a worthwhile bargain.

1998 Delphine de Margon Chardonnay,
Vin de Pays des Côtes de Thongue ★★ $
The wild and pungent nose offers fresh thyme, sweet basil, and other herbs. This is a full-bodied, earthy style with custardy, herbal flavors and a long minerally finish. A good wine, but not for those who demand lush fruit flavors.

1997 Les Jamelles Chardonnay,
Vin de Pays d'Oc ★ $
Nice tropical-fruit nose. Full and smooth tropical-fruit flavors. Medium bodied and refreshing.

1997 Mas de Bressades Roussanne-Viognier,
Vin de Pays du Gard ★ $
This wonderful little bargain has a nose of smoky nuts, apricot, and mango. It's medium bodied and lively, with apricot, nut, and toffee flavors and a fresh, clean finish.

1998 Réserve St-Martin Chardonnay,
Vin de Pays d'Oc ★ $
The pear, apple, and tropical-fruit nose has hints of mineral and mild herbs. This light, delightful wine has refreshing minerality and lively fruitiness on the finish.

RED WINES

1997 Les Clos de Paulilles, Collioure ★★★ $$
Collioure is the southernmost appellation in France. Some Collioures are blockbusters. This one is medium weight and sports a gamy nose full of slightly roasted, but mostly fresh raspberry aromas. Excellent, concentrated raspberry and plum flavors and suave tannin, with no one element overwhelming another.

1997 Château Valcombe, Costières de Nîmes ★★★ $$
Violets, huckleberries, raspberries, black olives, and a note of game on the nose. Concentrated plum and berry flavors with vibrant acidity giving them a boost on the finish.

1997 Cuvée de l'Arjolle Cabernet-Merlot, Vin de Pays d'Oc ★★ $$
The oak-influenced nose has spicy cloves, vanilla, coffee, cassis, and plum aromas. It has a creamy texture and concentrated, succulent cassis and chocolate flavors on the palate and finish.

1997 Domaine de Coussergues Syrah, Vin de Pays d'Oc ★★ $
Textbook southern Syrah nose of peppery spice, cassis, game, and black olives. On the palate, the wine is medium weight and lively with Indian spice and black currant flavors. A long finish.

1998 Château du Donjon Merlot, Vin de Pays d'Oc ★★ $
Blueberry, cherry, and blackberry flavors spurt from this wine as from just-bitten fruit. This Merlot is utterly beguiling.

**1998 Domaine de Gournier Merlot,
Vin de Pay des Cévennes-Uzège** ★★ $
Huge nose of violets, damson plums, and dried herbs. It's full-bodied with sweet, almost jammy blackberry flavors and a nice, tannic finish. A big mouthful of flavor for a very small price!

1997 Le Jaja de Jau Syrah-Grenache, Vin de Pays d'Oc ★★ $
A lovely nose of fresh boysenberries and blackberries nuanced with aromas of game, meat, and spice. Exuberant fruit is beautifully balanced by light tannin. The finish is long and satisfying.

1998 Château de Jau, Côtes du Roussillon-Villages ★★ $
A combination of spice, raspberry, leather, and underbrush graces the nose. This is an elegant, understated wine with the flavors perfectly balanced by tannin and alcohol—a relief after so many of 1998's Languedoc-Roussillon fruit bombs.

**1998 Domaine de la Madeleine Carignan,
Vin de Pays de l'Herault** ★★ $
Intensely concentrated cherry and blackberry aromas, along with herbs, earth, and minerals. The brash fruit flavors and strong tannin indicate that this youthful wine needs time to settle down.

1997 Mas de Bressades, Vin de Pays du Gard ★★ $
Aromas of cassis, green olive, licorice, vanilla, and gamy Syrah notes. Grenache (40 percent) contributes velvety texture and herbal raspberry flavors to the spicy cassis of the Syrah (60 percent). Some slightly charred, woody tannin on the finish, but the wine is still quite pretty.

1998 Réserve St-Martin Syrah, Vin de Pays d'Oc ★★ $
The aromatic and inviting nose is spicy, gamy, and varietally correct. This medium-weight wine is harmonious from beginning to end, with spicy cassis flavor, good tannin, and a smooth finish.

1998 Fortant de France Cabernet Sauvignon, Vin de Pays d'Oc ★ $

A light, simple, and delightfully quaffable Cabernet Sauvignon. It's also easy to find and to afford.

1997 Les Jamelles Merlot, Vin de Pays d'Oc ★ $

A cherry, roast-chestnut, and licorice nose precedes an attractively mellow wine full of cherry-jam and spice flavors. The wine has a hint of pepper in the finish.

1998 Réserve St-Martin Merlot, Vin de Pays d'Oc ★ $

Charming plummy aromas precede a simple wine with light, plummy flavors and surprising length of finish. A mellow, somewhat slight, but elegant little wine.

Loire valley

France's longest river, the Loire covers over 600 miles from its source in the Massif Central to its Atlantic terminus near Nantes. Along the way, it passes through subregions sporting a variety of soils and microclimates. First encountered are the Central Vineyards, famous for their distinctive Sauvignon Blancs from Sancerre and Pouilly-Fumé. Farther west, Touraine is renowned for its Cabernet Franc–based reds and for Vouvrays. Both sweet and dry Chenin Blancs, off-dry rosés, and fruity reds mingle in Anjou-Saumur, while dry Muscadet virtually blankets the Pais Nantais around Nantes.

This bewildering array of wines has two things in common: The Loire's cool climate imbues them with thrilling acidity and vivid fresh-fruit flavors, and the wines are virtually never oaked. These are among the most refreshing wines in the world and the most flexible at the table. And, although much Loire wine is destined for uncritical quaffing, throughout the valley are dedicated artisans, committed to making wines as complex, concentrated, and unique as great wines anywhere.

CHENIN BLANC

Based on its performance in the Loire, Chenin Blanc is considered one of the world's noble white grapes. Here it produces wines in four styles: Sparkling, dry, off-dry, and sweet to very sweet. All have Chenin's honey and flowers flavors and its blazing acidity, which makes them almost immortal. All can be excellent. The unique blue-schist soil of Savennières (sah-ven-yair) yields stony, lemony, dry, and occasionally off-dry wines. Vouvray and Montlouis produce all four styles, depending on the vintage. Vouvray is fruitier and more floral than Savennières; Montlouis is similar to Vouvray, but a bit lighter. Anjou and Touraine are regional appellations that produce simple, inexpensive Chenin Blancs. See page 231 for a discussion of Loire sparkling wines and page 254 for sweet Montlouis, Vouvray, and the luscious wines of the Coteaux du Layon.

ON THE LABEL

The level of sweetness is indicated by the following terms: *Sec* is dry; *demi-sec*, off-dry; *moelleux* means medium sweet to very sweet. *Doux* or *liquoreux* are rarely used terms for very sweet dessert-style wines. If you see none of these terms after the appellation Savennières, it's dry. But if a Vouvray or Montlouis label has no further designation, expect the wine to be made in the slightly off-dry style known as *sec tendre*.

at the table

Young, dry Savennières, Vouvray, and Montlouis make excellent aperitifs and complement mild fresh-water fish beautifully. In the Loire, salmon with *beurre blanc* is *the* match for a mature Savennières; its razor-sharp acidity makes the perfect palate cleanser between bites of the rich fish and richer sauce. Savennières works equally well with other oily fish. Off-dry Vouvray and Montlouis are remarkably good with mild curries, scallops, shrimp, and lobster.

the bottom line Unfashionability keeps a lid on prices. Small growers' Vouvrays offer good value at $15 to $20; those from leaders Foreau and Huet are priced a bit higher. Avoid most *négociant* Vouvrays. Montlouis costs a few dollars less, but you won't come across many. Savennières is one of the great undiscovered white-wine values at $12 to $25. Also look for generic Anjou and Touraine-Azay-le-Rideau.

WHAT TO BUY DRY CHENIN BLANC

1994	1995	1996	1997	1998
★★★	★★★★	★★★★	★★★	★★★

1996 Domaine des Baumards, Savennières ★★★★ $$

This remarkable Savennières sports strong notes of lanolin and beeswax that mingle with yellow plums, peaches, and wet stones. The palate has intense minerality and almost aggressively concentrated stone, quince, peach, and wax flavors. Blazing acidity enhances this polished, suave beauty and makes for a seemingly endless finish.

1995 Domaine de la Roche-aux-Moines, Savennières Becherelle ★★★ $$$

At first sniff, the only aromas are dried herbs, lemon sherbet, pepper, and mineral. Later peach fruitiness emerges. This powerfully acidic wine is not ready now, yet it has oodles of peach and lemon-drop flavors and nuances of bitter almond, herbs, and pepper. It also has a full-bodied, mineral finish. All indications are for a long life in the cellar and excellent development.

1997 Champalou Cuvée des Fondreaux, Vouvray ★★★ $$

The classic nose is an eruption of flowers, spices, peaches, apricots, and honey and brown sugar. The wine starts off-dry with notes of apricots, honey, brown sugar, and oranges but is absolutely dry on the finish due to good balancing acidity. Refreshing now, it will also age well.

1997 François Pinon Cuvée Tradition, Vouvray ★★★ $

Pinon's Cuvée Tradition is normally rather dry, but, because of the especially ripe grapes from the 1997 harvest, it is almost a demi-sec in this vintage. Huge aromas of apricot, kirsch, banana, and beeswax are entrancing. Sweet but with vibrant balancing acidity. Very full-flavored and very delicious.

1998 Domaine Bourillon Dorléans La Coulée d'Argent Vieilles Vignes, Vouvray ★★ $$

The aromas are classic—peach, flowers, and beeswax. Hints of nuts and spices on the finish. This particularly pleasant wine has just enough acidity to enhance its flavor.

1997 Marc Brédif, Vouvray ★★ $

The somewhat generic nose of peach and banana belies what's to come: a surprisingly sophisticated off-dry wine with perfect acid-sugar balance and understated flavors of peach, tangerine, lemon, and a bit of spice. It has a long finish, too.

MUSCADET

Light, refreshing, and moderately acidic, with subtle apple, nut, yeast, and mineral flavors, Muscadets (mus-cah-day) are fascinating wines. They are widely thought of as screachingly tart, but good Muscadets are well-balanced. Though vast swaths of mechanized vineyards produce oceans of supermarket swill, it is humbling to meet artisinal Muscadet growers who take their winemaking as seriously as anyone. Their finest bottles display the superb quality and endless variation in *terroir* characteristics (see page 17) associated with all great wines.

ON THE LABEL

The best wines include the words *sur lie* on the label, indicating that they were aged on their lees (dead yeasts). *Sur lie* aging adds a slight sparkle, protects against oxidation, and imparts a nutty, yeasty taste. The designation *Sèvre-et-Maine* attests that the wine came from the best part of the Muscadet region.

at the table

Raw oysters and Muscadet are classic, although in the Pais Nantais, oysters are served with the lighter, fruitier, and wincingly acidic Gros Plant. Muscadet partners steamed langoustines (crayfish), sole meunière, and other mild ocean- and river-fish dishes. Salads, crudités, and grilled vegetables all are lovely with Muscadet. And it's fine alone as a charming, light aperitif.

the bottom line   At $8 to $12, the best Muscadets deliver excellent value.

1997 Luc Choblet Clos de la Sénaigerie, Muscadet   ★ ★ ★ ★ $
The reticent nose has a delightful hint of Scotch whisky, of all things. This is a superb Muscadet. Brisk, minerally, and lively on the palate. Complex and concentrated apple, yeast, and mineral flavors carry through to a persistent finish.

1997 Domaine Brégeon Sur Lie, Muscadet de Sèvre-et-Maine   ★ ★ ★ $
A wonderfully harmonious Muscadet with a nose of minerals, yeast, and fresh pears. A touch of spritz enlivens the full, but perfectly balanced flavors. Snappy acidity and focused mineral and fruit flavors make this perfect for oysters.

1997 Clos des Briords Sur Lie Vieilles Vignes, Muscadet de Sèvre-et-Maine ★ ★ ★ $

Apples and pears mingle with minerals and hints of red fruits in the nose. Mellow and smooth with fruit and nut flavors and a hint of strawberry on the minerally finish. Another surprisingly full-bodied Muscadet from the 1997 vintage.

1998 Domaine les Hautes Noëlles Sur Lie, Muscadet Côtes de Grandlieu ★ ★ ★ $

Breezy mineral and green-apple aromas. Understated, lively apple, mineral, and herb flavors are wonderfully refreshing and surprisingly elegant. A very sophisticated Muscadet.

1997 Luneau-Papin Clos des Allées Sur Lie Vieilles Vignes, Muscadet de Sèvre-et-Maine ★ ★ ★ $

This outsize Muscadet has the weight of a white Burgundy, yet is perfectly balanced by bracing acidity. Its nose and flavors of apple, pear, almond, and mineral are clear and full leading to a long, complex finish.

1997 Marquis de Goulaine Sur Lie, Muscadet de Sèvre-et-Maine ★ ★ $

Aromas and flavors of nectarines, white grapes, yeast, and minerals in this textbook Muscadet. Much more concentrated than their white-label bottling and worth the extra dollar or two.

SAUVIGNON BLANC

The upper Loire Valley's cool climate and rolling hills produce some of the world's greatest Sauvignon Blancs. Sancerre and Pouilly-Fumé (poo-yee foo-may; no relation to Pouilly-Fuissé) are brisk, bracing white wines, immediately appealing for their mouthwatering citrus, gooseberry, herb, and fresh-cut grass aromas and flavors. In general, Sancerre is fruitier and tarter, Pouilly-Fumé, fuller bodied and more mineral in character. Both are for drinking young, but top wines from good sites can benefit from a year or two of cellaring. Look to Menetou-Salon, just west of Sancerre, for light, mineral Sauvignon Blancs, and further west to Quincy (can-see) for peachy, lower-acid versions.

ON THE LABEL

Sancerre's fruitiest wines are from the *commune* of Chavignol (one of 14 in Sancerre) , which has the right to put its name on the label. Also look for single-vineyard sites such as Les Monts Damnés, Clos du Chêne Marchand, and La Grande Côte.

at the table

We may drink more Loire Sauvignon Blancs with our meals than any other wine. They are perfect for the light cuisine we eat—right before the triple-chocolate cake. Field greens with warm goat cheese is made for Loire Sauvignon. Vegetables and herbs are naturals, and this is one of the few wines that can handle asparagus. Light, white fish, simply sautéed with lemon and capers or baked with herbs, chicken paillard with herbs and mustard, and shellfish, are all superb with Sauvignon. It makes a great aperitif, too.

THE BOTTOM LINE At their best, Sancerre and Pouilly-Fumé are among the finest Sauvignon Blancs in the world and deserve their $12 to $20 price tags. Unfortunately, there is all too much high-yield, thin junk not worth half that price. Quincy, and especially the up-and-coming Menetou-Salon, provide excellent, cheaper alternatives.

1998 Pascal Jolivet, Sancerre ★★★★ $$

The spectacularly penetrating nose of asparagus, citrus, and malt makes this a dead ringer for a New Zealand Sauvignon Blanc. Full and concentrated; yet brisk acidity keeps it refreshing. It wakes up the palate with grapefruit, lemon, and grassy flavors. Very long finish.

1997 Paul Thomas Chavignol Les Comtesses, Sancerre ★★★★ $$

A sophisticated, powerful, and complex wine that dishes up very full aromas and flavors of melons, figs, herbs, yellow plums, citrus, and caramel. They unfold slowly and seductively on a very long and intense finish.

1997 Thomas-Labaille Chavignol Les Monts Damnés, Sancerre ★★★★ $$

Aromas of peach, citrus, grass, mineral, and an intriguing hint of root beer. A huge Sancerre, balanced with ample acidity. The wine boasts an almost endless finish.

1998 Alain Cailbourdin les Cris, Pouilly-Fumé ★★★ $$

The very subtle nose hints at lemon and sage. And the full-bodied wine's citrus and mineral flavors open up slowly as the wine airs. This is a Sauvignon Blanc that will benefit from a year or two of cellaring.

1998 Domaine de Chatenoy, Menetou-Salon ★★★ $$

Aromas of pears, minerals, herbs, and pepper and a smoky, flinty note. The wine has remarkable minerality and vivacious acidity. A terrific wine whose flavors and impact persist on a long finish.

1998 Dauny Terres Blanches, Sancerre ★★★ $$
The classic but very full aromas include gooseberry, mineral, peach, and spice. Lovely tangy fruit flavors resolve into a smooth but lively finish. Big for a Sancerre, with just enough acid to keep it in balance.

1997 de Ladoucette, Pouilly-Fumé ★★★ $$
Good stuff! Right now the minerally, grapefruity nose is weak, but the palate shows excellent concentration. Refreshing, subtle citrus flavors, medium body, and a long finish.

1997 Régis Minet Vieilles Vignes, Pouilly-Fumé ★★★ $$
A big Sauvignon, with 13 percent alcohol and intense mineral and limestone flavors. At present, this young wine has more sheer palate impact than flavor, but it should bloom into something special with another six months to a year in the cellar.

1998 Jean Reverdy Vignoble la Reine Blanche, Sancerre ★★★ $$
Aggressive herbal, grapefruit, asparagus, and grass aromas. Full-bodied and lively. Very good, but not a fruity style. Flavors lean toward citrus pith, herbs, and grass.

1998 Hervé Seguin, Pouilly-Fumé ★★★ $$
Inviting lemon-lime aromas accented with the signature Pouilly-Fumé smoke and flint nuances. This medium-bodied wine's vibrant, lemonadelike quality and focused minerality make it particularly delicious.

1998 Domaine du Salvard, Cheverny ★★★ $
A little beauty with aromas of cut grass, hay, and gooseberries and vivacious citrus, gooseberry, hay, and mineral flavors. Full, yet bracing, amazingly long finish—make this your house Sauvignon!

1997 F. Tinel-Blondelet L'Arret Buffatte, Pouilly-Fumé ★★ $$
An unusual oaked style of Pouilly-Fumé. Vanilla and dill pickle aromas dominate the nose and remain to affect the melon and herbal flavors. Very good if you like the style.

1998 Domaine de Corbillières, Sauvignon de Touraine ★★ $
The beautiful fresh nose is very herbal, with lime, pear, and grass aromas. The palate is light bodied and zesty with lime zest, asparagus, mineral, and herb flavors and a lovely silky texture.

1998 Jean Tatin Domaine du Tremblay, Quincy ★★ $
Ample nose of peach, pear, white grapes, and limes. A very smooth and full wine; a mineral whiplash comes on strong in the finish .

CABERNET FRANC

The reds of the middle Loire get no respect. Writer after writer damns them with faint praise, likening them to Beaujolais. Rubbish! These medium-bodied reds have a complex perfume of strawberries, herbs, and bitter cherries; light tannin; and vibrant acidity that make them spectacular with food. They can mature for decades, retaining their fruit flavors and developing seductive tobacco and cedar tones. Wines from single-vineyard sites can be formidable. In general, Chinon is less tannic and earthier than St-Nicolas-de Bourgueil or Bourgueil, while Saumur-Champigny is the most frankly fruity.

on the Label

Almost every grower bottles a young vine (Jeune Vignes) *cuvée* and a Cuvée du Domaine, both of which are made for immediate imbibing. The best wines, made for aging, are from single-vineyard sites such as La Grande Vignolle (Saumur-Champigny), Grand Mont and Beauvais (Bourgueil), and Clos de l'Echo, Clos du Chêne Vert, and Les Picasses (Chinon).

at the table

Next time you're thinking Bordeaux, reach for a Loire red instead. Red meat is an obvious companion. Also try sausages or cold salads with shredded duck or lamb. The unobtrusive tannin of these Cabernet Francs will support poultry, like roasted or sautéed chicken or quail, that the more aggressive Bordeaux would overwhelm. Mild cow's-milk cheeses of the Loire and Brittany make winning matches as well.

the Bottom Line Does the word *bargain* get your juices flowing? How about *steal*? Young-vine wines and Domaine *cuvées* at $10 to $15 and top-vineyard wines at most around $25 put Loire Cabernet Francs among the best red-wine buys. In addition to value, there is some amazing quality in these bottles.

what to buy CABERNET FRANC

1994	1995	1996	1997	1998
★★	★★★★	★★★★	★★★	★★★

1997 Charles Joguet Clos du Chêne Verte, Chinon   ★★★★ $$$
Awesome aromas of sandalwood, cinnamon, nutmeg, red fruits, and leather are almost overwhelming. A concentrated, sensuously spicy masterpiece boasting an almost endless finish. Extraordinary.

1997 Domaine de Roche Neuves Terres Chaudes, Saumur-Champigny
★★★★ $$

Pungent red-berry and wild-animal aromas. Obvious new oak, but the wine has the concentrated fruit to stand up to it. The long, succulently fruity finish has velvety tannin and strong gamy nuances.

1996 Couly-Dutheil Clos de l'Echo, Chinon
★★★ $$

Aromas of strawberries, leather, underbrush, just-chopped herbs, and tobacco. The concentrated flavor of this medium-bodied wine is now subdued, with the tannin and acid holding sway. History shows that this wine blossoms beautifully with five to eight years of age.

1997 Taluau Cuvée du Domaine, St-Nicolas-de-Bourgueil
★★★ $$

Tremendous Cabernet Franc nose of strawberries, raspberries, and fresh herbs. Full of succulent fruit flavors, with persistent nutmeg and cinnamon on the finish.

1997 Domaine de la Chanteleuserie, Bourgueil
★★ $$

Earthy nose with smoky overtones. The flavors are plum and black cherry with a hint of bell pepper. A brawny wine with rambunctious tannin and a strong, earthy finish. It needs a few years to calm down.

1998 Clos Roche Blanche Cabernet de Touraine
★★ $

Aromas of violets, raspberry, and herbs. Focused fruit flavors are held in check by dry tannin. The long, fruity finish hints at more to come with time. Give this a year or two.

PROVeNCe

Paris•

PROVENCE

The playground of Europe's rich and famous, revered for its blazing beaches and azure sea, Provence is also home to some delightfully sunny wines. Infused with the scent of the ubiquitous fennel-and-herb-scented scrub known as garigue, these spicy, full-bodied reds and rosés offer a tantalizing taste of Provence's warm, laid-back life style.

Grapes and styles

The traditional grapes of southern France, Cinsaut, Carignan, and Grenache, are the foundation of most Provençal reds and rosés. However, Bandol, its one true great red, is made from at least 50 percent Mourvèdre, and modern-style wines usually have a measure of Cabernet Sauvignon and Syrah. Traditional whites tend to tire and oxidize easily, but the Rolle grape is proving successful at producing fresher-tasting wines.

BANDOL

Southeast of Marseilles and a few miles inland, a 900-hectare amphitheater spreads to the sun like a beachgoer's reflector. The late-ripening Mourvèdre flourishes here, producing full, long-lived wines redolent of Provençal garigue, spice, smoked meat, and black fruits. Provençal poets of the 18th century called Bandol bottled sunshine, and, 200 years later, it is still Provence's, and perhaps southern France's, finest red wine.

at the table

The Mourvèdre in Bandol gives it a smoked-meat note, an earthy-mineral bite, and assertive tannin that demand boldly flavored, rich foods. Try grilled leg of lamb rubbed with garlic and herbes de Provence, smoked ham, barbecued spareribs, and duck, goose, or pork confit. The gamy flavors often present in Bandol complement venison, wild boar, and other wild meats.

the bottom line

Bandols are not easy to find, but when you do, don't balk at the $20 to $30 price tag. Considering their quality and ability to develop complexity with age, the cost is more than fair.

what to buy BANDOL

1994	1995	1996	1997	1998
★ ★ ★	★ ★ ★	★ ★ ★	★ ★ ★	★ ★ ★ ★

1995 Domaines Bunan Mas De La Rouvière   ★ ★ ★ ★ $$
A big, full-bodied, predominately Mourvèdre wine with great fruit flavor combined with an intriguing earthiness. Aromas and flavors of lavender, rosemary, and baked stones. Lush, yet elegant. Stunning.

1997 Château de Pibarnon ★ ★ ★ ★ $$

About 90 percent Mourvèdre, a brilliant wine with lots of garigue and berry aromas. Huge, packed with velvety tannin and concentrated black currant and cherry flavors. Good now, it can develop well for decades.

1996 La Bastide-Blanche ★ ★ ★ $$

Mourvèdre makes up 50 percent of this wine; there's also a large helping of Grenache. Wonderfully varied aromas and flavors of blackberries, fur, violets, and lavender are overridden by tannin but will emerge with time. A rustic, unfiltered wine with game and stone notes in the finish.

OTHER RED PROVENÇAL WINES

Côtes de Provence, Coteaux d'Aix-en-Provence, and Coteaux d'Aix-en-Provence-les-Baux are the three generic appellations extending from just west of Marseilles to Cannes in the east. Scattered in their hilly, relatively cool microclimates are literally hundreds of quality-conscious *vignerons* producing some of France's most astonishing bargains. Traditional blends are interspersed with those sporting hefty doses of Cabernet Sauvignon and Syrah.

at the table

Cooler climates make these fruitier, more acidic, and less tannic than Bandols. A classic Provence pairing is chicken grilled over grapevine cuttings and dried fennel. No grapevine cuttings? Spicy roast chicken or simple mixed grills are also fine. With mature Provençal wines, the ambitious will want to try the likes of a Moroccan chicken-and-olive-based tagine or a lamb and prune stew spiced with cinnamon and cloves.

the bottom line Shop with confidence. Values abound from $10 to $20.

what to buy OTHER RED WINES

1994	1995	1996	1997	1998
★★★	★★★	★★★	★★★	★★★★

1995 Domaine Richeaume Cabernet Sauvignon, Côtes de Provence ★ ★ ★ $$$

A powerful wine with loads of black pepper on the nose along with black fruits, perfume, and rosemary. Notes of damp earth and wet fur make for a powerful mélange on the palate. Not for the faint of heart.

1996 Domaine Sorin, Côtes de Provence ★ ★ ★ $$

An explosion of fruity blackberry aromas presages the jammy blackberry and black-currant flavors. A last minute dose of tannin in the finish saves this from becoming cloying.

1997 Château de Roquefort la Poulpae,
Côtes de Provence ★ ★ $$

Still has a lots sulfur to absorb; it needs time in the cellar. The animal aroma suggests a lot of Syrah. Big, concentrated and intensely packed with cassis and garigue flavors; should blossom with time.

1993 Terres Blanches,
Coteaux d'Aix-en-Provence-les Baux ★ ★ $$

The blend of Grenache, Cinsaut, Mourvèdre, Cabernet Sauvignon, Counoise, and Syrah, all organically grown, gives this wine a plethora of varied fruit and spice aromas. A bit light on the palate with some notes of green olives, and a slightly abrupt, earthy finish.

1997 Château Routas Carignan, Coteaux Varois ★ ★ $

This is a lovely wine that's very Pinot Noir–like both in its pale purple-ruby color and in its light-bodied elegance. It finishes with a firm nip of tannin.

ROSÉ PROVENÇAL WINES

U.S. consumers have given rosés a bum rap, but Europeans know rosés are refreshing and extremely versatile with a wide array of foods. Rosés from Provence are fuller-bodied and drier than most of the world's pink wines. Drink them young while their delicate red-fruit flavors are still vibrant and fresh.

at the table

The many fish and shellfish soups and stews of the Mediterranean virtually demand Provençal rosés. The wines' acidity also allows them to stand up to rich or oily foods, such as fried calamari, brandade, chowders, and bisques. With their berrylike fruit flavors and earthy notes, they pair well with eggplant dishes, such as ratatouille and caponata, pasta with vegetables, grilled poultry, and pork. Don't forget salads and simple summertime lunches. Rosés also make perfect aperitifs

the bottom line When many consumers think pink, they think cheap. But these are serious wines, and the good ones are worth every penny of the $12 to $20 they cost.

1998 Domaines Ott Cuvée Marine, Bandol   ★ ★ ★ $$

Pale orange. This gutsy full-bodied, high-alcohol rosé tilts more toward powerful earth and mineral flavors than berrylike fruit. It takes a bit of time to open, but when it does it is superb.

1998 Château de Roquefort Corail, Côtes de Provence   ★ ★ ★ $

Pale cherry pink. Aromas of wild strawberries and hints of refreshing mint. Very fruity strawberry, raspberry flavors in a lively, medium-bodied package. Mint comes again on the lightly tannic finish.

1998 Domaine Sorin, Côtes de Provence   ★ ★ $$

A rosé with an enticing nose of black pepper, herbs, and raspberries and with lovely flavors of pepper, raspberries, and cherries. Spicy and refreshing.

RHÔNe valley

The northern and southern Rhône differ in almost every aspect, including soil, climate, grape varieties grown, and production methods used. Not surprisingly, the wines are very different as well. In fact, many experts consider the Rhône Valley to be two separate regions. One common denominator is that the Rhône Valley produces some of France's most robust and long-lived wines.

NORTHERN RHÔNE
RED WINES

In the north, steeply sloping, terraced vineyards on granite soil tower above the Rhône River. Here, in this narrow gorge, the noble Syrah ripens to yield tiny quantities of extraordinary wines. On the Rhône's steepest and warmest sites, Syrah reaches its zenith in the legendary wines of Côte-Rôtie, Cornas, and Hermitage. These are among our favorite wines in all of France.

GRAPES AND STYLES

● **Côte-Rôtie** is ravishingly aromatic, due in part to the addition of up to 20 percent of the white grape Viognier. The finest Côte-Rôties are silky textured with velvety tannin and a complex bouquet of black currants, flowers, pepper, and bacon fat. Côte-Rôtie translates as *roasted slope*.

● **Cornas** wines are 100 percent Syrah. Cornas (literally *scorched earth*) have more mouth-puckering tannin and fuller body than either Côte-Rôtie or Hermitage, and their flavors and aromas run to black cherry, spice, leather, and olives. They also need time to mellow.

● **Hermitage** If one had to construct a world-class vineyard from scratch, it would probably look like the great hill of Hermitage. Its perfect southern exposure produces massive but suave wines that were once known (before political correctness) as France's most masculine. Good Hermitage requires 10 to 20 years of cellaring to develop its multifaceted flavors of cassis and black plum augmented by notes of black pepper, anise, and roasted meat. Hermitage may contain up to 15 percent white grapes, but rarely does.

● **St-Joseph** and **Crozes-Hermitage** produce lighter wines that can be drunk earlier as the result of sandy soils, shorter fermentations, and widespread use of carbonic maceration. Crozes-Hermitage is often called baby Hermitage, but with rare exceptions, the resemblance is in name only.

AT THE TABLE

When they're young, Côte-Rôtie, Cornas, and Hermitage require robust foods to mellow their substantial tannin. Serve Côte-Rôtie with grilled meats, wild birds, and other game. Hermitage makes the perfect accompaniment to rare beef, lamb, and venison, while the earthier Cornas shines with stews and meats braised in red wine. They're all excellent foils to hard, sharp cheeses. As these wines shed their tannin and become more complex with age, serve them with plain grilled or roasted meats and softer, milder cheeses. Enjoy the lighter St-Joseph and Crozes-Hermitage with simple veal, pork, and turkey dishes, barbecued pork, and burgers.

THE BOTTOM LINE The northern Rhône accounts for a mere 5 percent of the Rhône's total production. There are just 200 producing hectares in Côte-Rôtie, and in a good year all of Hermitage may yield only as much wine as a single large

Bordeaux château. Because of that, along with the overall high quality of these wines, prices ranging from $30 to $65 for top wines look pretty good, especially when compared with those of other major regions. St-Joseph and Crozes-Hermitage can deliver excellent value at $12 to $20, if you stick to the best producers.

what to buy RED WINES

1994	1995	1996	1997	1998
★ ★ ★	★ ★ ★ ★	★ ★ ★	★ ★ ★	★ ★ ★

1997 Jean-Luc Colombo Les Ruchets, Cornas ★ ★ ★ ★ $$$
Made from ungrafted vines that are nearly 100 years old and aged in 70 percent new-oak barrels. Aromas of Indian spices, raspberries, cassis, and cocoa powder. Concentrated, polished, and elegant yet with a sub-tle, earthy edge of Cornas *terroir*. Its finish is quite long. This wine needs at least 10 years' aging.

1995 E. Guigal Brune et Blonde, Côte-Rôtie ★ ★ ★ ★ $$$
The classic cassis, green-olive, bacon-fat, and vanilla oak aromas are graced with hints of herbs and pepper. This elegant wine is full-flavored but restrained and has both a silky texture and an almost endless, gamy finish. It's a superb wine for the cellar, but it's so delicious now that you may not be able to keep your hands off it long enough for it to mature.

1997 Paul Jaboulet Aîné La Chapelle, Hermitage ★ ★ ★ $$$$
The nose is full of cassis and black olives along with, oddly for a La Chapelle, a strong aroma of coconut. The wine is concentrated, with mint, raspberry, and black-currant flavors. This La Chapelle is polished but unusually oaky. It usually needs 10 to 15 years to develop its potential, so time will tell.

1996 Domaine Jean-Michel Gerin Champin le Seigneur, Côte-Rôtie ★ ★ ★ $$$
Violet, cassis, and spicy oak aromas. There is great concentration of red- and black-fruit flavors, resulting in an elegant, succulent wine. The silky, voluptuous texture is its most beguiling feature. Drink now or hold for up to 10 years.

1997 Paul Jaboulet Aîné Domaine de Thalabert, Crozes-Hermitage ★ ★ ★ $$
The nose is classic: berry, cassis, game, tar, and green olive. This full-bodied wine is balanced with lively acidity and good tannin in the finish. Perfect Syrah—tangy and full flavored yet polished. It will improve for a decade.

to oak OR NOT to oak?

Two decades ago, Marcel Guigal brought new *barriques* to the northern Rhône. His stunning success with his markedly oaky, single-vineyard Côte-Rôties was a shock to many of the vintners in the region. The battle is still raging between traditionalists who feel oak has no place in Syrah and those, like Guigal and Jean-Luc Colombo in Cornas, who champion its use. Today you will find as many vanilla-scented, fruity, modern-style wines as you will more *terroir*-driven (see page 17), slow-developing traditional ones.

1996 Michel Ogier Cuvée Syrah La Rosine, Vin de Pays des Collines Rhodaniennes ★ ★ ★ $$

This is an aggressively gamy Syrah with strong bacon-fat and black-pepper aromas. Despite its humble category, Vin de Pays, it is a concentrated wine with full gamy flavors and some sharp acidity that quickly mellows as the wine sits in the glass. Three to five years in the bottle will do it wonders.

1998 Jean-Luc Colombo Les Forots, Côtes-du-Rhône ★ ★ ★ $

An unusual Côtes-du-Rhône made from 100 percent Syrah grown in Cornas. A big wine, with intense aromas of cassis, blueberries, and violets. On the palate, there's a taste of cocoa powder with subtle, gamy undertones. The wine is powerful, yet polished and elegant. This one needs time.

1996 Albert Belle Cuvée Louis Belle, Crozes-Hermitage ★ ★ $$

Lots of berry and violet aromas. A velvety texture and oaky vanilla flavors. There's a hint of pepper on the long finish. A nice, straightforward wine.

1997 Domaine les Chenets, Crozes-Hermitage ★ ★ $$

Full red-berry nose with some herbal, peppery notes. Light-to-medium bodied with good balance of flavor, acidity, and light tannin. It has a good long finish.

1996 Pierre Gonon, St-Joseph ★ ★ $$

A nose of strong, gamy aromas mingled with herbal notes. Succulent, with concentrated cooked berry, game, and black-olive flavors and prominent balancing acidity. The finish is long with flavors of leather, cassis, and violets. The gamy component may be a bit extreme for some.

SOUTHERN RHÔNE RED WINES

The Rhône river bursts free of the Alps' foothills below Valence and fans out onto the vast, sun-baked plain of the south. Its rocky, alluvial soils are home to a bewildering array of grapes, which go into wines that are generous and earthy. They have a deep, roasted-raspberry flavor along with peppery, herbal overtones—and, often, head-spinning alcohol. Of all Rhône wines, the south produces 95 percent, and 95 percent of that is red.

Châteauneuf-du-Pape is the most famous appellation of the southern Rhône and has the highest minimum alcohol requirement, 12.5 percent, of any wine in France. Many Châteauneuf-du-Papes easily top 15 percent. Yet their dense texture and full fruit flavors balance the alcohol, giving an impression of sweetness that makes even the 15 percenters appealing in their youth. Some Châteauneuf-du-Papes are made in a simpler style for early drinking, but the best develop magnificently over a decade or two.

grapes and styles

Most southern Rhône wines are blends based on Grenache. Grenache provides the raspberry and herbal flavors, but its high alcohol, low acidity, and tendency to oxidize mean that, unless held to ridiculously low yields, it needs help from other grapes to make balanced wines. The late-ripening Mourvèdre adds powerful tannin and a deep, meaty flavor; Syrah, acidity, intense cassis flavor, and subtle gamy notes. Use of these highly regarded grapes is on the rise, while Cinsaut, the traditional blending grape, is declining in popularity. Styles range from simple, grapey Beaujolais Nouveau–style Côtes-du-Rhônes and Côtes-du-Rhônes Villages to the lusty blockbusters from Châteauneuf-du-Pape. Among Crus other than Châteauneuf-du-Pape, Vacqueyras and Gigondas are also big, strapping wines, full and tannic on the palate with lush fruit flavors. Gigondas is a shade more mellow; Vacqueyras, slightly rustic and more tannic.

on the LabeL

You will find four basic classifications of southern Côtes-du-Rhône reds:

● **Côtes-du-Rhône** The basic wine of the southern Rhône, it accounts for 80 percent of the bottles of wine produced in this region.

● **Côtes-du-Rhône Villages** A total of 16 villages in the best parts of the southern Rhône have earned the right to this title by making better than basic wines. They may be labeled simply Côtes-du-Rhône Villages, indicating a blend from some or all of the villages, or they may carry a particular village name. This category can be a stepping stone to Cru status. Gigondas was elevated to its own appellation in 1971, and Vacqueyras followed in 1990. Cairanne is widely considered to be next in line for promotion.

● **Crus** These are the great appellations of the southern Rhône, led by the well-known Châteauneuf-du-Pape. They include Gigondas and Vacqueyras and the lesser-known Lirac and Tavel.

● **Satellite Appellations** Côtes du Lubéron, Côtes du Ventoux, and Coteaux du Tricastin flank the official southern Côtes-du-Rhône zone, and these areas produce similar wines that cost less.

at the table

Drink these quintessential Mediterranean wines with Mediterranean cuisines. Pair them with southern French dishes redolent of garlic, onions, leeks, and herbs. Tunisian couscous with *merguez* sausage, Turkish lamb kabobs, and Spanish paella are all exciting matches. The lighter Côtes-du-Rhônes and satellite wines cry out for burgers, barbecues, and beach parties. Maturing wines marry well with earthy wild mushrooms.

the bottom Line Southern Côtes-du-Rhône reds represent tremendous value with prices starting as low as $7. A new trend in Châteauneuf-du-Pape has many winemakers producing both a regular wine and a luxury *cuvée*. The problem is that the best juice is skimmed off for the costlier wine, robbing the regular *cuvée*. Therefore, at $25 to $35, regular Châteauneuf-du-Pape is no longer the compelling bargain it used to be. Some of the luxury *cuvées* can justify their $50 and up price tags, but beware. Many fall short. At $20 to $25, Gigondas take the prize as the most consistent wines and best values in the southern Rhône.

what to buy RED WINES

1995	1996	1997	1998
★★★★	★★	★★★	★★★★

1997 Domaine de Beaurenard Cuvée Boisrenard, Châteauneuf-du-Pape ★ ★ ★ ★ $$$

The nose is not yet aromatic. On the palate, however, this modern-style blockbuster already has intense fruit and spice flavors. The lively finish is superlong.

1995 Domaine les Paillières, Gigondas ★ ★ ★ ★ $$$

A blockbuster, but the aromas are not yet forthcoming. On the palate, the wine is spicy, with concentrated plum flavor and huge tannin. The finish is long and viscous. To reach its potential, the wine needs at least another five years.

1997 Domaine de Cayron, Gigondas ★ ★ ★ ★ $$

What an exciting bouquet this wine has: Violet, lavender, and raspberry aromas are accented by earthy, briary, minerally notes. The wonderfully concentrated fruit flavors easily balance the 14 percent alcohol. The finish offers Hungarian spices, good tannin, and astonishing length.

1996 Domaine de la Ferme St-Martin Cuvée Font de la Borry, Côtes-du-Rhône ★ ★ ★ ★ $$

A four-star Côtes-du-Rhône? You bet! Seductive dried violets, Indian spices, rosemary, and roasted raspberries combine in the wildly complex aromas. The flavors dance and unfold in skeins of fruits and spices. The wine is densely flavored yet seems light on the palate, proving great balance. To top it all off, the wine has a virtually endless, nicely fruity finish.

1996 Domaine Le Sang des Cailloux, Vacqueyras ★ ★ ★ ★ $$

A beautifully harmonious nose of plum, anise, pepper, and violets. The succulent plum, leather, and spice flavors are full yet admirably restrained. The wine is concentrated and has strong tannin. A gorgeous specimen.

1996 Château des Tours Réserve, Vacqueyras ★ ★ ★ ★ $$

Lots of pepper and dried spices—nutmeg, cinnamon, cumin—and roasted raspberry aromas jostle for attention in the untamed nose. A massive Vacqueyras, but all that flavor, tannin, and alcohol are in balance. The finish is spicy, long, and a bit wild. Terrific old-style Rhône at its blockbuster best.

1997 Château du Trignon, Gigondas ★ ★ ★ ★ $$

The nose of blackberry and violets is brightened by a note of lemon—like a squeeze on a fresh fruit salad. There's even a hint of gamy Syrah in the nose as well. This thrilling wine has black-raspberry flavor, velvety tannin, and seamless harmony of these elements with its acidity and alcohol content.

1997 Domaine du Galet des Papes Vieilles Vignes, Châteauneuf-du-Pape
★★★ $$$

Tobacco, raspberry, plum, and lavender aromas. Extremely concentrated flavors on the palate, with just a hint of pruney over ripeness. A massive, old-style wine that resembles a raspberry, prune, chocolate cordial seasoned with black pepper. It's superb.

1997 Les Hautes de Montmirail, Gigondas
★★★ $$$

Super-ripe berries on the nose. A modern, fruit-driven, international-style wine with lots of spicy fruitiness shot through with vanilla-oak flavors. An impressive and delicious red wine, but not one that has much Rhône character.

1997 Clos du Mont Olivet, Châteauneuf-du-Pape
★★★ $$

Dusty, earthy nose of licorice, raspberry, plum, and spice. Velvety texture with flavors of cinnamon, clove, garigue, and leather. A medium-bodied wine. Strong but velvety tannin and a long, spicy, earthy finish. A delicious, old-style Châteauneuf-du-Pape.

1997 Clos de l'Oratoire des Papes, Châteauneuf-du-Pape
★★★ $$

Spice and garigue aromas with a slight barnyard note thrown in. The raspberry flavor is not so roasted in character, nor is the alcohol content so high, as in many of the 1997 Châteauneuf-du-Papes. This is a medium-weight wine, with lively acidity and fruitiness in the finish.

1997 Château des Tours Réserve, Côtes-du-Rhône
★★★ $$

Scents of baked stones, roasted raspberries, and wild garigue along with an animal note. The raspberry, spice, and game flavors are intensely concentrated and complex, and the tannin strong and dry. A powerful, full-bodied wine, not for the faint of heart.

1996 J. Vidal Fleury, Côtes-du-Rhône
★★★ $

This is textbook, traditionally styled Côtes-du-Rhône offering perfectly balanced aromas and flavors of berries, herbs, spices, and a dash of intangible excitement. The venerable *négociant* house of Vidal Fleury was recently purchased by Guigal, but we prefer this wine to the Guigal offering.

1998 Domaine L'Ameillaud, Vin de Pays de Vaucluse
★★ $

Spicy plum, raspberry, and game nose. Nicely balanced flavors of raspberry, spice, and garigue. This lovely little wine finishes with good tannin.

1997 Domaine de la Janasse, Côtes-du-Rhône ★ ★ $
This monster Côtes-du-Rhône has a huge nose of fruit, spice, leather, and earth along with a blast of alcohol. It's full-flavored as well, with big raspberry and black-cherry flavors and leathery overtones. A strong, tannic finish.

1996 Michel Picard, Côtes-du-Rhône ★ ★ $
Roasted-raspberry flavor and medium weight, with enough alcohol content to balance the concentrated flavor. Its lively Rhône spiciness carries right through the long finish. What a pleasant surprise to find such a nice wine from a high-volume *négociant*.

1997 Domaine St-Luc, Coteaux du Tricastin ★ $$
Raspberry nose. A simple, tasty wine with cherry flavors, gentle tannin, and a fruity finish. A good everyday, bistro wine.

1996 E. Guigal, Côtes-du-Rhône ★ $
A polished, modern-style wine with concentrated roasted-raspberry flavor and light earthy accents. Simple, tasty, and eminently quaffable.

1997 Paul Jaboulet Aîné Parallel 45, Côtes-du-Rhône ★ $
The nose is spicy, while the flavors emphasize straightforward cherry and raspberry with mild spicy notes. Light tannin on the finish. Mellow, lush, and attractive.

RHÔNE WHITE WINES

Whites make up only 5 percent of the Rhône's production, but winemakers and consumers the world over are developing an infatuation with them. Production and export are increasing, giving consumers the opportunity to enjoy more of these unique wines.

grapes and styles
The suddenly fashionable Viognier has been widely touted as the next big white variety, leading to an explosion of plantings from California to Australia. Yet so far it has failed to achieve elsewhere the exotic peach and honeysuckle aromas and sheer voluptuous hedonism of that produced in the appellation Condrieu. Drink Condrieu young to appreciate its youthful fruitiness. White Côtes-du-Rhônes and Châteauneuf-du-Papes, made from Grenache Blanc and Clairette, offer intriguing, full-bodied, earthy alternatives to overpopular whites, such as Chardonnay. The very rare white Hermitage is unmatched in the virtually ageless power of its nut, peach, and honey flavors.

at the table

Let Condrieu be the star by showcasing it against simple dishes. Sautéed mild fish, crab, shrimp, or scallops will highlight its heady aromatics. White Côtes-du-Rhônes and Châteauneuf-du-Papes pair well with foods that have similar earthy flavors. Wild mushrooms, root vegetables, garlic, and bitter greens all are fine foils. If you are lucky enough to have a bottle or two of old white Hermitage, don't complicate the matter with food. Two glasses and a good friend should be all that's necessary.

the bottom line
Because of their limited availability, white Rhônes are expensive. Condrieu averages from $30 to $60, and quality is notoriously spotty. White Côtes-du-Rhônes and Châteauneuf-du-Papes cost a bit more than their red counterparts, yet are often surprisingly good values. If you can find one, a white Hermitage will set you back at least $50.

1997 Domaine Jean-Michel Gerin Coteau de la Loye, Condrieu ★★★★ $$$
Full, toasty oak and sweet honeysuckle and apricot on the nose. Enough body to balance the high alcohol content. Excellent.

1997 Paul Jaboulet Aîné Blanc Le Chevalier de Sterimberg, Hermitage ★★★★ $$$
Complex nose of apricot, caramel, hazelnut, orange zest, hot stones, and earth. This full-bodied wine has intense palate impact and slightly bitter hazelnut, peach-pit, and mineral flavors. Balancing acidity drives the long peachy, nut flavored finish. Drink now or wait 20 years.

1996 Albert Belle Blanc, Hermitage ★★★ $$$$
Minerals, pine, and herbs mingle in the nose. A suave wine with a currently shy core of concentrated peach, herb, and nut flavors. Its long mineral finish and excellent balance of flavor and alcohol content bode well for 10 to 20 years of life.

1997 Domaine de la Charbonniere Blanc, Châteauneuf-du-Pape ★★★ $$$
Herbal, piney, talc, and lemon-custard nose. The flavors are mostly neutral, but attractive with faint nuances of herbs, stones, and gunflint that carry all the way through the long finish. Right now, this wine is more about texture and harmony of components than taste. With some cellaring, however, the flavors should develop nicely.

1997 Vieux Mas des Papes Blanc, Châteauneuf-du-Pape ★★ $$$

Nut, apple, and pear aromas. A deliciously fruity style, featuring apple, pear, orange, and nut flavors. There's lively acidity, orange-peel flavor, and a strong mineral streak on the finish.

1997 Château Le Devoy Martine Blanc, Lirac ★★ $$

Vivacious acidity enlivens the stone, honey, and peach flavors. Medium bodied and deliciously concentrated. An elegant example of a white Rhône.

southwest
france

Paris ·

SOUTHWEST
FRANCE

Pyrenees Mts.

The southwest is France's single most exciting newly emerging wine region. Its scattered appellations hold fascinating wine discoveries—as well as breathtaking views of the high Pyrenees. Exploring the wines will reward you with compelling values of striking individuality.

grapes and styles

The districts abutting Bordeaux to the east and south use the same grape varieties to produce lighter versions of Bordeaux's wines. Look to Bergerac for some good values in reds and to Côtes de Duras for refreshing, peachy Sauvignon Blancs. Moving south, the indigenous Tannat, as tannic as its name implies, is the principal grape of the appellation Madiran, the source of an especially full-bodied, ageworthy red with great depth of flavor. Cahors, made mostly from Malbec with its tannin moderated by Merlot, ranges from grapey nouveau-style wines to richly fruity, firmly tannic powerhouses. Jurançon is home to intriguingly spicy white wines made from the Petit Manseng and Gros Manseng varieties.

at the table

Use Bergerac reds and Côtes de Duras whites as you would their Bordeaux counterparts (see page 26). Simple Cahors can be gulped with picnics and bistro meals, while sturdier versions demand robust meats like braised lamb shanks or venison stew. An aged Madiran, a cold winter night, and cassoulet—the belly-busting casserole of white beans with duck or goose confit, sausages, lamb, and pork—is a preview of heaven.

THE BOTTOM LINE Since southwestern wines are virtually unknown, bargains abound. Bergeracs and Côtes de Duras cost $8 to $12, Cahors $10 to $18, Madirans $12 to $20. Jurançon starts around $10.

SOUTHWESTERN WHITE WINES

1998 Domaine du Mage, Vin de Pays de Côtes de Gascogne ★★ $

A delightful blend of Ugni Blanc and Colombard, with aromas of flowers and peaches. On the palate, it is shockingly full-bodied and full of make-you-smile peach and fruit salad flavors. Refreshing and fun.

1998 Plaimont, Vin de Pays de Côtes de Gascogne Colombelle ★★ $

This delightful and versatile quaffer has an earthy, herbal, peppery nose with a lovely Sauvignon Blanc–like quality. Lively sweet melon, lemon, and herb flavors resolve into a clean, refreshing finish. A gentle and thoroughly likeable wine.

1997 Les Vignes Retrouvées, Côtes de Saint Mont ★★ $

Floral, almondy aromas with hints of papaya and pineapple. Surprisingly concentrated pineapple and papaya flavors explode on the palate and last long after the wine is swallowed.

SOUTHWESTERN RED WINES

1995 Chapelle Laurette, Madiran ★★★★ $$

This intense wine has a huge and entrancing nose of roasted chestnuts, grilled meat, shoe polish, dried herbs, and black-cherry jam. Dense and powerful with a thick, velvety texture and meaty flavors. Stunning.

1996 Domaine Capmartin Vieille Vignes, Madiran ★★★ $$

Powerful, meaty nose with generous oak spiciness and notes of iron, smoke, and roasted plums. Full-bodied, with huge tannin and deep, earthy, gamy, meaty flavors. Oaky vanilla flavors currently dominate the finish. This wine's tannin will allow it to age well.

10 most overLooked wines

Today's most fashionable wines are powerful, fruity, oaky, and dry. Delicacy and finesse go unappreciated, and anything even imagined as sweet causes wrinkled noses. But open-mindedness can lead you to incredible values among overlooked gems.

1. ALSACE WINES: Pinot Gris, Pinot Blanc, Muscat, and Gewürztraminer
Perception Sweet, sweet, sweet.
Reality Dry, full-bodied, and refreshing.

2. CHABLIS
Perception California jug wine.
Reality The best Chardonnays in the world.

3. CHAMPAGNE
Perception Special occasions only.
Reality Great with salads, sushi, and fried food.

4. FINO SHERRIES
Perception Your great-aunt's drink.
Reality Nothing is better with tapas or with soups.

5. GEWÜRZTRAMINERS
Perception Love it or hate it.
Reality Always wonderful with spicy foods.

6. LOIRE VALLEY CHENIN BLANCS
Perception Simple quaffer.
Reality Some of the finest and longest-lived whites.

7. LOIRE VALLEY REDS: Chinon, Bourgueil, St-Nicholas-de-Bourgueil, Saumur-Champigny
Perception Insignificant.
Reality Among the most delicious, food-friendly wines.

8. MADEIRAS
Perception Stuffy, stodgy.
Reality Perhaps the most complex wines in the world.

9. RIESLINGS German, Austrian, Alsace, and Australian
Perception Alsace in spades.
Reality Any bit of sweetness balanced by scintillating acidity.

10. ROSÉS
Perception Soooo unsophisticated.
Reality Tasty and refreshing.

1995 Château la Coustarelle Grande Cuvée Prestige, Cahors ★ ★ ★ $$

Strong aromas of vanilla, licorice, and cooked red and black fruits. Spicy, dark-berry flavors are freshened by vibrant acidity, but elevated tannin suggests the need for a few years of aging. The concentrated fruit will easily outlast the tannin. Good long finish.

1995 Château de Triguedina, Cahors ★ ★ ★ $$

Made from 70 percent Malbec, 20 percent Merlot, and 10 percent Tannat. Meaty, earthy, gamy nose. Completely traditional vinification. Beautifully restrained and concentrated. Big, furry tannin and lots of fruit on the long finish. Excellent.

1996 Château Barréjat Tradition, Madiran ★ ★ ★ $

The shy nose slowly reveals anise, smoked-meat, and berry aromas. Smooth on the palate with bracing acidity enhancing concentrated berry flavors framed by big tannin. Finish is definitely tannic, but with a strong core of pure fruit.

1993 Château Crouseilles, Madiran ★ ★ ★ $

Spicy grilled-meat and plum aromas. Intense, spicy flavors, including roasted-plum and smoked and grilled meat. A long and tannic finish. Will mellow nicely.

1998 Yvon Mau Ecocert, Bergerac ★ $

This organically grown wine has very fresh raspberry aromas and flavors with a touch of black pepper. Its low acidity makes it quite soft and easy to drink. Very pretty.

1996 Segnieurs du Perigord, Bergerac ★ $

Nose of fresh-turned earth, minerals, and black-currant jam. Light, and zesty, this has good depth of flavor and a berry-flavored finish augmented by nice strong tannin.

ITALY

Italy is the world's largest producer of wine (a distinction shared in some years with France) and the largest supplier to the United States. As recently as 20 years ago, Italy was known only for a few widely distributed commercial wines, such as Chianti, Soave, and Valpolicella. Lackluster quality was the rule. Today's Italy offers a stunning array of wines in every imaginable style and price range. Quality has never been higher, and importers unearth exciting new wines every day.

grapes and styles

The modern era of winemaking hit northeastern Italy in the mid 1970s and spread like wildfire throughout the country. For better or worse, in every region, subtlety, elegance and complex *terroir* (see page 17) characteristics are being challenged by the current fashion for lush, straightforward, fruit-driven wines markedly influenced by new oak. Italy's greatest wines are her reds based on Nebbiolo, Sangiovese, and Aglianico, and they are smoother, fruitier, and more approachable than ever. Most, however, still benefit from long-term aging. Lighter reds made from such grapes as Barbera, Dolcetto, Montepulciano, and Sangiovese are made for early consumption. The majority of Italy's whites are based on Trebbiano, and refreshingly acidic describes them best, but look to the northeast for distinctive and fruity white varietals, Tuscany for oaked Chardonnays, and the south for hefty whites made from Greco and Fiano. Many sparkling (see page 228) and dessert (see page 261) wines are made, as well.

During more than 2,000 years of winemaking, Italian wines have evolved as the perfect complement to Italy's amaz-

ing cuisine. That's why so many Italian wines have high acidity and a dry, palate-cleansing finish. These attributes can make the wines difficult to drink solo, but few of the world's vinous offerings are better with food.

ON THE LABEL

Though the sheer variety of Italian wines can be intimidating, most employ the common European geographic system of labeling. Many of the wines, such as Nebbiolo delle Langhe or Trebbiano d'Abruzzo, use geographic labeling in combination with varietal. The grape variety appears first, then *from the* or just *from*, and last the region or appellation. The Friuli-Venezia Giulia region, with its varietal labels, is an exception. The Alto Adige, also known as the Südtirol because of its strong Germanic influence, is particularly quirky in the way it labels its wines. Here you can find the same wine with both an Italian- and a German-style label.

northwest italy

For the U.S. consumer, northwest Italy means Piedmont, the rugged foothills of the Alps where fog, truffles, and red wine are the specialties. Piedmont's famous big reds, Barolo and Barbaresco, rank among the greatest wines in the world. Its lighter Dolcettos and Barberas number among the most versatile. Neighboring Lombardy makes fine reds, too, especially in the Valtellina district. These wines are similar to Piedmont's Barolos and Barberescos, but much lighter. Whites of the northwest include Piedmont's refreshing, limelike Gavi and the mellower, appley Arneis. Piedmont also produces a most delightful sparkler, Moscato d'Asti (see page 228).

BAROLO & BARBARESCO

The powerful Barolo and the more elegant Barbaresco have been dubbed the King and Queen of Italian Wines. Together, the growing zones for these red wines comprise a relatively small 1,700 hectares surrounding the town of Alba. Both are based on Italy's finest variety, Nebbiolo (neb-b'YOH-lo). This late-ripening grape, high in acidity, sugar, and tannin, has the rare ability to accurately transmit subtle nuances from soils and sites.

As in Burgundy, the vineyards are many, and the ownership, fragmented. Winemakers typically produce tiny quantities of wines from small plots in numerous sites. The high demand for these few bottles makes them hard to find and usually very expensive.

Before the 1980s, tannin dominated Barolos in their youth, making two decades or more of cellaring necessary. The wines often retained their severe tannin even when fully mature. But now, shorter maceration, later picking, less time aging in wood, and widespread use of new-oak barrels have resulted in many smoother, less tannic wines with an emphasis on the delicate fresh strawberry and cherry flavors of Nebbiolo.

at the table

Barolos and Barbarescos, with their high tannin, high acidity, and powerful flavors, are the quintessential partners for robust meat dishes. Pair them when young with game stews and roasts, particularly venison. These wines often have smoky, earthy notes reminiscent of white truffles, making them ideal with mushrooms of all kinds. When aged and mellow, the wines show off their complex flavors with braised veal, such as osso buco, with simple grilled steak, or with a cheese course.

the Bottom Line

Prices for the superb 1995 and 1996 Barolos and Barbarescos, which are hitting the market this year, have exploded—in some cases doubling the cost of the 1994s. Many basic *cuvées* from top producers cost $40 to $50, while some single-vineyard wines will set you back $75 to $100 or more. Limited production, high demand, and tight supply are conspiring to drive prices even higher.

What to Buy BAROLO & BARBARESCO

1990	1991	1992	1993
★★★★	★★★	★★	★★★

1994	1995	1996	1997
★★	★★★★	★★★★	★★★★

PRODUCERS AND THEIR WINES

ALDO CONTERNO ★★★★ $$$$
One of the first to combine new and old techniques, resulting in wines of depth and complexity that retain their fruit flavors for many years. Aldo Conterno avoids new oak. LOOK FOR Barolos from the vineyards Bussia Soprana, Vigna Cicala, and Vigna Colonnello.

GIACOMO CONTERNO ★★★★ $$$$
Powerful, concentrated, tannic Barolos made for long-term cellaring. They develop magnificently. LOOK FOR Barolos Monfortino, Monfortino Riserva, and Cascina Francia.

ANGELO GAJA ★★★★ $$$$
Brilliant Barbarescos. Polished, concentrated wines with a touch of spiciness from deft use of new oak. Branched out to Barolo in 1988. LOOK FOR the Barbarescos Sorí Tildin and Sorí San Lorenzo and the Barolo Sperss.

BRUNO GIACOSA ★ ★ ★ ★ $$$$

A staunch traditionalist. Tannic in youth, these wines take many years to develop the tar, rose-petal, eucalyptus, and dried-strawberry flavors for which Barolo and Barbaresco are famous. LOOK FOR Barbaresco from the vineyards Santo Stefano and Asili, Barolos from the vineyards Villero and Falletto di Serralunga.

BARTOLO MASCARELLO ★ ★ ★ ★ $$$$

As traditional as they come: long maceration, no new oak, no individual *cru* bottlings. Almost impossible to find, but extraordinary. LOOK FOR Mascarello makes only one Barolo simply labeled Barolo. If you find it and have a good cellar for aging, buy it.

VIETTI ★ ★ ★ ★ $$$$

Often referred to as an enlightened traditionalist, Vietti tames the typical power of Barolos without losing it. Its wines also clearly reflect their *terroir* (see page 17). LOOK FOR Barolos from the vineyards Rocche, Lazzarito, and Brunate.

PAOLO SCAVINO ★ ★ ★ $$$$

Superbly cultivated grapes and skillful use of new oak combine to make these among the best of the modern-style Barolos. LOOK FOR the Barolos Bric dël Fiasc, Cannubi, and Rocche dell'Annunziata.

CERETTO ★ ★ ★ $$$–$$$$

Tannic, fairly old-style Barolos and Barbarescos that are widely available. LOOK FOR Barolos from the Prapò and Bricco Rocche vineyards and Barbarescos from the vineyards Asili and Faset.

DOMENICO CLERICO ★ ★ ★ $$$–$$$$

An early experimenter who has settled into a moderately modern style. LOOK FOR the two Barolos Ciabot Mentin Ginestra and Pajana.

MARCHESI DI GRESY ★ ★ ★ $$$–$$$$

These stubbornly traditional Barbarescos are marvels of subtlety and silky elegance, aging beautifully for decades. LOOK FOR the Barbarescos Martinenga, Camp Gros Martinenga, and Gaiun Martinenga.

CARRETTA ★ ★ ★ $$$

Medium-bodied, very traditional wines that require time to gain aromatic complexity—and always retain some of their tannic bite. Excellent values. LOOK FOR the Barolo Cannubi.

PRODUTTORI DI BARBARESCO ★ ★ ★ $$$

The finest cooperative in the area and perhaps the best in Italy. Excellent values in surprisingly high-quality Barbarescos. LOOK FOR the Barbarescos Asili and Rabajà.

FONTANAFREDDA ★★ $$$–$$$$

A large house producing textbook, traditional Barolos in a relatively light style. Excellent values. LOOK FOR Barolos from the vineyard plots La Rosa and San Pietro.

TERRE DEL BAROLO ★★ $$$

A large co-op capable of turning out solid, well-priced Barolos in the better vintages. LOOK FOR basic Barolo and Rocche.

OTHER TOP-NOTCH PRODUCERS

Elio Altare *(Barolos Arborina and La Morra)*, Pio Cesare *(Barolo, Barolo Ornato, Barbaresco)*, Corino *(Barolos Vigna Giachini and Rocche)*, Manzone *(Barolo Gramolere)*, Marcarini *(Barolo Brunate)*, Giuseppe Mascarello *(Barolo Monprivato, Barbaresco)*, Massolino *(Barolos Parafada and Margheria)*, Moccagatta *(Barbaresco)*, Prunotto *(Barolos Bussia, Cannubi, and Ginestra; Barbarescos Montestefano and Rabajà)*, Renato Ratti *(Barolos Marcenasco and Rocche)*, Giuseppe Rinaldi *(Barolo Brunate)*, Sandrone *(Barolo Cannubi Boschis)*, Seghesio *(Barolo La Villa)*, Voerzio *(Barolo Cerequio)*

OTHER NEBBIOLO -BASED WINES

For those without the patience or the cellar to age Barolos and Barbarescos, earlier-maturing Nebbiolos make a lot of sense. North of Alba, Gattinara (gah-tee-NAH-rah), where Nebbiolo is known as Spanna, produces medium-to-full bodied, somewhat rough wines. The lighter-bodied Valtellina is produced on a narrow band of south-facing slopes overlooking the Adda River in northeastern Lombardy. In addition, look for simpler regional wines bottled as Nebbiolo delle Langhe or Nebbiolo d'Alba from famous Barolo and Barbaresco producers.

at the table

These wines make excellent restaurant choices. Their medium weight won't overwhelm food, and they are usually drinkable even in current vintages. Try them with such light meat and game dishes as grilled chicken, roasted pheasant, or veal chops with mushrooms. Since the wines are fruitier and less tannic than Barolos and Barbarescos, they marry well with pasta and risotto, again especially those with mushrooms or light meat sauces.

the bottom line   Collectors and label-drinkers focus their attention on the high-profile Barolos and Barbarescos and virtually ignore these less-known wines. Bargains abound. Gattinaras and Valtellinas can be found for under $25, while you can find basic Nebbiolos for between $10 and $15.

1995 Rainoldi, Valtellina Superiore Grumello   ★ ★ ★ ★ $
This ravishingly elegant wine has a superb nose of raspberry, plum, earth, and spice. Medium in weight, it offers concentrated, lip-smacking fruit flavors and complex notes of tobacco, truffle, and earth. Though it's enjoyable now, it will truly blossom with five years of aging.

1997 Bruno Giacosa, Nebbiolo d'Alba   ★ ★ $$
Spice, earth, truffle, and rose aromas. Classic, aggressive Nebbiolo acidity and alcohol is allied with good tannin and complex flavors of leather, truffle, strawberry, and rosé. This young wine needs a few years to mellow.

1996 Monchiero Carbone Srü, Roero   ★ ★ $$
This single-vineyard, 100 percent Nebbiolo takes a while in the glass for its aromas to become apparent. When they do, however, there's a classic nose of strawberries, roses, truffles, and eucalyptus. The prominent tannin suggests this would profit from a year or two in the cellar.

1991 Nervi, Gattinara   ★ ★ $$
Fascinating rustic aromas of iron, animal fur, herbs, meat, and roasted raspberry are this wine's best attributes. Chunky and a bit foursquare in character, it has slightly stewed flavors.

1995 Rainoldi, Valtellina   ★ ★ $
A nose of raspberry, strawberry, and spice with hints of leather. This zingy, medium-bodied wine's berry and mushroom flavors will be lovely in two to five years.

1996 Vallana, Spanna Colline Novalese   ★ $
Gentle, stewed red-fruit aromas and overripe berry flavors abound in this slightly rough, robust crowd pleaser. For those who like gutsy red wine with lots of flavor, this is a consistent bargain.

BARBERA & DOLCETTO

The Piedmontese save their treasured Barolos and Barbarescos for special occasions; their daily wines are the lighter and fruitier Barberas and Dolcettos. Barberas have mouthwatering acidity, a vivid blackberry flavor, and virtually no tannin. All Barberas used to be consumed young, but recently more serious styles, matured in new oak and made for aging, have become popular. Dolcetto literally means *little sweet one*, a reference to the grapes not the wine, which is dry. Light to medium in body with fresh cherry and herb flavors, Dolcettos have moderate tannin and a dry, slightly bitter bite on the finish.

at the table

Barbera is the ultimate pizza and pasta-with-red-sauce wine. Given the popularity of these two in the United States, why Barbera isn't our number one import is beyond us. Barbera's acidity also contrasts well with rich meats, cutting the fat and refreshing the palate. Dolcetto is equally at home with pizza and pasta, but its modest tannin allows it to partner with poultry, meat sauces, and light meats as well.

the Bottom Line Five years ago, Dolcettos and Barberas were commonly available for under $10. Alas, those days are gone. Today you can expect to pay at least $10 to $15, with *barrique*-style Barberas at $20 or more. The spectacular 1997 vintage represents good value even at these high prices.

what to Buy   DOLCETTO & BARBERA

1990	1991	1992	1993
★★★★	★★★	★★	★★★

1994	1995	1996	1997
★★	★★★★	★★★★	★★★★

1997 Giacomo Conterno, Dolcetto d'Alba   ★★★★ $$
Explosive aromas of black cherry, blackberry, and spice. Wow! This wine features powerfully concentrated black-cherry flavors with the classic Dolcetto whiplash of bitter nuttiness on the finish. An extraordinary wine.

1997 Sorì Paitin, Dolcetto d'Alba   ★★★★ $$
A nose of super-ripe black plums and cherries presages a rush of cherry and blackberry flavors. This wine is succulent and has the perfect amount of tannin balanced nicely by the fruit flavors. The finish goes on and on.

1997 Veglio, Dolcetto d'Alba ★ ★ ★ ★ $$

This is a truly fabulous Dolcetto d'Alba. The wine is tremendously fruity and dense, and yet it is suave and polished. Its focused fruit flavors fairly explode on the palate. The texture is silky, as is the long finish.

1997 Vietti Tre Vigne, Barbera d'Alba ★ ★ ★ ★ $$

A huge nose of cherry, earth, and mineral aromas. The intense cherry, blackberry, and plum flavors are stunningly concentrated, and these great-big fruit flavors more than balance the good acidity. What a year!

1995 Pietro Barbero La Vignassa, Barbera d'Asti ★ ★ ★ $$$

The earthy blackberry aromas mingle with spiciness from oak and scents of Brazil nuts. Mouthwatering acidity just enhances the already concentrated fruit flavors. The wine has a velvety texture from barrel aging.

1998 F. Boschis Pianezzo, Dolcetto di Dogliani ★ ★ ★ $$

Lovely, classic bitter-almond and cherry nose. Cherry flavor tangos with slightly astringent Dogliani tannin in this refreshing, simply delicious Dolcetto.

1997 Castelvero, Barbera del Piedmonte ★ ★ ★ $

A spectacular year for Barbera, in which tremendously full fruitiness balances Barbera's unstoppable acidity. This wine hits you with a blast of incredibly succulent fruit flavor and nuances of smoke and mushrooms.

1997 Cordero di Montezemolo, Dolcetto d'Alba ★ ★ $$

First of all, there are captivating cranberry and herbal scents on the nose. On the palate, this is a bracing, light-bodied style of Dolcetto that features delicate yet crystal-clear red-berry, cherry, and herbal flavors.

1997 La Sera Il Cielo, Barbera d'Alba ★ ★ $$

A lovely ruby color sets the stage for unusual and intriguing pepper, smoked-meat, and beef-jerky aromas. Fruit flavors greet you on the palate immediately and stay right through the deliciously refreshing finish.

1996 Vicara Rubello, Monferrato ★ ★ $$

This wine boasts a plethora of sweet red-cherry flavor and herbal notes along with the high acidity that gives the wine its classic northern Italian briskness. The flavors and acidity make it a terrific food wine. It's 90 percent Barbera and 10 percent Cabernet Sauvignon and Nebbiolo.

WHITE WINES OF NORTHWEST ITALY

The pale, light-bodied Gavi, based on the Cortese grape, has a distinct limelike flavor and good acidity. It may be labeled as Gavi, Cortese di Gavi, or Gavi di Gavi. The hidden treasure of Piedmont is Roero Arneis (roh-AIR-oh ahr-NAY'z), which at its best has complex apple and nut flavors buttressed by palate-cleansing acidity.

at the table

Like many of Italy's white wines, those of Piedmont are refreshing and light bodied, so they pair well with foods of similar description. Try them with shellfish, mild finfish, and simple chicken dishes. These whites are particularly good foils for roasted vegetables, antipasti, and salads. Gavi also works well as an aperitif, though in Italy no wine is ever served without food. Instead, beverages specifically designated as aperitifs, such as Cinzano and Campari, are offered before the meal.

the bottom line Good Gavis are pricey at between $15 and $20. Roero Arneis, at a few dollars more, usually offers better value.

1997 Vietti Arneis, Roero ★★★★ $$
Spicy, nutty, appley nose. Tremendously concentrated apple and nut flavors are highlighted by vivid acidity. An amazing white wine with a great mineral and fruit finish.

1997 La Spinetta Chardonnay, Piedmont ★★★ $$$
The Chardonnays of Piedmont tend to be far less oaky than those of Tuscany. La Spinetta's excellent example is vibrant and beautifully concentrated.

1997 Broglia La Meirana, Gavi di Gavi ★★ $$
Classic limelike Gavi nose with notes of hay and grass. Lovely, lively lime flavor. Brisk and light with a refreshing finish.

1998 Monchiero Carbone Arneis, Roero ★★ $$
Apple, herb, and earth nose with a hint of spice. Earthy flavors. Lowish acidity due to the hot summer in 1998. Very good with food.

1997 La Scolca White Label, Gavi ★★ $$
Some bruised-apple flavor along with the classic and lively lime and minerals. Fuller than most Gavis. Very good.

NORTHeast italy

TRENTINO-
ALTO ADIGE

FRIULI-
VENEZIA
GIULIA

Adda River   VENETO

Rome

The regions of Friuli-Venezia Giulia, Trentino-Alto Adige, and the Veneto share a moderately cool climate that is ideal for the production of light, refreshing white and red wines. Historically, the whites were earthy in flavor and aromatically neutral. Lately the trend has shifted toward more fruitiness and complexity.

FRIULI-VENEZIA GIULIA, usually shortened to simply Friuli, is home to wines from an array of international and traditional Italian grape varieties. Pinot Grigio, Pinot Bianco, Tocai Friulano (toh-KIE free-oo-LAH-no), and Sauvignon Blanc head the list of whites, which also includes Chardonnay, Riesling, and Gewürztraminer. Reds from Cabernet Sauvignon, Merlot, and Pinot Nero can be good in years when conditions permit the grapes to ripen fully before harvest. Look for wines made from the uniquely minerally and potentially long-lived Refosco grape.

TRENTINO-ALTO ADIGE produces vibrant, aromatically complex white wines from the same varieties as Friuli. Riesling and Gewürztraminer play more prominent roles here, and you'll find some of the best Müller-Thurgau made anywhere. These ski-country wines are as exhilarating as fresh-powder snow. The region also produces traditional reds from Teroldego and Schiava grapes.

THE VENETO is familiar to most consumers for its oceans of thin Soave, Valpolicella, and Bardolino. Overproduction has debased the names, but excellent, concentrated examples abound. Sweet *recioto* wines are a specialty of the region— powerful reds and a few whites, made by air-drying the grapes to concentrate their sugar. Those labeled Recioto della Valpolicella are sweet; those labeled Amarone (ah-mah-ROE-neh) are dry.

at the table

The light, high-acid whites of Italy's northeast are excellent with salads and finfish and superb with shellfish. Try one with clams *oreganato*. The reds, again light bodied and tart, make wonderful partners for salami and other cured meats, as well as for pizzas, chicken, and pasta with a simple tomato sauce. Amarones should be enjoyed either with well-aged hard cheeses, such as Parmigiano-Reggiano, very full-flavored stews, or game. Sweet *recioto* wines are best after a meal, alone or with walnuts.

the bottom line

This is wonderful territory for refreshing, fruity whites. Many are great values at $8 to $20, though some top bottlings are shockingly expensive. Reds are spottier, with some compelling values but many wines made from unripe grapes are not worth the price. For Soaves and Valpolicellas, pay the extra dollar or so for those marked Classico; they're worth it. Amarones will run $30 to $50 or more, but, nevertheless, the best are good value.

WHITE WINES

1997 Tiefenbrunner Feldmarschall von Fennerzu Fennberg Müller-Thurgau, Alto Adige ★★★★ $$$

Complex aromas of talc, mineral, spring flowers, white grapes, and peaches. This is a remarkably concentrated wine with lots of intriguing flavors. Talc, peach, spice, and herbs all echo on the long, minerally finish. An extraordinary Müller-Thurgau.

1997 Pojer e Sandri Müller-Thurgau, Trentino ★★★ $$

Lovely grapey, floral, lemon-lime nose with a touch of peach. Concentrated flavors lean toward the floral, with a sophisticated streak of minerality on the finish.

1997 Peter Zemmer Gewürztraminer, Alto Adige ★★★ $

Exciting, in-your-face rose, litchi, and peach nose. The matching flavors are simply delicious. A bit of spritz adds to the liveliness. A great value.

1996 Vie di Romans Sauvignon Blanc Vieris, Friuli ★★ $$$

The nose features pepper, celery, and thyme. It's medium bodied and has a dominant taste of toffee. This big wine (the alcohol is 13 percent) is short on Sauvignon Blanc character but long on mellow flavor.

1998 Gini Soave Classico Superiore Salvarenza, Veneto ★★ $$

Remember those orange-colored, peanut-shaped, banana-flavored candies? That's the nose. Quite full flavored for a Soave, with a strong mineral component that nicely balances the candied elements of this wine.

1998 Puiatti Pinot Grigio, Collio ★★ $$
Faint but clear peach aromas with hints of mineral. Quite full-bodied, with nutty, mineral flavors and the fairly high alcohol content typical of the year.

1998 Kris Pinot Grigio delle Venezie ★★ $
Lovely lemon-orange and fresh-almond scents lead to lemony, nutty flavors with an accent of orange peel. Much fuller than in past vintages. Its typical minerality asserts itself on the tasty finish.

1998 Santi Pinot Grigio Vigneto Sortesele, Trentino ★★ $
Neutral nose hints at quinine. Nicely concentrated mineral, citrus, and gently nutty flavors. Good fruit flavor carries through into the brisk, minerally finish. Quite good.

1998 Peter Zemmer Pinot Grigio, Alto Adige ★★ $
Fresh, peachy, slightly spicy nose reminiscent of Gewürztraminer. Excellent peach, nut, and earth flavors. A full-bodied style, with lively acidity. Long finish.

1998 Zenato Pinot Grigio, Veneto ★★ $
Aromas of toasted nuts and vanilla. Full, mellow, and nutty with creamy-vanilla and toast flavors. Low acidity for a Pinot Grigio.

1998 Cavalchina Bianco di Custoza, Veneto ★ $
Light, floral aromas. Refreshing with modestly concentrated apple and almond flavors. Lively acidity on the long, slightly earthy finish.

1998 Eno Friulia Pinot Grigio, Friuli ★ $
Classic nut and peach-skin nose. Peach, banana, and nut flavors with a bit of enlivening spritz. This refreshing wine finishes with hints of banana.

1998 Villa del Borgo Pinot Grigio, Grave del Friuli ★ $
Nice, slightly candied floral and nutty aromas. Peachy flavors are nicely concentrated for the money. Good body and a long, fruity finish make this a fine value.

Red Wines
1993 Allegrini
Amarone Recioto della Valpolicella ★★★★ $$$
Don't be fooled by the misleading label; the wine is dry. It has heady, almost overwhelming aromas of roasted raspberries, leather, and

herbs. This is a huge wine, so thick, so high in alcohol, and so powerful that it almost hurts to drink it now. In 15 years, however, it will be
spectacular.

1995 Masi Campofiorin Ripasso, Valpolicella ★★★★ $$

Masi invented this style of Valpolicella, which is refermented on the
lees of Amarone. This example has a classic baked-cherry and plum
nose with hints of leather, herbs, spice, and bacon fat. The full-bodied flavors and velvety texture are consistent from beginning to
end. A finishing note of chocolate is like dessert after a splendid
meal. The price makes this a steal.

1993 Le Ragose Amarone della Valpolicella ★★★ $$$

Beautiful mulberry, roasted-cherry, and chestnut nose. It gives an
impression of freshness, with little of the oxidized aromas typical of
older styles. Medium-bodied, tannic, and fruity.

1995 Santi Proemio Amarone
della Valpolicella ★★★ $$$

An elegant, lighter-than-usual style of Amarone featuring well-balanced bitter-chocolate and raspberry flavors, excellent concentration, and a long, lingering raspberry finish.

1996 La Prendina Merlot, Lombardy ★★★ $$

Right away, the inky ruby color tells you this is a serious wine. The
smoky, mysterious nose has hints of game and powerful scents of
black fruits. Concentrated plum flavor, gentle tannin, and tart, spicy
accents lead to a mouthwateringly refreshing finish.

1995 Acinum, Valpolicella Classico Superiore ★★★ $

What a buy! This unusual Valpolicella is made from 100 percent
Rondinella grapes and has a wonderfully intense cherry-blackberry
flavor and intriguing notes of earth and spice.

1997 Mazzi, Valpolicella Superiore ★★ $$

Lovely violet perfume and cherry aromas on the enticing nose.
Cherry and blackberry flavors and tangy acidity make this wine particularly attractive.

1998 Santi Solane, Valpolicella Classico ★★ $

Inviting nose of bitter cherries and herbs. This light-bodied, bracing
wine has delicate but concentrated cherry flavor balanced by a lovely tang. Long palate-cleansing finish.

1997 Villa del Borgo Merlot, Grave del Friuli ★★ $

Bracing aromas of cherries and plums to begin. It's a light-bodied
and delightfully lively Merlot, with full cherry flavors.

tuscany

TUSCANY

Montalcino

Rome

Clearly central Italy's most important wine region, Tuscany, with its great Sangiovese-based reds, lays strong claim to being the vinous heart of all of Italy, as well as its cultural center. The Sangiovese wines range in style from charming, everyday quaffers to serious, long-lived cellar treasures that rival the masterpieces in the museums of Siena and Florence. Quality has come light-years from the not-so-far-away days of paint-stripper Chiantis in straw-covered flasks.

grapes and styles

Tuscany's important red wines, Chianti, Brunello di Montalcino, Rosso di Montepulciano, Vino Nobile di Montalcino, Carmignano, and most of its Super Tuscans, are based on Sangiovese (san-joh-VAY-zeh). Not a blockbuster grape, Sangiovese generally produces elegant, medium- to full-bodied wines with dried cherry and herb flavors and a refreshingly dry, nutty finish. Sangioveses age beautifully and are among the best wines in the world to accompany food.

Tuscany led Italy's movement toward international styling when the early *barrique*-aged Cabernet Sauvignon and Cabernet Sauvignon–Sangiovese blends, which became known as Super Tuscans, wowed the wine world with their lush fruit and unabashed oak flavors. Over the last 20 years, many of Tuscany's wineries have embraced that style, sparking much debate and controversy among winemakers and critics alike. Today, the pace of change has slowed, but, as in Piedmont, the issue seems settled: Delicious modern and traditional wines exist side by side.

Tuscany's best white is the almond-scented Vernaccia di San Gimignano. We prefer to avoid the heavily oaked Chardonnays that are the current favorites of many Tuscan producers. The traditional dessert wine Vin Santo (see page 261) is a specialty of the area.

at the table

The basic Chiantis and Rossos that are drunk young burst with charming, tart-cherry flavor and are perfect for light foods like simple chicken and pasta dishes and with soft, mild cheeses. Chianti Classicos, the fuller bottlings among the Rossos, and the lighter of the Riserva wines are better suited to roasted meats, grilled vegetables, and firm cheeses. The more serious Riserva Chiantis, Brunellos, and Vino Nobiles are best when aged. Then their mature flavors and aromas of spice, chestnuts, and dried flowers can be savored with red meats, game, and aged hard cheese. Because many of the Super Tuscans sport a powerful fruitiness and flashy oak, show them off against steak or roasts.

CHIANTI

Tuscany's most important wine, Chianti, is also by far its most widely produced. The basic wines are drunk young and are priced for everyday consumption. They offer lively herbal and cherry flavors and a light, food-friendly texture. The more significant wines include single-estate, single-vineyard, and Riserva bottlings, the last of which receive extra aging before release. All these full-bodied, mouth-filling reds are made for cellaring, during which they develop their silky synthesis of acidity, flavor, and tannin, along with complex nuances of dried violets, spice, and mushrooms.

Traditionally, Chiantis are blended wines, with Sangiovese as the mainstay. Small percentages of Canaiolo, Mammolo, and the whites Trebbiano and Malvasia used to be included. As tastes have changed, so has the *uvaggio* (blend). New laws eliminate the requirement of white grapes and allow 100 percent Sangiovese Chiantis. For blends, Mammolo is out, but, for modern-style producers, Cabernet Sauvignon is in. Traditional producers avoid the use of new oak, but many new-style Chiantis spend time in small barrels, which gives them a creamy texture and marked vanilla notes.

Chianti is grown in seven individual zones on the hills between Florence and Siena. Chianti Classico (a zone, not a quality designation) is at the heart, surrounded by Rufina, Montalbano, Colli Senesi, Colli Fiorentini, Colli Aretini, and Colline Pisani. Classico's wines are the most concentrated and most consistent in quality. They are closely followed by Rufina's lively, elegant, age-worthy wines and the fuller of Colli Senesi's wines, which offer great values.

THE BOTTOM LINE After four mediocre harvests, prices soared with the excellent 1995 and 1996 vintages. Now comes 1997, perhaps the greatest year in a generation, so expect sticker shock. Even basic Chiantis that cost $6 to $7 two years ago are now $8 to $10. Many Classicos are $15 to $20, and Riservas $20 and up. Look to Rufina and Colli Senesi for relative bargains.

WHAT TO BUY CHIANTI

1990	1991	1992	1993
★★★★	★★★	★★	★★★

1994	1995	1996	1997
★★★	★★★★	★★★	★★★★

1997 Badia Coltibuono, Classico ★★★★ $$
This is one of our favorite old-style Chiantis. Densely colored and packed with cherry, herb, and anise flavors, its definite acid and tannin will give it at least 10 years of life. Look also for Badia's older Riservas.

1997 Castellare, Classico ★★★★ $$
Beautiful cherry and plum flavors. Tremendously concentrated and quite powerful for a basic Chianti, but the flavor and alcohol are in superb balance from the beginning to the mouthwatering, cherry-flavored finish.

1995 Monsanto Riserva, Classico ★★★★ $$
Here's our kind of Chianti. Made in a stubbornly traditional style—quite tannic, with a distinctly earthy and herbal character unobscured by new oak. There is a magnificent core of concentrated, kirsch-like cherry flavor waiting to burst forth given 5 to 10 years of aging.

1996 Castello di Nipozzano Riserva, Rufina ★★★ $$
Acidity rules now, but an impressive core of cherry that echoes long and loud on the currently tart finish promises much. The wine will be lovely with five years of age.

1996 Colognole, Rufina ★★★ $$
An exciting, on-the-button Sangiovese nose of bitter cherry, earth, mineral, truffle, and sandalwood. A bracing, beautifully archetypal Chianti Rufina.

1996 Dievole, Classico ★★★ $$
The mellow nose includes classic leather and tobacco nuances along with its smoky plum, black-cherry, and mineral aromas. Concentrated red-fruit flavors, excellent acidity to keep them lively, and a tannic finish. Medium-to-full bodied.

1996 Villa Antinori Riserva, Classico ★ ★ ★ $$

Antinori's flagship wine has a beautiful nose first of violets, leather, red fruits, herbs, and earth and then of cherries and smoke. A classic Chianti made in a dry, restrained, understated style.

1997 Villa Cafaggio, Classico ★ ★ ★ $$

Invigorating minty notes waft in the cherry and raspberry nose. Full, clear, and tangy boysenberry flavor and medium body. Some dry tannin on the finish. Give it two to three years to harmonize.

1997 Selvapiana, Rufina ★ ★ ★ $

A Rufina Chianti from a family famous since the early 19th century for ageworthy Riservas and single-vineyard wines. Enticing cocoa, nutmeg, and red-berry aromas, and a mélange of berry, leather, and earth flavors. The finish is refreshingly brisk yet attractively mellow.

1995 Castello Di Verrazzano Riserva, Classico ★ ★ $$

The inviting nose of this Chianti offers a little bit of chocolate and cedar along with its black cherry. The flavors blossom nicely on the palate and fade languidly in the long finish. Yes, the family-owned estate dates back to the famed explorer.

1996 Isole Olena, Classico ★ ★ $$

This decidedly modern-style Chianti is a big wine with lots of tannin, and perhaps too much oak for some, but the black-pepper and full red-fruit flavors linger in a long, persistent finish.

1997 Rocca delle Macìe, Classico ★ ★ $$

A focused wine, with full, if a bit simple, cherry flavor and lively acidity. A refreshing, delicate style of Chianti. Beautiful balance of flavor, acidity, and alcohol content.

1997 Geografico, Colli Senesi ★ ★ $

Nice nose of dried cherries, earth, and spices. A light, fairly simple but fruity Chianti with cherry flavors and a classic, pleasingly bitter almond finish.

1998 Renzo Masi, Rufina ★ ★ $

This vivacious, light, and delicious Chianti has a classic nose of bitter wild cherries and tart fruity flavors with a pleasing herbal edge. Sipping the wine is like biting into a fresh cherry.

1997 Melini Borghi d'Elsa, Chianti ★ $

Just what Chianti-in-the-straw used to be when it was good: a simple, easy-drinking wine, with cherry flavor and lively, palate-cleansing acidity.

SUPER TUSCANS

In the late 1960s and early 1970s, some Chianti winegrowers became frustrated with restrictive laws that they felt prevented them from experimenting and perhaps making their best wines. In particular, they wanted to try blends using Cabernet Sauvignon, an unsanctioned grape. The problem was that if one used prohibited methods or grape varieties, the resulting wine would be declassified to Vino da Tavola and theoretically sell for a very low price.

Nonetheless, the Marchesi Incisa della Rochetta forged ahead, standing the wine world on its ear with his intense, lavishly oaked Cabernet Sauvignon–based Sassicaia. Other vintners rushed to follow, and these celebrated wines were soon dubbed Super Tuscans. Far from being cheap, they were among the most expensive wines Italy had ever seen. Their triumphant makers put Vino da Tavola on the labels like badges of honor.

Super Tuscans often have some Cabernet Sauvignon or Merlot in the blend and are aged in small new-oak barrels to give them spicy flavors and a lush, velvety texture. Some wines are 100 percent Sangiovese, an option also not permitted under old law. In 1992, the Italian government finally faced reality and amended the Chianti laws to embrace some of these wines, and in 1996 created new DOCs, such as Bolgheri, for others. Another welcome change is that today these wines are being made in every price range.

tHE Bottom LINE Expensive limited-edition Super Tuscans continue to proliferate, but fortunately, so too do good wines that can now be found for as little as $15. Just five years ago, $30 was the price of admission. The most famous names continue to be sought after, hard-to-find wines that will set you back $50 or more.

wHat to BUY SUPER TUSCANS

1993	1994	1995	1996	1997
★★★	★★★	★★★	★★★	★★★★

1996 Tignanello ★★★★ $$$$
This 80 percent Sangiovese, 20 percent Cabernet Sauvignon wine has aromas of cassis, black cherry, Asian spices, smoke, animal fur, vanilla, and violets. The powerful tannin, the concentrated smoky cassis and cherry flavors, and the oakiness are all in magnificent balance.

1996 Villa Cafaggio San Martino ★★★★ $$$

This 100 percent Sangiovese aged in French oak sports a gorgeous, ruby-purple color and a nose of vanilla from the oak and super-ripe cherries. Good tannin accompanies the concentrated, intense flavor. The wine has a long finish. Given five to seven years aging, it will be fabulous.

1993 Castellare I Sodi San Nicolo ★★★ $$$

A 100 percent Sangiovese wine that has a classic, to-die-for nose of bitter wild cherry and just-chopped herbs. It is elegant, with beautiful, concentrated cherry flavor and fine tannin that last through the long finish. Give this one another few years.

1994 Cennatoio Mammolo ★★★ $$$

A blend of 70 percent Merlot and 30 percent Sangiovese that seems to maintain better balance through its lavish oak treatment than most. It has succulent cherry and chocolate flavors, a full-bodied, unctuous texture, and a long, velvety finish. Bravo!

1996 Tenuta la Calcinaie ★★★ $$$

A blend of Sangiovese and Merlot. Dusty, earthy nose with oak currently overshadowing aromas of plum, cherry, and blueberry. This has superbly concentrated cherry flavor, accented by notes of plum, chocolate, and herbs. The finish is long, tannic, and refreshingly tart. Give this complex wine at least five years.

1997 Renzo Masi I Pini ★★ $$

Made from 50 percent Sangiovese and 50 percent Cabernet Sauvignon. Has an almost black, purple color. Aromatic nose of plums and berries, with hints of vanilla. This medium-bodied blend has zesty currant, cherry, and plum flavors, with an attractive note of bitter chocolate and a long silky finish.

OTHER SANGIOVESE -BASED WINES

BRUNELLO DI MONTALCINO, Tuscany's finest wine, is grown south of the Chianti zone on the hillsides surrounding the town of Montalcino, where the hot, dry climate produces fully ripe, concentrated grapes. Made entirely from a unique clone of Sangiovese, Brunellos are tannic, full-bodied, serious reds for aging. Buy them when finances allow and save them for 10 to 20 years. You will be rewarded with wines that are slightly spicy on the palate and velvety on the tongue, with an admirably harmonious balance of tannin, acidity, alcohol, and varietal flavor.

ROSSO DI MONTALCINO is a recent creation by Brunello wine-makers who needed a wine they could sell for early drinking, while consumers wait for their Brunellos to mature. Made in a medium-bodied style, the best of these are sensational mouthfuls of pure Sangiovese flavor.

VINO NOBILE DI MONTEPULCIANO is fuller bodied than Chianti, lighter than Brunello, and rarely rises to the elegance of either. Some well-made, ageable examples exist, but, in many Vino Nobiles, rustic tannin overwhelms the flavor.

CARMIGNANO must always have a bit of Cabernet Sauvignon blended into the wine; whereas use of Cabernet is optional for Chiantis, and only some include it. Thus Carmignanos are fuller bodied than most Chiantis, with more cassislike Cabernet flavor.

THE BOTTOM LINE Brunellos are expensive and their current fadishness is driving prices higher. Basic bottles are hard to find for less than $30, with $45 a more typical starting point. Riservas, whether big names or small, will often cost $70 or more, and only the best are worth it. On the other hand, Rossos, available from $15 to $25, usually offer good value. Vinos Nobile can be had for $20 to $30 but rarely merit even that. Carmignanos are bargains, with many regular bottlings priced at $20 or less.

WHAT TO BUY OTHER SANGIOVESE-BASED WINES

1992	1993	1994	1995	1996	1997
★★	★★★	★★★	★★★★	★★★	★★★★

1993 Tenuta Friggiali, Brunello di Montalcino　　★★★★ $$$
A wine with wonderful smoky-chocolate and wild-cherry aromas and flavors. It's full-bodied, and its tannin, acid, flavor, and alcohol are in beautiful balance. A long finish.

1997 Giovanni Dei, Rosso di Montepulciano　　★★★★ $$
Blackberry, plum, and cherry flavors. Deliciously mellow and polished, with excellent concentration and a long finish. A beautiful wine.

1993 La Gerla, Brunello di Montalcino　　★★★ $$$
Spice, chocolate, herb, and roasted-cherry nose. The wine sports delicious, spicy cherry, chocolate, and leather flavors and a velvety finish. This is ready to drink.

1997 Angelo Sassetti Pertimali, Rosso di Montalcino ★★★ $$$

Herbal, earthy, peppery notes season cooked-cherry aromas in the nose. A refreshing yet full fruity style. Incredible harmony of flavor and tannin makes this wine a standout.

1997 Altesino, Rosso di Altesino ★★★ $$

Known for long-lived Brunellos, Altesino also makes this blend of Sangiovese and about 10 percent Cabernet Sauvignon to drink earlier. A strong but vibrant wine, earthy and full of violet and leather scents.

1995 Artimino, Carmignano Riserva ★★★ $$

Menthol, eucalyptus, and fennel scents play off those of cassis, plum, and black cherry. A full wine, with plummy, chocolaty flavors tinged with tobacco, herbs, and minerals. Well balanced by full tannin. Long, fruity, tannic finish.

1995 Fattoria d'Ambra, Carmignano ★★★ $$

A beautiful wine; wonderfully complex violet, blackberry, and earth aromas and the same flavors. On the palate, it is silky in texture with a harmonious elegance that continues right through the long finish.

1996 Nottola, Vino Nobile di Montepulciano ★★★ $$

Judicious use of large Slavonian oak casks, which impart less flavor and tannin than small casks, allows the vivid raspberry flavors to shine brightly. Nuances of nuts and violets add to the complexity of this wonderful wine.

1997 Il Poggione, Rosso di Montalcino ★★★ $$

Underbrush, spice, and tobacco aromas mingle with plum, cassis, and black cherry. Full tannin and tart acidity focus and enliven the fruit flavors in a mouthwatering, modern-style wine.

1995 Avignonesi, Vino Nobile di Montepulciano ★★ $$

A little game, dried flowers, and perfume aromas mingle with the scents of black fruits. This complex, medium-bodied wine has a lovely, long finish that carries its flavors well.

1996 Tenuta Trerose, Vino Nobile di Montepulciano ★★ $$

An up-and-coming estate with one foot rooted in tradition and the other firmly placed in contemporary winemaking. This vibrant Vino Nobile is a mellow wine with full cherry flavor and smooth tannin.

1995 Monte Antico Red Tuscan Table Wine, Tuscany ★★ $

Hillside-grown Sangiovese grapes help make this wine a little blockbuster of sprightly, concentrated dried-cherry and berry flavors well balanced by spicy oak.

OTHER CENTRAL ITALIAN WINE REGIONS

EMILIA-ROMAGNA
UMBRIA
MARCHES
ABRUZZI
Rome
LATIUM
Appennines Mountains

The six regions of central Italy are divided by the Apennines mountains—Tuscany, Latium, and Umbria to the west; Emilia-Romagna, the Marches, and Abruzzi to the east. Among red grapes Sangiovese dominates in the western regions, gradually yielding to the robust and fruity Montepulciano in Abruzzi. Lambrusco is a force in Emilia-Romagna. The ubiquitous Trebbiano produces oceans of mostly neutral whites that slake thirsts in the bars and trattorias of Rome, Bologna, and beyond. Watch as well for new-style wines from recent plantings of Cabernet Sauvignon, Syrah, Merlot, and Chardonnay.

ABRUZZI produces inexpensive quaffing wines in vast quantities. Just about every Italian restaurant in the U.S. serves red Montepulciano d'Abruzzo and white Trebbiano d'Abruzzo as its house wines.

EMILIA-ROMAGNA, the agricultural heartland of Italy, is known for Lambrusco, familiar to Americans as a low-alcohol, bubble-gum flavored, sweet and fizzy wine with a screw cap. Look for the dryer cork-sealed versions drunk in Italy. They are far superior. Also be on the lookout for new varietals made from Chardonnay and Cabernet Sauvignon. Albana di Romagna is the only traditional white of interest.

LATIUM (Lazio in Italian) boasts a wonderful harvest of Malvasia and Trebbiano, which merge in their light, easy-drinking Frascati. The better wines have more Malvasia, and many have a zesty hint of spritz.

MARCHES is undergoing a resurgence of quality, not only in its bracing herbal Verdicchio but also in its full and fruity reds. Rosso Cònero and Rosso Piceno, both blends of Sangiovese and Montepulciano, are worth seeking out.

UMBRIA is famous for its Orvieto. Light, tart, and dry or *amabile* (off-dry), Orvieto is a blend of Trebbiano and Malvasia. A few notable Sangiovese-based reds are produced as well.

at the table

The refreshing Verdicchios, Frascatis, dry Orvietos, and Trebbianos d'Abruzzo are perfect with salads, light fish, and shellfish. Try an Orvieto *amabile* with fresh fruit. If you can find a traditional Lambrusco, you will be amazed at how its acidity and light tannin balance the richness of Prosciutto di Parma or Bolognese sauce. The simple Montepulcianos d'Abruzzo are great hamburger and pizza wines, while the classier Rossos Piceno and Conero are of much more interest with meat, pasta, and white truffles.

the bottom Line Many of these wines offer reasonable value at bargain-basement prices. It's worth it, however, to pay the extra dollar, or two or three, necessary to get a wine from one of the best producers.

WHITE WINES

1998 Antinori Chardonnay Castello della Sala, Umbria ★★★ $$
Pear, lemon, peach, vanilla, and marmalade nose. This is a medium-to full-bodied Chardonnay. Lovely, creamy texture and full fruit flavors with some obvious vanilla oakiness, particularly on the finish.

1997 Salviano Orvieto Classico, Umbria ★★★ $
Old-style Orvieto: earthy, nutty, slightly oxidized nose. Full nutty flavors and powerful alcohol. Impressive.

1997 Umani Ronchi Verdicchio Casal di Serra, Marches ★★★ $
A big wine for a Verdicchio, with surprisingly explosive peachy aromas and flavors. Unusual for a wine of this type, it needs a year or two of aging in the bottle to come together.

1997 Colli Amerini Chardonnay Rocca Nerina, Umbria ★★ $$
This 100 percent Chardonnay, grown on volcanic soil in a mountain clime, has full varietal flavor and a generous amount of toasted French oak, yet a refreshing finish.

1996 Colonnara Bianco, Marches ★★ $
Delicious Verdicchio with a lovely, slightly floral nose that gives way to zingy lemon-lime acidity and bushel baskets of peach and apricot flavors.

1998 Falesco Poggio dei Gelsi Est! Est!! Est!!! di Montefiascone, Latium ★★ $
Lovely aromas of honey, nuts, and citrus are the prelude to this surprisingly fruity and full-bodied wine. The wonderful fresh-orange and cooked-peach flavors are refreshingly offset by a palate-cleansing hint of bitter nuttiness in the finish.

1997 Sartarelli Verdicchio dei Castelli di Jesì Classico, Marches ★ $
Neutral, slightly herbal nose. Light herbal and earthy flavors are refreshing. An excellent wine for mild fish.

Red Wines

1995 Colle Picchioni Vigna del Vassallo, Lazio ★★★ $$$
The Cabernet Sauvignon, Cabernet Franc, and Merlot from the Vigna del Vassallo, planted in 1946, are used for this *cuvée*. A velvety, full-bodied wine, with a lovely fragrance of violets and toasted oak.

1997 Le Terrazze Rosso Conero, Marches ★★★ $$
This typical blend of Sangiovese and Montepulciano is terrific. It has unusually concentrated red-fruit flavors, lively acid, and a velvety texture. Very sophisticated for this emerging region.

1997 Lungarotti San Giorgio, Umbria ★★ $$$
This Cabernet and Sangiovese blend is on the oaky side, but there are lovely chocolate and cherry flavors, and a long and subtle finish.

1996 Pieve del Vescovo Lucciaio, Umbria ★★ $$
Since superstar consultant Riccardo Cotarella took over as winemaker at Pieve dei Vescovo, quality is skyrocketing. This 80 percent Sangiovese wine has intense berry flavors. Aging in French *barriques* has softened the tannin, making this wine great drinking right now.

1996 Cantina Tollo, Montepulciano d'Abruzzo Colle Secco ★ $
This wine is left on its skins longer than Tollo's other two Montepulcianos, making it deeply colored and full in body. A year in large Slovenian oak casks has made it particularly smooth and mellow.

1998 La Carraia Sangiovese dell'Umbria ★ $
A 100 percent Sangiovese wine that is bursting with raspberry flavors and hinting at black pepper. It's a great value, one that's just right to drink young. Also be on the lookout for La Carraia's bracing Orvieto.

1998 Falesco Vitiano, Latium
★ $

Falesco Vitiano blends equal amounts of Merlot, Cabernet Sauvignon, and Sangiovese to create a wine buoyant with strawberry flavor, a taste of cherry candy, and a slight spritz.

1996 Terrazzo Esino Rosso, Marches
★ $

Simple and tasty, this may just be the perfect pizza and pasta wine. Don't look for complexity, just a cherry-flavored, easy-drinking, everyday wine offering excellent value.

SOUTHERN ITALY & THE ISLANDS

Like the Languedoc-Roussillon a decade ago, southern Italy is poised for a breakthrough. Even now, as pioneering importers comb its regions for outstanding bargains, the area is shedding its long-standing and well-deserved reputation for low-quality, high-alcohol wines. A host of fascinating wines is being produced from ancient grape varieties, and quality is improving dramatically as increased interest attracts new money.

APULIA (Puglia in Italian) produces full-bodied, robust reds, such as Salice Salentino, from Negroamaro, Primitivo, and other lesser varieties. The values from this region are tremendous.

BASILICATA, Italy's instep, is known for the powerful Aglianico del Vulture made from grapes grown on the slopes of the extinct volcano Mount Vulture. A tannic, quality red that requires age.

CALABRIA is dominated by cheap and cheerful reds. Some excellent values made from the Gaglioppo grape in the Cirò zone are now commonly available.

CAMPANIA is the source of some of Italy's greatest wines, grown on the hills around Avellino. The red Taurasi made from the Aglianico grape is intense, tannic, complex, and long lived. Greco di Tufo and Fiano di Avellino are dry whites of distinctive character and longevity.

SARDINIA has highly aromatic, floral whites made from the Vermentino grape; these are the island's most exciting wines. The best reds are from the Cannonau (Grenache) grape.

SICILY, known primarily for Marsala and sweet Moscato wine, is also home to two major regional brands, Corvo and Regaleali. Both offer excellent values.

at the table

Aglianico's tannin needs the contrast of red meat or hard Pecorino Siciliano cheese. The full-bodied white Greco di Tufo, with its almond and honey flavors, favors firm-fleshed fish and sautéed veal or pork, while the more delicate Fiano di Avellino, also from Campagnia, complements flaky fish, shellfish, and roasted chicken. The full-bodied red wines of the islands, with their earthy fruitiness and balancing acidity, are ideal with the traditional Mediterranean cuisines that are based on garlic, tomatoes, olives, and pungent herbs. Serve them with antipasti, pasta or chicken with tomato sauce, or herb-infused grilled meats. Vermentino's exotic floral scent is well suited to the assertive flavors of citrus-dressed legumes and grilled shellfish or poultry.

the bottom line Southern Italy offers tremendous values. Not only are the prices extraordinarily low, quality is skyrocketing with each new vintage. Many excellent, even ageworthy wines can be had for less than $12 per bottle. Top bottlings rarely exceed $20.

White Wines

1997 Mastroberardino Greco di Tufo, Campania   ★ ★ ★ $$

Classic Greco aromas of honey, roasted nuts, and peaches. This full-bodied, earthy, thick-textured wine is chock full of peach-stone flavors that echo on a long, honeyed finish. A wine that needs robust food.

1997 *Terre Dora di Paolo Fiano di Avellino, Campania* ★ ★ ★ $$
A complex nose consisting of nuts, mushrooms, peaches, and floral notes. This dry, full-bodied wine has good balancing acidity for its hazelnut, mineral, and mushroom flavors. It has a long, lingering finish.

1998 *Argiolas Vermentino di Sardegna, Sardinia* ★ ★ $$
Hugely aromatic earthy, floral, and hay nose. This dry, medium-bodied wine has assertive floral flavor balanced by citruslike acidity. A good long finish.

1997 *Caputo Lacryma Christi Bianco, Campania* ★ ★ $$
These "tears of Christ" have aromas of toasted nuts and a whiff of pears. Quite dry, this medium-bodied wine serves up a little prickle of spritz, flavors to match the nose, and just the right acidity.

1997 *Villa Maltilde Falerno del Massico, Campania* ★ ★ $$
From the Falanghina grape grown on volcanic soil and much praised by the Latin poet Virgil. Nuts, candied citron, and a bit of smokiness on the nose. Full on the palate with mineral and earth flavors and good balancing acidity.

1998 *Botromagno Gravina Bianco, Puglia* ★ ★ $
This full-bodied, buttery wine has an exotic, perfumed nose of lemon rind and quince. On the palate, its earthy lemon flavor and good acidity balance the full texture.

1997 *Corvo Bianco, Sicily* ★ $
Herbal and vanilla tones to the nose. Dry and smooth with citrus flavors and good, palate-cleansing acidity in the finish.

1998 *Regaleali Bianco, Sicily* ★ $
Apple and pear nose. This smooth, dry, medium-bodied wine is simple but good from aroma through finish.

RED WINES

1995 *D'Angelo Aglianico del Vulture, Basilicata* ★ ★ ★ ★ $$
Grown on the hillsides of Mount Vulture at 1,600 feet, this brilliant wine has an intense bouquet of red cherries, cherry pipe tobacco, anise, and flowers. Full tannin and an electric nerve of acidity give persistence to the complex, concentrated flavors. Balance of flavor, tannin, acidity, and alcohol auger well for long-term aging.

1994 *Mastroberardino Taurasi Radici, Campania* ★ ★ ★ $$$
Bitter cherries, plums, violets, and a whiff of wet cement all mingle in the complex nose. Concentrated, with intense fruit flavors and big but smooth tannin. Give this one a decade.

1995 Librandi Duca Sanfelice Ciro Riserva, Calabria ★★★ $$

Enticing floral, pine-sap, and pipe-tobacco aromas. This wine has a complex red-fruit character, and, repeating the nose, is tinged with pine, flowers, and tobacco. It has moderate weight, ample tannin, heady alcohol, and a smoky finish. Give this time in the bottle to develop its full potential.

1997 Apollonio Primitivo Terragnolo, Puglia ★★★ $

Impressive black color and a fabulous nose of blackberries. This powerful, full-bodied wine has concentrated blackberry flavor, strong tannin, and a long, polished finish.

1993 Taurino Notarpanaro Rosso del Salento, Puglia ★★★ $

Intense fragrance of bitter black cherries, raw almonds, and flowers. Full and smooth in the mouth with flavors of toasted nuts and cherries. Moderately long, tannic finish.

1995 Venusto Aglianico del Vulture, Basilicata ★★★ $

Concentrated aromas of earth, black plums, leather, and roses. The similar flavors are enlivened by refreshing acidity and framed by velvety, mouth-coating tannin.

1997 Grotta del Sole Lacryma Christi Rosso del Vesuvio, Campania ★★ $$

A charming wine made from Piedirosso and Olivella grapes grown on the slopes of Mt. Vesuvius. Cherry, apple, and caramel in the nose, along with a whiff of smoke from the volcanic soil. Good tannin and lively acidity carry the smoky cherry flavors into a sustained and fragrant finish.

1996 Argiolas Perderas Monica di Sardegna, Sardinia ★★ $

Beet and bitter black-cherry aromas make a fascinating combination. Dry tannin, spice, leather, and earth flavors enhanced by good acidity. Made from the Monica grape, which is unique to Sardinia.

1996 Cantele Primitivo Salento Rosso, Puglia ★★ $

Alluring anise, chocolate, vanilla, caramel, plum, and blackberry aromas. Ample tannin and acidity buttress the berry flavors. The dry finish mellows with exposure to air.

1994 Cantele Salice Salentino Riserva, Puglia ★★ $

A fascinating nose of caramel, raw almonds, black plums, and earth. Full on the palate, where concentrated bitter black-cherry and almond flavors are balanced by the sweet notes of pipe tobacco on the finish.

1997 Regaleali La Segreta Rosso, Sicily
★★ $

Made predominately from the Nero d' Avola grape, which gives the dark-cherry, spice, and floral notes to the nose. Dry and reminiscent of a cinnamon-spiced cherry pie on the palate, this wine is a pleasure to sip with or without food. Good acidity, moderate tannin, and a long finish contribute to making this a consistent value.

1997 San Francesco Ciro, Calabria
★★ $

Made entirely from the Galioppo grape of ancient Greek origin. Intense aromas of leather, tobacco, and dried figs are echoed in the flavors. Medium bodied, with strong tannin and enlivening acidity, this is a wine that complements food well.

1996 Duca di Salaparuta Corvo Rosso, Sicily
★ $

Vanilla aromas from oak are apparent in the nose, along with underlying spice, smoke, and red-cherry scents. Dry but smooth, with clear earth, smoke, and spice flavors.

IBERIAN PENINSULA

Spain and Portugal have produced traditional red and white table wines for centuries, but both countries entered the 1980s ill prepared for a rapidly modernizing wine world. From Spain, only Rioja enjoyed any consumer recognition, and even today many wine lovers would be hard pressed to name a single table wine from Portugal. Yet, things are stirring now, and the Iberian peninsula is emerging as a source of myriad bargains along with a few bona fide, world-class treasures. Iberia's famous fortified wines, Port, Sherry, and Madeira, are discussed on pages 239, 234, and 244 respectively. For Cava, Spain's delightful sparkler, see page 227.

SPAIN

As recently as 20 years ago, to most oenophiles the only Spanish wines of any importance were Rioja and Sherry (see page 234). Today, from Spain's cool mountain foothills to its searing central Meseta, excellent wines are being crafted from both traditional and international grape varieties. For wine lovers stunned by the exploding prices of classics like Bordeaux, Burgundy, and Barolo, exploring Spanish possibilities offers great, and tasty, rewards.

Wine growing regions

RÍAS BAIXAS
VINHO VERDE
DOURO
Oporto
Douro R.
Douro R.
DÃO
BUCELAS BAIRRADA
Ribatejo
Alentejo
Extramadura
Lisbon
JEREZ
PORTUGAL

NAVARRA
Pyrenees Mts.
RIOJA
SOMONTANO **Barcelona**
Duero R.
RUEDA
RIBERA DEL DUERO
Madrid
PRIORATO
PENEDÈS
LA MANCHA
VALENCIA
VALDEPEÑAS
JUMILLA
SPAIN

MADEIRA

0 km 25 50
0 km 50

Grapes and styles

Tempranillo, the base for Riojas and Ribera del Dueros, is Spain's quality red grape. The most widely planted red grape is Garnacha (Grenache), which produces intensely fruity wines with enormous alcoholic clout, as well as some very fine rosés. It is also a major component of the Rioja blend. Among whites, Albariño, the one true standout, yields tart, appley, medium-to-full bodied wines. Foreign grape varieties are increasingly popular for blending and on their own. Currently, styles run the gamut from very traditional to ultramodern, fruit driven, new-oak influenced wines.

On the Label

For the most part, Spain employs geographic labeling. Albariño, the grape of Rías Baixas, is one exception. Its name is featured as often as the region. The terms *Vino Joven* and *Sin Crianza* indicate wines bottled within a year after the vintage. Red Crianza wines age in oak casks and then in bottles a minimum of two years altogether, while Reserva and Gran Reserva age at least three and five years respectively. Aging requirements are reduced by one year for white and rosé wines.

RIOJA

Not only Spain's best known red, Rioja (ree-oh-ha) is arguably its finest. Yet Rioja is having an identity crisis due to the sweeping changes wrought by the "quiet revolution" of the eighties. Traditionally, long aging in small American oak casks produced gentle red wines with hints of leather, barnyard, spices, violets, and coconut and white wines redolent of paraffin, lemon, and varnish.

Today, young, fruity reds and straightforward, aromatic whites offer fashionable alternatives to the classics. Both are the result of less time aging in wood and modern, temperature-controlled fermentation. The spreading use of French oak barrels and the Cabernet Sauvignon grape is further blurring Rioja's regional character. Many of the international-style wines are superb, but it would be a shame if Rioja lost the heritage of its traditional wines. Not only are they unique, but they are also among the greatest and most pleasurable wines in the world.

The best red Riojas are blends. Tempranillo is the base, providing fragrance, color, and tannin, while Garnacha gives full fruitiness and boosts the alcohol level. Small amounts of Mazuelo (Carignan) and Graciano contribute acidity, longevity, and additional fragrance and tannin. Whites are usually pure Viura, only occasionally blended with some Malvasia and Garnacha Blanca.

at the table

Elegance and good balance of flavor, acidity, tannin, and alcohol give Riojas wide-ranging versatility with food. Reds traditionally accompany grilled pork and roasted lamb. Both old-style whites, with their oaky, oxidized character, and mature reds go beautifully with tapas, such as cured ham, sautéed mushrooms in garlic and olive oil, roasted peppers, or chorizo sausage. The simpler Crianzas are good choices for turkey, hamburgers, and steaks. Modern white Riojas complement both seafood and poultry dishes, and they're perfect for paella.

the bottom line Rioja is one of the few of the world's great wines that is truly ready to drink when it is released. It's worth paying for. The better Reservas offer good value in the $15 to $30 range, with many Crianzas available at under $15.

what to buy RED RIOJA

1991	1992	1993	1994
★★★	★★	★★	★★★★

1995	1996	1997
★★★★	★★★	★★★

RED RIOJA

1995 CUNE Contino Reserva ★★★ $$$
Beautiful dark-ruby color. Nose has cherry, chocolate, and roasted-raspberry aromas mixed with leather and toffee. Mouth-filling, leathery cherry flavors and a long, velvety finish.

1990 La Rioja Alta Viña Ardanza Reserva ★★★ $$$
Lovely garnet color. Developed now, with mature, pronounced aromas of leather, spice, and strawberries. The strawberry, plum, and vanilla flavors are balanced by lively acidity that propels the long, spicy finish. An excellent Reserva that's ready to drink.

1994 Baron de Oña Reserva ★★★ $$
Clear, intense spice, caramel, strawberry-jam, and cocoa aromas. The palate follows through with finely focused flavors, good tannin, brilliant acidity, and a medium-long finish.

1992 Marqués de Cáceres Reserva ★★★ $$
This wine has a surprisingly youthful nose of blackberries, cedar, and peppercorns to complement its berry and underbrush flavors. Its excellent concentration augers well for further improvement as it ages in the bottle.

1989 Marqués de Cáceres Gran Reserva ★★★ $$
Cinnamon, crushed strawberries, and vanilla on the nose. Warm, inviting flavors of concentrated black currants, framed by dusty tannin and brisk acidity evolve into a long, smooth finish. Has further aging potential due to its balance, character, and intensity.

1989 Bodegas Montecillo Viña Monty Gran Reserva ★★★ $$
A fragrant nose of dried currants, cedar, and vanilla. This full-bodied, robustly fruity wine has admirable acidity and gentle tannin in perfect balance. It has a long finish and will continue to improve.

1992 Bodegas Faustino Martinez Faustino I
Gran Reserva ★ ★ $$$

An almost opaque, deep-garnet color. Cassis, black-cherry, spice, and vanilla aromas lead into cooked-berry flavors with some leather and subtle barnyard notes. The finish is full of fruit, and it has lip-smacking acidity.

1994 La Rioja Alta Viña Alberdi Reserva ★ ★ $$

Intense, appetizing strawberry and coconut aromas. The wine is medium bodied, has fairly mild but noticeable tannin, and sports lively acidity that accentuates the nice fruit flavors. A medium-length finish.

1996 Bodegas Bretón Loriñon
Crianza ★ ★ $

The complex nose offers an initial whiff of game, followed by aromas of roasted berries, caramel, cedar, toasted coconut, and vanilla. Full of berry flavors, this mellow, velvety wine finishes with a lingering, spicy aftertaste.

1996 CUNE Viña Real Crianza ★ ★ $

This wine is brisk and medium bodied in a spicy Burgundian style. The taste is almost like that of a Pinot Noir but spicier, with lovely, concentrated blackberry, leather, and spice flavors. It's a little gem, an elegant wine.

1996 Bodegas Montecillo
Viña Cumbrero Crianza ★ ★ $

On the nose, there are penetrating aromas of cedar, cherry, and spices. This mellow, medium-weight wine has zesty acidity balancing its spicy berry and plum flavors. Readily available and always a good value.

WHITE RIOJA
1997 CUNE Monopole ★ ★ $$

A concentrated nose of coconut, apple, cocoa, and vanilla. Very creamy in the mouth with a ramrod of acidity that drives the oaky, appley flavors through the long finish. Unusual, but very good. This is one of the few traditional, American-oak-aged white Riojas left on the market today.

1998 Marqués de Cáceres ★ ★ $

Made from 100 percent Viura grapes grown in the Rioja Alta, this wine features heady aromas of flowers, herbs, and lime peel. The wine is dry, with a silky texture and concentrated flavors of marzipan, fresh bread, and flowers. The flavors are enhanced by the lemon-lime acidity.

1997 Bodegas Montecillo Viña Cumbrero ★ $

Subtle toasted-bread and lemon-peel aromas. A silken texture and moderate viscosity with flavors of apples and pears. This easy-to-find wine sports a hint of spice on the finish.

1998 Bodegas Paternina Banda Dorada ★ $

Yeast, earth, and apples meld harmoniously on the nose. A refreshing, medium-bodied wine with fruity flavors of ripe cantaloupe sprinkled with lime juice. Delicious!

RIBERA DEL DUERO

The breakthrough for Ribera del Duero (ree-BAIR-ah del doo-EH-ro) came with the glowing reviews of the 1982 and 1983 Pesqueras by the influential American wine critic Robert Parker. A rush of new investment and wineries followed his plaudits, making the region one of the most exciting, if somewhat inconsistent, in Spain today. The wineries Vega Sicilia and Pesquera are the engines of the Ribera del Duero, which produces impressively concentrated red wines with a happy harmony of flavor, acidity, tannin, and alcohol. The primary grape is Tempranillo. Some wineries use up to 25 percent Cabernet Sauvignon and Merlot. Many of the wines see lavish amounts of new oak.

at the table

The power and strength of these reds stand up to bold flavors. In northern Spain, roasted whole lamb and suckling pig are specialties that are often served with Dueros because they soften the wines' assertive tannin. Back home in the American kitchen, roast beef, steak, leg of lamb, and lamb chops are more realistic pairings. Vegetarians will love Ribera del Dueros with grilled portobello mushrooms or eggplant. They also accompany marinated olives and salty, firm cheeses beautifully.

THE BOTTOM LINE   You may need a second mortgage for Vega Sicilia and Pesquera's top wines, but most Ribera del Dueros are in the affordable category, between $18 and $35. Given the region's generally high quality, the wines are excellent buys.

WHAT TO BUY   RIBERA DEL DUERO

1993	1994	1995	1996	1997	1998
★★	★★★★	★★★★	★★★★	★★★	★★★

1994 Bodegas Alejandro Fernandez Pesquera Reserva Especial   ★★★★ $$$$
Big, enveloping aromas of leather, chocolate, coconut, vanilla, dark plums, cassis, and spices. On the palate, the wine has a satiny texture, snappy acidity, and fullness as a result of lots of glycerine. The finish is long and has a note of iron-rich, mineral soil.

1981 Bodegas Vega Sicilia Unico   ★★★★ $$$$
Still some youthful floral, blackberry, and chocolate aromas mingle with leather, coffee, toffee, and spice. Slightly oxidized flavors and rough tannin betray old-style winemaking, but there's no denying the tremendous concentration, huge body, and amazing length of finish. Very expensive but worth the experience.

1996 Bodegas Alejandro Fernandez Pesquera   ★★★★ $$$
Intense, intriguing chocolate, blackberry, plum, and anise aromas. A full-bodied wine with a velvety texture and dense, complex flavors of blackberries and plums accented by notes of iron, earth, spice, and pine resin. Definitely made for long-term aging.

1995 Hacienda Monasterio   ★★★ $$$
Huge aromas of anise, blackberry, and butterscotch. Lush fruit flavors are framed by smooth but ample balancing tannin. The wine has a lovely, velvety texture and finishes with the savor of dark chocolate.

1996 Condado de Haza   ★★★ $$
The nose oozes blackberry, toast, and thyme aromas with an intriguing, briny note. This gorgeous wine is dense and concentrated; yet it is quite elegant in a modern, polished style. Its explosive, red-berry fruit flavors on the palate carry through the long finish, with a nice note of chocolate coming through at the end as well.

1995 Viña Mayor Crianza   ★★ $
A nose of plums and raspberries leads to fruity flavors with hints of spices. The wine is medium bodied and has good flavor concentration, powdery tannin, and a pleasantly dry finish.

OTHER SPANISH RED WINES

Spain is exploding with new red wines and updated versions of old ones. In the region of Navarra, Cabernet Sauvignon and Merlot are joining the traditional Garnacha and Tempranillo and to produce exciting wines. The Somontano zone in northeast Spain boasts wines from the indigenous Moristel grape as well as modern-

style wines from French varieties. Heady, Garnacha-based blockbusters from the Priorato district in Catalonia have achieved cult status and stratospheric prices. Look to the established Penedès district in Catalonia for more elegant wines from local grapes, often blended with foreign varieties. Valencia, Jumilla, Extremadura, and the central Meseta regions of La Mancha and Valdepeñas are all emerging as excellent sources of well-made values.

THE BOTTOM LINE A number of Spain's new reds are also her best bargains. Prices range from $6 to $15 for many of the wines from Jumilla, Extremadura, La Mancha, Navarra, and Somontano. Prioratos, however, are in very high demand and are priced accordingly. Expect to pay $40 to $60 for many of these monsters.

1996 J. M. Fuentes Gran Clos de Fuentes, Priorato   ★★★★ $$$
Voluptuous black cherry, cinnamon, and floral aroma. So full flavored and bodied, you almost need a spoon for the velvety-textured berry flavors. Massive, yet high alcohol, tannin, and acidity are all in balance.

1997 Vinicola del Priorat Onix, Priorato   ★★★ $
Made from Carignane and Garnacha. Dense, spicy, black-raspberry, cassis, and vanilla aromas. A burly wine with substantial tannin, high alcohol content, and concentrated, roasted-berry, pepper, and spice flavors.

1995 Miguel Torres Cabernet Sauvignon Gran Coronas Reserva, Penedès   ★★ $$
Big nose of cassis, plums, bell pepper, earth, and some animal fur. Snappy cassis flavor. The wine has good concentration, but the fla-

vors are overridden by acidity and tannin right now. If past vintages are any guide, this just needs a few years to mellow.

1992 Vallformosa Vall Fort Gran Reserva, Penedès ★★ $$

Made from Tempranillo with a dollop of Cabernet Sauvignon. A bouquet of smoke, autumn woods, strawberries, and spice. The finish is medium length and sports a note of coconut.

1998 Bodegas Agapito Rico Carchelo, Jumilla ★★ $

Made from 50 percent Monastrell (Mouvèdre), 30 percent Tempranillo, and 20 percent Merlot. A fragrant cherry and spice nose, rambunctious spice and berry flavors, and strong, dry tannin. Though delicious now, it could use a year in the bottle.

1992 Bodegas Julián Chivite Gran Feudo Reserva, Navarra ★★ $

Hints of leather and red-berry fruit on the nose. A bracing style with spicy strawberry flavors and palate-cleansing acidity.

1996 Bodegas Guelbenzu, Navarra ★★ $

Black peppercorn and mixed berry aromas exude a "drink me" fragrance. Full-bodied, with mouthwatering fruitiness, it's a delicious wine that will only improve. But why wait when its youthful charm is so seductive now?

1996 Bodegas INVIOSA Lar del Barros, Tierra de Barros ★★ $

A nose of black peppercorns, strawberry jam, and spices leads to a light-to-medium bodied wine with smooth berry and spice flavors and a hint of leather on the finish.

1998 Bodegas Pirineos Moristel, Somontano ★★ $

Made from 100 percent Moristel grapes. Assertive aromas of loganberry, spice, and chocolate. The wine is medium bodied, with zesty acidity, smooth tannin, and, in the finish, a note of earth.

1994 Allozo Crianza, La Mancha ★ $

Penetrating aromas of blackberries and new oak's vanilla and spice. Simply delicious berry flavors are framed by gentle tannin and mild acidity. A superb everyday red.

1998 Bodegas Colegiata Farina, Toro ★ $

Aromas of black-currant preserves tinged with a gamy note. The wine is full and jammy with mild tannin, refreshing acidity, and a bit of high-alcohol heat in the spicy finish.

OTHER SPANISH WHITE WINES

Galicia's cool, coastal Rías Baixas district produces Spain's finest whites. These Albariño-based wines are intensely aromatic, refreshingly tart, and appley, and yet some can be surprisingly full in body. In the Rueda district of Castile, the Verdejo grape is prized for its herbal fragrance and medium body. Whites from the Penedès are also respected for their aroma, body, and acidity.

at the table

Galicia is renowned for its shellfish, and the Rías Baixas district's Albariño, with its citruslike acidity and mineral earthiness, is a sublime match. Mussels cooked in white wine, sautéed sea scallops, steamed lobster or crab, and clams on the half shell all sing when served with Rías Baixas wines. Albariño's vibrant flavors also pair well with Cantonese dishes. The herbal aromas of Rueda's Verdejo make it a natural with seafood and chicken dishes flavored with herbs. Weightier whites from the Penedès can handle spicy tapas and creamy sauces. Try Penedès with *patatas Catalana*, the traditional fried potatoes of the region.

THE BOTTOM LINE Albariño is Spain's most expensive white wine, at $10 to $22, but it's also the country's most consistent. The better ones offer terrific value. Other Spanish whites, with the exception of many Riojas (page 112), can be downright cheap, with prices starting as low as $5, but they're spotty in quality.

1998 Martin Codax Albariño, Rías Baixas ★★★ $$
An Albariño that has a floral, appley bouquet accented with a flinty note. These aromas are followed by vibrant apple and citrus on the palate, along with a lively mineral edge. These flavors make the wine ideal with light salads or seafood of any kind. Well worth the effort to find.

1998 Bodegas Morgadío Albariño, Rías Baixas ★★★ $$

Enticing aromas of almonds, honeydew, and minerals lead into melon, peach, and honeysuckle flavors. The combined tingle of spritziness, buttery texture, and snappy acidity create an intriguing interplay of contrasting tactile sensations on the palate.

1998 Bodegas Angel Rodríguez MartinSancho, Rueda ★★★ $

A medium-bodied, creamy-textured wine made from 100 percent Verdejo, with a vivid fragrance of flowers and pears, concentrated pear and nut flavors, and lively balancing acidity. It finishes with medium length.

1998 Bodegas As Laxas Albariño, Rías Baixas ★★ $$

Made from 100 percent Albariño. Earthy nose with slight floral and baked-apple notes. On the palate, focused lime and honeydew flavors. This wine has the full body and refreshing acidity typical of Albariño.

1998 Burgans Albariño, Rías Baixas ★★ $

Enveloping aromas of tropical fruit lead to similar full flavors. This easy-drinking wine is refreshing and finishes with a long floral note. As good as many a more expensive Albariño.

1998 Sumarroca Chardonnay, Penedès ★★ $

This young Chardonnay has shy aromas of apple and melon and the flavor of yeasty, fresh-baked bread, which recalls its recent fermentation. Only a bit of burn from a high-alcohol content detracts from an otherwise delightful wine.

1997 Torres Viña Sol, Penedès ★★ $

Made from 100 percent Parellada, a grape native to Catalonia, this wine has an earthy aroma tinged with lemon and blossom. On the palate, there's the flavor of earth and an invigorating zestiness, as vibrant acidity brings out the tastes of lemon-lime and apple.

1998 Viñedos de Nieva Blanco Nieva, Rueda ★★ $

Flowers, raw almonds, and minerals mingle in a fascinating bouquet. Creamy textured and medium in body, this wine has intense, but at the moment muted, muskmelon and mineral flavors. At this point, high acidity is at the fore.

1998 Bodegas Nekeas Vega Sindoa Viura-Chardonnay, Navarra ★ $

Aromas of pear and dominant oak. Abundant oak makes the wine a bit dry and bitter, but good acidity, nutmeg and butterscotch flavors, and a silky texture make amends.

SPANISH ROSÉ WINES

Americans have long snubbed rosés in general as uncool, but now these wines are on the comeback trail. Don't overlook the deliciously dry, and fruity, food-friendly pink wines that come from Spain. Navarra is the prime source for good rosés, but Rioja and the Ribera del Duero will reward you with some fine, enjoyable examples, as well.

at the table

The beauty of rosés is that they have both the lively acidity characteristic of white wines and the full fruitiness of red wines. The combination makes them incredibly versatile with food. Spain's rosés are perfect for tapas or mixed hors d'oeuvres. Their mild tannin and balancing acidity contrast well with smoked or cured meat, such as serrano ham, and with grilled or fried fish. They are great summertime wines, and they're the ideal accompaniment to salads, light first courses, and sandwiches,

the bottom line   Spain's rosés are cheap. Take advantage of the many refreshing, tasty wines available for $12 or less.

1997 Julián Chivite Gran Feudo Rosado, Navarra ★★ $
First, there's the brilliant pink hue. Then, stunning aromas of strawberries and spices. Concentrated and dry with a mouthwatering tang of strawberrylike acidity, this just may be the perfect warm-weather wine.

1998 Bodegas Muga Rosado, Canarias ★★ $
Gorgeous pale salmon in color, this dense and full-bodied rosé serves up delicious aromas of strawberries, herbs, smoke, and black pepper. The wine is bone-dry, with concentrated berry-fruit flavors and a grown-up streak of earthiness on the finish. This is a terrific picnic wine.

1998 Marqués de Cáceres Rosado, Rioja ★ $

Salmon pink. Mixed berries, cinnamon, and bramble mingle on the nose. Light-to-medium bodied, this refreshing rosé tastes of luscious sun-ripened berries right through the finish.

PORTUGAL

Until recently, Portugal's red and white wines had little to offer beyond a cheap buzz. Entering the 1990s, its reds were astringent and lacking in fruit, its whites either sweet and simple or oxidized and dull. Most successful were the mass-produced rosés Lancers and Mateus. European Union membership in 1986 brought increased investment, and Portuguese wines have steadily improved. Now, Portugal is an excellent source of a variety of sturdy, bargain-priced red and white wines. And, of course, Portugal has long made two of the world's great fortified wines, Port and Madiera (see pages 239 and 244).

grapes and styles

The majority of Portugal's best reds are medium-bodied blends employing such native grapes as Touriga Nacional, Tinta Roriz (Tempranillo), and Baga, though Cabernet Sauvignon and Merlot are showing up more and more frequently. Portugal's most popular white, the invigorating Vinho Verde is usually blended, but versions based solely upon Alvarinho (Albariño) are on the increase.

on the label

The terms *Reserva* and *Garrafeira* indicate wines of superior quality. Reserva wines must pass a tasting panel. Garrafeiras, in addition, must be aged a minimum of two years in barrel and one in bottle for reds, six months in each for whites. Don't trust vintage dates on wines older than 1986. Rules were looser before Portugal joined the European Union, and pre-1986 wines sometimes contained either blends of vintages or wine from a much more recent year than the one stated on the label.

PORTUGUESE RED WINES

As Portugal's wine revolution continues, it is producing ever more distinctive wines, under more technologically advanced conditions, with fresher fruit flavors and with better balance of the basic elements—flavor, acidity, tannin, and alcohol—than it ever has before. Nonetheless, these red wines still retain enough of their earthiness to keep their characteristic identity and their rustic charm.

at the table

Though Portuguese reds are medium weight with good acidity, their brawny flavors make them work best with robust food. Dão wines made in part from Touriga Nacional, and Bairrada made from Baga grapes both cut the richness of fried, cured, or smoked meats. Douro blends, made from the same grapes as Port, stand up to grilled, spicy sausages and poultry or veal dishes with garlic, onions, and tomatoes. Garrafeiras from the Douro, Dão, Ribatejo, and Alentejo pair well with game and lamb.

the bottom line

The quality of Portuguese red wines has increased faster than have their prices, making for excellent values. Many bottles can be found for under $12. Expect to pay more for Reservas, Garrafeiras, and a few top names.

1997 Luis Pato Vigna Barossa, Bairrada ★ ★ ★ $$$
Fragrant floral, black-cherry, and cinnamon aromas nearly jump from the glass. Spicy cherry flavors are focused by lively acidity and moderate, smooth tannin. This truly fine wine has a long finish with strong notes of chocolate.

1995 Caves São João Porta Dos Cavaleiros, Dão ★ ★ ★ $
A full fragrance of dried cherries, cassis, and rich soil. Strong tannin, medium body, intense fruitiness, and a long finish. Needs more time to develop fully.

1995 Caves Aliança Quinta da Terrugem, Borba ★ ★ $$$

Seductive aromas of anise, mocha, blackberries, and fresh-ground black peppercorns. The dry tannin and full body are balanced by lip-smacking acidity and concentrated blackberry flavor laced with new-oak vanilla. Still needs time.

1996 Quinta do Casal Branco Falcoaria, Almeirim ★ ★ $$

Made from Trincadeira Preta and Castelhão Frances grapes, giving it an intoxicating nose of black cherry, plum, and anise. New-oak aging contributes aromas of vanilla. The wine has dusty tannin and cherry and chocolate flavors.

1996 Quinta do Cotto Montez Champalimaud, Douro ★ ★ $$

Predominant aromas of wet earth, cooked plums, and pungent spices. The wine is medium bodied, and it has a somewhat astringent, tannic finish.

1996 Quinta Sociedad Agricola São Domingos Torna Grande, Douro ★ ★ $$

Intense anise, blackberry, and dark-plum aromas fill the nose. Full-bodied and flavored with lots of dusty tannin and lively acidity that brings out the spicy black-cherry flavors and carries them right through the finish. A big wine!

1995 Les Domaines Barons de Rothschild Dom Martinho, Alentejo ★ ★ $$

A nose of prunes, pungent spice, leather, and smoke. This smooth, tasty, medium-bodied wine has a slightly hot and short finish due to high alcohol content.

1996 Caves Aliança Particular, Dão ★ ★ $

Aged in oak barrels, this wine has a nose of lively cherry, vanilla, and new-oak spice that begs you to take a sip. Medium body, bracing acidity, and a delightful aftertaste of spice and smoke.

1996 Cockburn Serradayres, Ribatejo ★ ★ $

Aromas of new leather, spice, and cotton candy. Fruity and fairly full in the mouth where moderate tannin and warming alcohol join in a very satisfying way.

1996 Quinta da Aveleda Charamba, Douro ★ ★ $

Earth, plum, and blackberry aromas. Concentrated, similar flavors, along with notes of spice and pine resin. Medium bodied with a good balance of flavor and alcohol content.

1996 Quinta das Maias Reserva, Dão ★★ $

Intensely spicy nose of black pepper, cinnamon, berries, and vanilla. This velvety textured wine tastes of strawberries and vanilla cream. Some drying oak tannin should mellow with a little bottle age to allow a modest beauty to emerge. Made predominantly from the obscure Jaén grape.

1996 Quinta dos Roques Reserva, Dão ★★ $

This wine is made from a blend of Touriga Nacional, Jaén, Tinta Roriz, Tinto Cão, and Alfrocheiro Preto grapes and is aged in new French oak. Full, intense aromas of chocolate, plums, and spices on the nose. A medium-bodied wine with gentle tannin and concentrated fruit flavors. The strong flavors are well balanced by exhilaratingly punchy acidity.

1996 Jose Maria da Fonseca Periquita, Terras do Sado ★ $

Pungent spice, earth, and animal aromas carry through into the pleasingly bitter-cherry flavor. On the finish, a pleasant whiff of woodsmoke joins the other scents. This wine is consistently good and is widely available.

portuguese white wines

Bracing acidity, low alcohol content, citrus and earthy mineral flavors, and a slight prickle of carbonation make Vinho Verde (VEEN-yoh VAIR-day) delightfully refreshing. The Vinho Verdes bottled for export are usually medium sweet, but versions drunk in Portugal can be raspingly dry. Look also for the exotic Dão whites made in part from the Encruzado grape and also for the zesty Arinto-based wines of Bucelas. Perhaps most promising of all are the Bairradas, which are based on the Maria Gomez grape. Portuguese white wines are generally made from a blend of grape varieties.

at the table

On its own turf, Vinho Verde is served with all types of fish, particularly shellfish. The wine's rapierlike acidity easily cuts through the oiliness of rich fish, such as tuna and salmon. The off-dry versions that we get in the U.S., with their slightly mellower acidity, quench the thirst nicely when paired with Indian and Southeast Asian cuisines. Use them as you might a German Kabinett *halbtrocken* as a match for other somewhat spicy food, too. Portuguese whites other than Vinho Verde have the body to pair well with firm-fleshed fish like swordfish, poultry, and pork.

the bottom line
A few Vinho Verdes have pierced the $8 mark, but most remain firmly below, making them excellent values. Other Portuguese whites are also reasonably priced.

1998 Quinta da Aleveda Loureiro da Aveleda, Vinho Verde
★ ★ ★ $

Loureiro means laurel leaf in Portuguese, and indeed this wine does smell of laurel, along with minerals and flowers. Suspended carbon dioxide adds the typical spritz of small bubbles, as well as a high-acid snap to the concentrated flavors. A very good example of a single-varietal Vinho Verde.

1997 João Pires Dry Muscat Branco, Terras do Sado
★ ★ ★ $

A delightful nose of fragrant grapes, muskmelon, and flowers. There are similar flavors on the palate, with brisk, balancing acidity. Medium bodied. This is a consistently remarkable wine for both quality and value.

1998 Quintas de Melgáco Alvarinho, Vinho Verde
★ ★ $$

Aromas of fresh-baked bread, apples, and marzipan. Dry and full-bodied, this wine resembles Spanish Albariños with their high-alcohol power more than it does typical blended Vinho Verde versions. A slight sparkle, zesty acidity, and a creamy texture complete the sensation.

1997 Quinta da Romeira Arinto, Bucelas
★ ★ $

Made from the Arinto grape, which retains its acidity even in hot climates. An intriguing nose, with aromas of chalk, lemon peel, and spice mingling in the nose. The wine is full and creamy, with brisk balancing acidity and a medium-length, spicy finish. Arinto shows great promise for Portugal.

1997 Quinta do Casal Branco Terra de Lobos Branco, Ribatejo ★ $

Apple, just-mown grass, and citrus-peel aromas. Dry, with green-apple-like acidity, lemon flavors, and excellent balance of acidity, flavor, and alcohol content.

1998 Sociedade Agricola de Santar Casa de Santar Branco, Dão ★ $

Subtle aromas of apple, pear, and nutmeg fill the nose. On the palate, the wine is quite dry, with a silken texture, medium body, and flavors of fresh bread, melon, and citrus. A moderately long finish.

barca velha

When Ferreira's master blender Fernando Nicolau de Almeida decided in 1952 to make a dry red table wine in the searing Douro, the task was daunting. There was no electricity, so blocks of ice were transported from Oporto to control the fermentations' heat. Other technology was rudimentary as well, but as it improved, so did the wine, and Barca Velha is now lauded as Portugal's finest. A blend of about 60 percent Tinta Roriz (Tempranillo), with Touriga Nacional, Touriga Francesa, and Tinta Barroca, Barca Velha is aged in new Portuguese-oak casks and only declared in exceptional years. It is a powerful, yet elegant, red, with a deep mulberry and chocolate fruit character and peppery tannin. Ferreira holds it at the winery until it is ready to drink. Barca Velha is expensive, retailing for about $75 a bottle but its second wine, Reserva Especial, is about half the price.

GERMANY

Once wines from Germany were as exalted as those from Bordeaux and Burgundy, but following World War II a flood of cheap, sugary exports torpedoed the reputation of German wines. Today, in great measure due to the efforts of a few dedicated importers, Germany's wines are once again on the upsurge in the U.S. In fact, wine drinkers worldwide are discovering the thrilling interplay in German wines — heady fruit aromas and flavors, electric acidity, and subtle sweetness.

grapes and styles

The finest German whites are invariably Rieslings, but wines made from Weissburgunder (Pinot Blanc), Grauburgunder (Pinot Gris), Gewürztraminer, Scheurebe, and Silvaner grapes are common. Müller-Thurgau is the staple grape for branded wines, such as Liebfraumilch. Most of the 22 percent of German wines that are red are produced from Spätburgunder (Pinot Noir). German wines run the gamut of styles from light to full and from dry to achingly beautiful, lusciously sweet dessert wines. Dry whites are common in Germany, but those most often exported have some residual sugar. This sweetness is always offset by mouthwatering acidity, making the wines tangy and refreshing. They're rarely oaked, and most are low in alcohol. Like the wines of Burgundy, they have the uncanny ability to transmit the unique flavors from their *terroir* (see page 17).

on the label

The German wine label can be intimidating, but it actually presents a lot of information in a clear and organized manner. As with most wines, the producer, or winery, is your most valuable piece of information, followed in importance by the vintage. Also, the region is clearly stated, giving you a clue as to the style.

With the finest wines, you will typically find four words on two lines in the middle of the label, presented in the following order. First is the town from which the wine came. The "er" ending means *coming from* or *belonging to* just as it does in English (think Londoner or New Yorker). The second word is the name of the vineyard. Simple so far, and typical of a geographic label, such as one from Burgundy. The second line states the grape variety, and, finally, something no other label tells you: the ripeness level, or *prädikat*, of the grapes when picked.

Of the four general categories of German wine, only the top two are exported:

QUALITÄTSWEIN *bestimmter Anbaugebiete* (quality wine from a specific region, or QbA) Often labeled simply Qualitätswein. The grapes must be those approved for use in the wines of the particular region, but chaptalization (the addition of sugar during vinification to increase the final alcohol content of the wine) is permitted.

QUALITÄTSWEIN MIT PRÄDIKAT (quality wine with distinction, or QmP) This top category is further classified based on the level of sugar in the grapes at harvest, which tells you how flavorful, aromatic, and concentrated the wine will be and is usually an indication of its sweetness as well. The last three classifications below are generally dessert wines (see page 257).

● **Kabinett** The lightest and most delicate wines. Usually dry or slightly sweet.

● **Spätlese** The grapes for this category are picked late for additional ripeness, and therefore more flavor and body. Usually off-dry or somewhat sweet, though can be dry.

● **Auslese** The late and selectively picked grapes used here may be botrytis affected or not. Usually sweet and full-bodied with concentrated flavors.

● **Beerenauslese** (BA) Very late-harvested and individually picked grapes go into these luscious and sweet wines. The grapes are usually botrytis-affected

● **Trockenbeerenauslese** (TBA) Individual grapes harvested so late that they have been shriveled to raisins by botrytis make wines that are unctuous and rare.

● **Eiswein** For these intense wines, the grapes are not affected by botrytis but are picked and pressed when frozen. Very sweet with pure, vivid fruit flavor and scintillating acidity.

Two more terms may indicate the sweetness level:

TROCKEN Dry, up to 9 grams residual sugar per liter.

HALBTROCKEN Half-dry, 10 to 18 grams residual sugar per liter.

PRODUCER   VINTAGE   VINEYARD

TOWN

VARIETY   RIPENESS LEVEL   REGION

at the table

First let us dispel the myth that German wines cannot be drunk with meals because they are sweet. In fact, they are among the most agreeable partners for food you will find anywhere. Their bracing, palate-cleansing acidity and absence of heavy oak allow them to pair beautifully with myriad cuisines. Drier styles, like the *trockens* and *halbtrockens,* are perfect with lean, white fish, with chicken, and with pork. Sweeter styles marry well with fruity sauces and with salsas and are amazing with Asian and fusion cooking as their sweetness offsets the saltiness and cools the heat of chilies. The hotter the dish, the sweeter the wine should be. Vinegary salad dressings destroy most wines, but German Riesling handles them well. The low alcohol levels make German wines perfect lunchtime and aperitif wines.

mosel - saar - ruwer

The forbiddingly steep vineyards of the Mosel and its tributaries the Saar and Ruwer produce many of Germany's most delicate Rieslings. With only 7 to 8 percent alcohol, their bracing acidity thrusts the fruit flavors into high relief, giving the wines a refreshing, yet complex character unequaled anywhere in the world. Their classic aromas are those of citrus fruit and zest, blossoms, and apples, to which the

porous, heat-retaining, blue-slate soils of the region contribute a unique mineral or wet-stone nuance. Of the Mosel zones, the Middle is generally considered superior to the Upper and Lower. The wines from all three are the fruitiest of the overall region Mosel-Saar-Ruwer and usually have the fullest flavors and aromas, while those of the cooler Saar are steely and lighter on the palate. Ruwer wines often have nuances of black currant and herbs. Nearly all Mosel-Saar-Ruwer wines come in traditional green, flute-shaped bottles.

the bottom Line   In relation to their quality and production cost, the prices of Mosel-Saar-Ruwer wines are almost laughably low, most ranging from $10 to $25 for good Kabinetts and Spätleses, less for simple Qualitätsweins (QbA). Ausleses from good producers will generally cost from $25 to $50, but a few highly sought-after wines can run even more.

what to Buy   MOSEL-SAAR-RUWER

1994	1995	1996	1997	1998
★★★★	★★★★	★★★★	★★★	★★★

PRODUCERS AND THEIR WINES

EGON MÜLLER, Saar   ★★★★ $$–$$$$
The acknowledged master of the Saar produces ageless botrytised masterpieces from the vineyards Wiltinger Braune Kupp and the renowned Scharzhofberg. LOOK FOR anything you can find.

JOH. JOS. PRÜM, Middle Mosel   ★★★★ $$–$$$$
Rieslings that are spritzy, sweet, and difficult to read when young. Buy on faith; with 10 years age, they become breathtakingly complex and elegant. LOOK FOR anything from the Wehlener Sonnenuhr vineyard.

**C. VON SCHUBERT
MAXIMIN-GRÜNHÄUS, Ruwer**   ★★★★ $$–$$$$
Black-currant, grapefruit, peach, and herb flavors mingle in these refreshingly tart, slatey, sophisticated, long-aging Rieslings. Expensive and well worth it. LOOK FOR anything from the Abtsberg or Herrenberg vineyard.

FRITZ HAAG, Middle Mosel   ★★★★ $$–$$$
Elegance and harmony are Haag's hallmark. He is a master at eliciting Brauneberg's signature pear, slate, and apple-blossom aromas. LOOK FOR wines from the Brauneberger Juffer-Sonnenuhr vineyard.

DR. LOOSEN, Middle Mosel   ★★★ $–$$$$
Large-scale wines that can seem outsized for the Mosel. Extremely concentrated flavors in wines from late-picked, low-yield vines. LOOK FOR anything you can find, especially Erdener Prälat Auslese.

JOH. JOS. CHRISTOFFEL, Middle Mosel   ★ ★ ★ $$–$$$
Concentrated and multidimensional Rieslings with strong varietal and soil characteristics. LOOK FOR anything you can find, especially wines from the Erdener Treppchen vineyard.

REINHOLD HAART,
Middle Mosel   ★ ★ ★ $$–$$$
The finest producer in the village of Piesport and one of the most consistent on the entire Mosel. Succulent wines redolent of peach, apple, slate, and spice. LOOK FOR anything from the Piesporter Goldtröpfchen vineyard.

WILLI SCHAEFER,
Middle Mosel   ★ ★ ★ $$–$$$
Astonishing slate, citrus, and peach flavors, along with blossom aromas and precise reflection of vineyard characteristics. LOOK FOR wines from the Graacher Domprobst vineyard are best, but anything you can find.

DR. F. WEINS-PRÜM, Middle Mosel   ★ ★ ★ $$–$$$
Underrated producer making delicate, lime-blossom, slate, and apple scented Rieslings from the great vineyards of the villages Wehlen and Graach. LOOK FOR wines from the vineyards Wehlener Sonnenuhr and Graacher Himmelreich.

ZILLIKEN, Saar   ★ ★ ★ $$–$$$
A source for classic Saar Rieslings: steely, with razor-sharp acidity. Zilliken produces great dessert wines in botrytis years. LOOK FOR wines from the Saarburger Rausch vineyard.

Less expensive
Bernkasteler Doctor

The Mosel's Doctor vineyard above Bernkastel combines a perfect site for Riesling with ideal soil for the superb grape. The Doctor is the most recognizable vineyard name in Germany, and its wines among the most costly. For a relatively inexpensive taste of the Doctor, look to the Bernkasteler Badstube, a small *grosslage*, or group of vineyards, consisting of five superb, contiguous sites, including the Doctor. When its wines are made entirely of grapes from the Doctor, they will be marked as such, but when a label specifies only Bernkasteler Badstube, the wine *may* have some of the Doctor's grapes in it and at the least will be from exceedingly similar vineyards.

SELBACH-OSTER, Middle Mosel ★★★ $–$$$

Excellent house whose estate wines feature creamy texture from lees contact and a strong soil signature. Also produces great values under its J. & H. Selbach *négociant* label. LOOK FOR wines from the Zeltinger Sonnenuhr vineyard.

OTHER TOP-NOTCH POSSIBILITIES

The producer is followed by particularly recommended vineyards in parentheses.

MIDDLE MOSEL Willi Haag *(Brauneberger Juffer and Brauneberger Juffer-Sonnenuhr)*; Heribert Kerpen *(Wehlener Sonnenuhr)*; von Kesselstatt *(Josephshofer and Bernkasteler Badstube)*; Schloss Lieser *(Niederberg Helden)*; Merkelbach *(Ürziger Würzgarten and Erdener Treppchen)*; Wegeler Erben *(Bernkasteler Doctor)*

RUWER Karlsmühle *(Kaseler Nies'chen and Lorenzhöfer Mäuerchen)*; Karthäuserhof *(Eitelsbacher Karthäuserhofberg)*; von Kesselstatt *(Kaseler Nies'chen)*

SAAR von Hövel *(Oberemmeler Hütte and Scharzhofberger)*; von Kesselstatt *(Scharzhofberger)*; von Othegraven *(Kanzemer Altenberg)*; Schloss Saarstein *(Serriger Schloss Saarsteiner)*

pfalz

Berlin

PFALZ

Warm enough to grow figs and palm trees, the Pfalz produces the Rhine's most flavorful and full-bodied wines. They have spicy, aromatic tropical-fruit flavors along with earthy notes. Riesling reigns on the east-facing slopes and mixed soils behind the villages of Deidesheim, Wachenheim, Forst, and Ruppertsberg, with the Scheurebe, Gewürztraminer, Pinot Gris, and Rieslaner varieties represented as well. A raft of lesser grapes such as Müller-Thurgau and Kerner dominate the vast flatlands of the region. Quality has surged in the Pfalz in the last decade, as young winemakers experiment freely and slumbering old estates awaken. In addition to classic sweet styles, the region is an excellent source of both powerful dry whites and spicy, fruity reds.

WHY **SONNENUHR** IS IN SO MANY MOSEL VINEYARD NAMES

Fanciful sundials, or *sonnenuhr*, dating back to the 18th and 19th centuries, pepper the steep vineyard sites of the Mosel. Some are more than two stories tall, and, even from across the river, vineyard workers could easily see the shadows they cast and thus keep track of the time. Over the decades, these sundials, became incorporated into some of the Mosel's most famous vineyard names, such as the Wehlener Sonnenuhr, Brauneberger Juffer-Sonnenuhr, and Zeltinger Sonnenuhr recommended here.

THE BOTTOM LINE Bottles from the Müller-Catoir winery will set you back a bit, but everyday Pfalz wines are priced at about the same level as those of the Mosel, generally in the $10 to $25 range. Some very good values can be found.

WHAT TO BUY PFALZ

1994	1995	1996	1997	1998
★★★	★	★★★★	★★★	★★★

PRODUCERS AND THEIR WINES

MÜLLER-CATOIR ★★★★ $$–$$$$

Polished, intensely concentrated, fruity wines made from Riesling, Rieslaner, Scheurebe, Gewürztraminer, and other grapes. Wine-maker Hans-Günther Schwarz is a driving force in the region. LOOK FOR anything you can find.

KOEHLER-RUPRECHT ★★★★ $$–$$$

Relatively high-alcohol and high-acid dry wines with spicy tropical-fruit flavors and a strong mineral edge. Wines from this producer are idiosyncratic but great. LOOK FOR wines from the Kallstadter Saumagen vineyard.

BÜRKLIN-WOLF ★★★ $$–$$$$

Revived and on the rise since 1994, Bürklin-Wolf makes powerful, ageworthy Rieslings, both sweet and dry. LOOK FOR Forster Kabinett, Wachenheimer Spätlese, and Ruppertsberger Gaisböhl.

REICHSRAT VON BUHL   ★ ★ ★ $$-$$$$

Another resurgent old estate like Bürklin-Wolf, von Buhl produces understated, yet full-bodied and fruity, sweet Rieslings, Scheurebes, and Gewürztraminers from the great vineyards of the villages of Forst and Deidesheim. LOOK FOR wines from the Forster Ungeheuer, Kirchenstück, and Forster Jesuitengarten vineyards.

BASSERMANN-JORDAN   ★ ★ ★ $$-$$$

The third of the resurrected "killer B's" (Bürklin-Wolf, von Buhl, and Bassermann-Jordan), this one leaped forward when superstar winemaker Ulrich Mehl joined the winery in 1996. Vibrant peach, pineapple, and mineral flavored wines. LOOK FOR Kabinetts and Spätleses from the village of Deidesheim.

PFEFFINGEN   ★ ★ ★ $$-$$$

Superelegant, subtle, and delicate yet spicy Rieslings, Scheurebes, and Gewürztraminers from the top sites in the village of Ungstein. LOOK FOR Spätleses and Ausleses from the Ungsteiner Herrenberg vineyard.

LINGENFELDER   ★ ★ $-$$$

Inconsistent of late but capable of great Rieslings, Scheurebes, and Spätburgunders (Pinot Noirs) from the sandy vineyards surrounding the town of Freinsheim. LOOK FOR wines from the Goldberg or Musikantenbuckel vineyard.

RHEINGAU

Berlin

RHEINGAU

Blocked in its northward course by the Taunus Mountains, the Rhine River jogs due west for 30 miles near Wiesbaden. Along the north bank of this stretch, the perfect southern exposure, protected from the wind at its rear by the mountains, produces grapes that make wine with an excellent acidic bite. This is the Rheingau, and over 80 percent of its gently sloping, loamy vineyards are planted in the noble Riesling grape.

Some of Germany's finest Spätburgunders (Pinot Noirs) come from here, as well. Rheingau wine, much of it dry, usually needs time to reach its potential in bouquet and flavor; when young, it frequently gives only a hint of what's to come. In recent decades, many of the Rheingau's aristocratic flagship estates have failed to make the most of their great possibilities, but a cadre of young, quality-conscious winemakers may yet succeed in reclaiming the region's historic place as the greatest wine-producing area in Germany.

THE BOTTOM LINE Reputation has made Rheingau wines among the priciest in Germany. Kabinetts can cost over $20; Spätleses, over $30. The few best are worth it, but look to other regions for better values.

WHAT TO BUY RHEINGAU

1994	1995	1996	1997	1998
★	★★	★★★	★★★	★★★

PRODUCERS AND THEIR WINES

ROBERT WEIL ★★★★ $$–$$$$
The leading estate in the Rheingau, and possibly all of Germany. Spectacularly complex, concentrated, ageworthy Rieslings, both dry and sweet, from the Kiedricher Gräfenberg vineyard. LOOK FOR anything you can find.

GEORG BREUER ★★★ $$–$$$$
Breuer is a leading proponent of dry Rieslings. His citric, minerally wines can be downright harsh in their youth. Give them time. LOOK FOR wines from the Rauenthaler Nonnenberg, Rüdesheimer Berg Schlossberg vineyard, and his blend, Montosa.

JOHANNISHOF/H. H. ESER ★★★ $$–$$$
Elegant, minerally, full-bodied Rieslings that can lean toward the sweet side when young. Tremendous value. LOOK FOR Kabinetts and Spätleses from the Vogelsang, Hölle, and Goldatzel vineyards.

FRANZ KÜNSTLER ★★★ $$–$$$
Complex, fruity wines that are full in flavor and body whether dry or sweet. This producer is one of the Rheingau's new stars. LOOK FOR anything you can find.

JOSEF LEITZ   ★ ★ ★ $–$$$

A source for small amounts of barrel-aged, artisanal Rieslings. Superconcentrated and minerally, with lovely, balanced fruit flavor and acidity, they require time to blossom. LOOK FOR anything you can find.

BARON VON KNYPHAUSEN   ★ ★ $$–$$$

Subtle, harmonious wines with classic Rheingau character and excellent acidity. A sleeper. LOOK FOR Kabinetts from the Erbacher Steinmorgen vineyard and Spätleses from the Kiedricher Sandgrub and Erbacher Marcobrunn vineyards.

RIESLING REIGNS AGAIN

In 1996, for the first time since 1972, Riesling overtook the prolific Müller-Thurgau and became Germany's most widely grown grape. Plantings of Riesling increased by 130 hectares while Müller-Thurgau lost about 730, reflecting declining sales of Liebfraumilch and other brand-name wines so popular in the 1970s. Now, sales of high-end estate Rieslings are surging.

RHEINHESSEN

Berlin

RHEINHESSEN

The warm and gently rolling Rheinhessen is Germany's largest grape-growing area. Much of its 26,000 hectares is given over to Müller-Thurgau, Silvaner, and Kerner, and other lesser grapes that are made into sweet, commercial wines without much character. Liebfraumilch, much of it of lamentable quality, is the Rheinhessen's largest volume wine. Along the Rhine River, however, a continuous five-kilometer amphitheater of steep, southeast-facing slopes known as the Rheinterrasse produces some of Germany's finest Rieslings. These wines are mellower than those of the Mosel or Rheingau, and the unique red-clay soil adds a meaty, smoky tang to their succulent peach and orange flavors. In the late 1980s, much of the Rhein-terrasse was replanted in the sweeping vineyard reorgani-zation known as *flurberinigung*. Today the vines are once again old enough to produce the superb wines that made the Rheinhessen famous.

tHe BottoM LINe   The great wines of the Rheinterrasse struggle to maintain their pricing power as lesser wines from the region undermine the reputations of the best. Some Rheinterrasse Kabinetts can be had for under $10. Spätleses usu-ally don't exceed $20. Excellent values.

wHat to Buy   RHEINHESSEN

1994	1995	1996	1997	1998
★★★	★★	★★★★	★★★	★★★

PRODUCERS AND tHEIR WINES

GUNDERLOCH ★★★★ $$–$$$$
Superb, intensely peach, guava, and spice flavored sweet and dry Rieslings from the Nackenheimer Rothenberg Vineyard. Stunning Beerenausleses and Trockenbeerenausleses. LOOK FOR anything you can find.

ST. ANTONY ★★★ $$–$$$
Harmonious, concentrated dry wines made mostly from Riesling and Weissburgunder (Pinot Blanc). LOOK FOR any wines from the Niersteiner Pettenthal or Niersteiner Hipping vineyard.

FREIHERR HEYL ZU HERRNSHEIM ★★★ $–$$$
Dry and off-dry Rieslings and Weissburgunders (Pinot Blancs) from some of the Rheinhessen's top sites. Subdued when young, these wines reward cellaring. LOOK FOR Spätleses and Ausleses from the Niersteiner Pettenthal or Brudersberg vineyard.

J. U. H. A. STRUB ★★ $–$$$
Riesling Kabinett, Spätlese, and Auslese from both great (Oelberg, Orbel, Pettenthal, Hipping) and lesser (Brückchen, Paterberg) sites. LOOK FOR all wines represent excellent value.

other german wine regions

Berlin
MITTELRHEIN
NAHE
FRANKEN

The mineral-based soil of the Upper Nahe yields the most complex Rieslings of all; they're like a cross between those of the Mosel and the Rheingau. Smooth, exuberantly fruity wines are found in the Lower Nahe. Scattered, steep slate vineyards in the Mittelrhein produce vibrant Rieslings akin to those of the Mosel. Silvaner is treated as a quality grape in Franken, where it is vinified into dry, full-bodied, wines of similar weight to white Burgundies.

producers and their wines

DÖNNHOFF, Upper Nahe   ★★★★ $$–$$$
If we had to pick our one "desert island" wine, it might be one of Helmut Dönnhoff's stunningly complex bottlings from the Niederhäuser Herrmannshöhle or Oberhäuser Brücke vineyard. LOOK FOR anything you can find.

TONI JOST, Mittelrhein   ★★★ $$–$$$$
Magnificent honeysuckle and orange scented, sweet Rieslings from the Bacharacher Hahn vineyard. LOOK FOR anything you can find. Beerenausleses and Trockenbeerenausleses if you can afford them.

JULIUSSPITAL, Franken   ★★★ $$–$$$
The top-quality estate of the region produces dry Silvaners of power and elegance that age nicely for a decade or more. LOOK FOR wines from the Würzburger Stein and Würzburger Innere Leiste vineyards.

OTHER TOP-NOTCH POSSIBILITIES
The producer is followed by particularly recommended vineyards, and sometimes classification as well, in parentheses.
FRANKEN Burgerspital (Würzburger Stein); Fürstlich Castell'sches Domänenamt (Casteller Bausch and Kugelspiel)

MITTELRHEIN J. Ratzenberger *(Steeger St. Jost and Bacharacher Wolfshölle vineyards)*; Weingart *(Bopparder Hamm Feuerlay)*
NAHE Crusius *(Traiser Bastei and Schlossböckelheimer Felsenberg)*; Diel *(Dorsheimer Pittermännchen and Goldloch)*; Kruger-Rumpf *(Münsterer Dautenpflänzer)*; Prinz zu Salm *(Schloss Wallhausen Kabinett)*; Schonleber *(Monziger Frühlingsplätzchen)*

tHe WORLD's most veRsatILe WINes

Bracing acidity stands out as the first requirement for vinous versatility at the table. Acidity enhances the taste of food, just like a squeeze of lemon juice, and refreshes the palate, readying it for the next delicious bite. Restrained flavors help, and, in red wines, moderate or low tannin is another plus. These requirements exclude some famous wines, but include many lesser luminaries that offer far more opportunities for exciting matches.

1. GERMAN RIESLING Works with cuisines not really developed with wine in mind, such as Asian or fusion.

2. ALSACE PINOT BLANC Our default wine. Almost every food harmonizes with this charmer.

3. CHABLIS Because it's not over-oaked, this is the best of all Chardonnays with food.

4. LOIRE VALLEY SAUVIGNON BLANC Even goes with the foods that are hardest of all to match—asparagus and artichokes.

5. CHAMPAGNE What other wine goes with eggs?

6. BEAUJOLAIS For parties, picnics, and simple meals, it's the ultimate all-purpose wine.

7. PINOT NOIR One of the few red wines that can partner fish as well as red meat.

8. LOIRE VALLEY RED WINES More acidic, less tannic, and thus more adaptable than either Cabernet Sauvignon or Bordeaux.

9. BARBERA Italians drink Barbera more often than any other red wine.

10. RIOJA Its moderate acidity breaks the rules of versatility; yet Rioja is fine with most everything.

AUSTRIA

At this moment, Austria is Europe's most exciting wine country. Nowhere is there a more vibrant community of young, competitive, increasingly worldly grape growers and winemakers striving for the highest possible standards. The average citizen can debate Austrian wine the way the French dissect dinner or Americans a box score. The variety of wines is mind-boggling, the quality as high as it is in wines from anywhere.

grapes and styles

The white Grüner Veltliner (GROO-ner felt-LEE-ner), Austria's most widely planted grape, covers over 30 percent of the vineyards. From this variety, Austrian vintners produce an impressive range of styles—from bracing, light, dry, uniquely herbal and peppery wines to sweet, honeyed masterpieces. Riesling is the top-quality grape. Austrian Rieslings have some of the perfumed delicacy of Germany's and some of the spicy power of those from Alsace. Welschriesling (vel'sh-REECE-ling), Weissburgunder (Pinot Blanc), Grauburgunder (Pinot Gris), and Sauvignon Blanc make excellent dry wines. Deliciously fruity reds are made from Blauburgunder (Pinot Noir), Blaufränkisch, Zweigelt (Zvi-gelt), and St-Laurent. And Austria bottles some of the finest sweet dessert wines in the world (see page 259).

Austrian winemakers avoid the medium-sweet style favored in Germany, preferring either very dry or obviously sweet wines. Whether dry or sweet, Austrian wines have an intense mineral quality that is especially evident in the persistent, almost adamant finish.

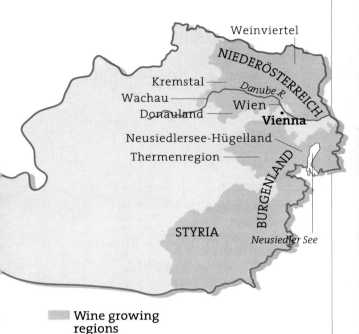

Wine growing
regions

on the Label

As with Germany, Austria's wines are labeled by both geography and grape variety. Wachau and Kremstal are the most important areas for quality white wines, Burgenland for reds and sweet wines. Austria classifies its wines in much the same manner as Germany, using the *prädikats* Kabinett through Trockenbeerenauslese (see page 130). But for each of these levels of ripeness, Austrian wine law requires a higher level of sugar at harvest, and thus, in every category, Austrian wine is fuller bodied and more intense than its German counterpart. An additional two terms unique to Austria, Ausbruch and Strohwein, are names of particular types of sweet wines (see page 259). The Wachau, which has some of the most stringent quality standards anywhere, uses its own three-tiered system. Steinfeder indicates the lightest wines; Federspiels are medium bodied; and Smaragd is used for the fullest, fruitiest wines. They are roughly equivalent to Kabinett, Spätlese, and Auslese respectively.

at the table

Wines made from Grüner Veltliner can be surprisingly full-bodied and have a distinct herbal flavor that makes them particularly adept with green salads and vegetables. Choose the lighter Grüner Veltliners for vegetables and freshwater fish. Wines from Wachau labeled Federspiel or Smaragd are big enough to be paired nicely with chicken, veal, and pork. Match Rieslings with fish, Asian cuisine, pork, chicken, veal, shellfish, and sushi. Some can be quite powerful, and these can easily partner full-flavored dishes.

the bottom line   Quantities are limited, and strong demand for Austrian wines in their own country keeps prices high. Grüner Veltliners start around $15, Rieslings around $20. Both can easily top $40. Wines from the best producers are worth their cost at all price levels.

what to buy WHITE WINES

1994	1995	1996	1997	1998
★★	★★★	★★★	★★★★	★★★

Lower austria

The largest of Austria's wine regions, Lower Austria (Niederösterreich) consists of five subregions: Wachau, Kremstal, Donauland, Weinviertel, and Thermenregion. They follow the sinuous course of the Danube as it slithers free of the Alps and carves a series of steeply sloping amphitheaters. Some of the world's most thrilling white wines come from the precipitous, rocky vineyards of the Wachau and Kremstal.

producers and their wines

WILLI BRÜNDLMAYER   ★★★★ $$$–$$$$
Delicate and harmonious, yet intensely concentrated Rieslings and Grüner Veltliners from some of the best slopes in the Kremstal.

Among the world's greatest Rieslings. LOOK FOR Anything you can find, especially Rieslings from the Zöbinger Heiligenstein vineyard.

F. X. PICHLER ★★★★ $$$–$$$$
Extraordinarily powerful, concentrated, and complex Grüner Veltliners and Rieslings from the Wachau. In warm years, such as 1997, they are positively Olympian. Pichler's almost cultlike following can make their wines hard to find. LOOK FOR Grüner Veltliner, Grüner Veltliner Smaragd M, Riesling von den Terrassen, and Riesling Kellerberg Smaragd.

FRANZ PRAGER ★★★★ $$–$$$$
One of the great names in the Wachau. Franz Prager's wines are an amazing synthesis of power, elegance, and clear fruit flavors. LOOK FOR Riesling Klaus Smaragd, Riesling Kaiserberg Smaragd, Riesling Steinriegl Federspeil, and Grüner Veltliner Hinter der Burg Federspeil.

LOIMER ★★★ $$–$$$$
Lush, modern style emphasizing full fruit flavors in medium-bodied, low-acid wines. Improving with every vintage. LOOK FOR Grüner Veltliner from the Spiegel and Spiegel Alte Reben vineyards, Grüner Veltliner Langenloiser, and Riesling Steinmassl.

FAMILIE NIGL ★★★ $$–$$$
Really coming on strong in the last few years—1997 was their break-through vintage. These are full-bodied, deeply fruity white wines, packed with spice and minerals. LOOK FOR Riesling Hochäcker and Grüner Veltliner Alte Reben.

HIRTZBERGER ★★★ $$–$$$
Franz Hirtzberger was one of the original members of the Vinea Wachau association, formed to promote quality wines in the region. Astonishingly elegant, minerally whites from great sites. LOOK FOR Riesling Singerriedl Smaragd, Grüner Veltliner Rotes Tor Smaragd, Grüner Veltliner Honivogl Smaragd, and Pinot Gris Pluris.

DINSTLGUT LOIBEN ★★ $–$$$
An excellent co-op in the Kremstal, producing terrific values in deli-cious, straightforward, fruity white wines. LOOK FOR Riesling Kremser Pfaffenberg and Grüner Veltliner Ried Loibenberg.

BERGER ★★ $–$$
Large production results in excellent values in basic varietal wines from the Kremstal zone. Clear, tart fruit flavors are the rule here. LOOK FOR Liters of Grüner Veltliner from this maker are one of Austria's greatest values.

BURGENLAND

Located in the extreme east of Austria, on the border with Hungary, Burgenland's vast, shallow lake called Neusiedler See generates enough humidity to guarantee the development of noble rot and thus the production of luscious dessert wines virtually every year (see page 259). To the west of the lake, is the rolling Neusiedlersee-Hügelland (hill country) where many of Austria's finest red wines are made.

PRODUCERS AND THEIR WINES

ALOIS KRACHER ★★★★ $$$–$$$$
A stunning array of spectacular botrytised sweet wines made from Chardonnay, Welschriesling, Scheurebe, and Weissburgunder. Also a wonderful dry white called Days of Wine and Roses. LOOK FOR Anything you can find. Superb wines.

WILLI OPITZ ★★★ $$$–$$$$
Wonderfully inventive producer of sweet wines. Opitz developed a particular type of Strohwein called Schilfwein (the grapes are dried on reeds—*schilf* in German). He has also experimented with botrytised red dessert wines. LOOK FOR Anything you can find; the wines are excellent, but it's the adventure that's most fun.

HEIDI SCHRÖCK ★★★ $$–$$$$
Fascinating varietal wines from an unusual array of grapes including Muscat, Weissburgunder, Grauburgunder, Zweigelt, and, of all things, Hungary's Furmint. Also produces marvelous Ausbruchs and Trockenbeerenausleses. LOOK FOR Weissburgunders, Furmints, Ausbruchs, and Trockenbeerenausleses.

ERNST TRIEBAUMER ★★★ $$–$$$$
Known to his friends as E.T., Triebaumer's wines are celestial as well. He specializes in intensely focused, powerful wines from Austria's three big red grapes, Blaufränkisch, Zweigelt, and St-Laurent. LOOK FOR Blaufränkisch Ried Gmark.

UMATHUM ★★★ $$–$$$$
Many feel Josef Umathum is Austria's finest red-wine maker. Umathum emphasizes delicacy, pure perfumes, complex flavor, elegance, and harmony. LOOK FOR Blauburgunder and Zweigelt.

HEINRICH ★★ $$

A specialist in fruity red wines made from the cherry and licorice scented Zweigelt. Drink these young. Also makes a good value Weissburgunder. LOOK FOR Zweigelt and Weissburgunder.

OTHER AUSTRIAN REGIONS

The region of Styria (Steiermark) lies in southeastern Austria, just south of Burgenland. Welschriesling is the principle grape, but red wines are produced as well. Wien is Austria's smallest region, surrounding the capital, Vienna. Most of its production is guzzled as refreshing, just-made wine in the city's many wine bars known as *heurigen*. Next to none is exported.

TEMENT, STYRIA ★★★ $$–$$$

Exceptional, extremely elegant Sauvignon Blancs and Muscats from steep, chalky single-vineyard sites containing vines over 50 years old. LOOK FOR Sauvignon Blancs and Muskatellers (Muscats) from the Zierreg, Graznitsberg, and Wietlisch vineyards.

SCHLUMBERGER, WIEN ★★ $$–$$$

A very highly regarded producer of widely available, traditional-method sparkling wines made from Welschriesling and other local grapes. LOOK FOR NV Brut Champenoise Cuvée Klimt.

WIENINGER, WIEN ★★ $$–$$$

Fritz Wieninger produces his share of quaffing wines for the *heurigen* but is renowned for powerful, Burgundian Chardonnays and Pinot Noirs. LOOK FOR Chardonnay Classique and Blauburgunder Select.

**OTHER TOP-NOTCH PRODUCERS
FROM THROUGHOUT AUSTRIA**

Emmerich Knoll *(Riesling Schütt Smaragd)*, Kollwentz *(red and sweet wines from Burgenland)*, Mantlerhof *(super Rieslings from the Kremstal)*, Nikolaihof *(Rieslings and Grüner Veltliners from the Steiner Hund and Vom Stein vineyards)*, Rudi Pichler *(Grüner Veltliner Wösendorfer and Riesling Terrassen Smaragd)*, Pockl *(Burgenland Zweigelts)*, Erich Salomon *(powerful Kremser Rieslings)*, Familie Zull *(excellent Grüner Veltliners)*

CALIFORNIA

Since around 90 percent of U.S. wines come from California, we're fortunate that they have never been better than they are today. These are quintessential warm-climate wines—powerful, tannic, high in alcohol, and packed with full, in-your-face fruit flavors. They're not always subtle, but California's best wines offer as much impact and enjoyment as any in the world.

grapes and styles

Americans love Chardonnay, and California obliges, producing it in a wide range of styles and in prodigious quantities. Sauvignon Blanc is the perennial also-ran; yet, with its charming fruitiness and balancing acidity, it's better with food than Chardonnay. Cabernet Sauvignon, a mainstay of Bordeaux, is California's most aristocratic red. The powerful Cabs from Sonoma and Napa are revered throughout the world. Fruitier, less-tannic Merlot is all the rage, but Pinot Noir, the notoriously finicky red grape of Burgundy, is soaring in popularity. Zinfandel can't be beat for its berry fruit intensity, and we're betting on Syrah to become the state's next big red.

These well-known grapes are only part of the story. There are more grape varieties in commercial production in California than anywhere else in the world. Experimentation, innovation, and competition are a way of life in California. Look for interesting new wines, both varietals—Viognier, Marsanne, Pinot Gris, Pinot Blanc, Cabernet Franc, Barbera, Nebbiolo, Sangiovese, Grenache, Mourvèdre, and others—and blends of these varieties of grapes.

on the Label

In the United States, wines are named after grape varieties, rather than grape-growing regions as in Europe. By law, if a grape name is used on a label, the contents must be made from a minimum of 75 percent of that variety. If the wine comes from an American Viticultural Area (AVA), it must con-

NAPA

SONOMA

LOS CARNEROS

Russian
River
Valley

Russian R.

SANTA BARBARA
• Santa Barbara
• Los Angeles

Wine growing
regions

tain 85 percent. Generic labeling has no such constraint, and so American Chablis, for example, which takes its name from the district of Burgundy, famed for its phenomenal Chardonnay, may contain any grape variety and be made in any style (despite much protest by the French). Don't take the term *reserve* seriously; it has no legal meaning and may appear on both high- and low-end bottles.

MERITAGE Prestigious, expensive Bordeaux-style blends of two or more grape varieties often do not use as much as 75 percent of any one grape, which makes labeling them as varietals illegal. Until recently either a generic name, such as Red Table Wine, or an invented proprietary name was the only option for these wines. To improve the market image and retain the flexibility to adjust the blend as necessary each year, wine makers adopted the word *Meritage*.

Meritage is trademarked by the Meritage Association, and wineries wishing to use the name must belong to the association and comply with its rules. Only grapes of Bordeaux origin—Cabernet Sauvignon, Merlot, Cabernet Franc, Malbec, and Petit Verdot for reds; Sauvignon Blanc, Sémillon, and Muscadelle for whites—may be used. In addition, blends identified as Meritage must be the winery's best and most expensive wines. Many restaurants also use the term as a category in their wine lists for all U.S. wines made in the Bordeaux style.

meritorious meritages

Ten fine examples of Bordeaux-style blends available at prices ranging from $30 to $90. Some of the wineries are members of the Meritage Association (see above) and are entitled to use the term Meritage on their labels .

1. Dominus Estate, Napa ★ ★ ★ ★
2. Flora Springs Trilogy, Napa ★ ★ ★ ★
3. Opus One, Napa ★ ★ ★ ★
4. Joseph Phelps Insignia, Napa ★ ★ ★ ★
5. Cain Vineyards Cain Five, Napa ★ ★ ★
6. Carmenet Meritage Moon Mountain Estate, Sonoma ★ ★ ★
7. Dry Creek Vineyard Meritage, Dry Creek Valley ★ ★ ★
8. Guenoc Langtry Meritage, Napa ★ ★ ★
9. Kendall-Jackson Meritage Cardinale, California ★ ★ ★
10. Niebaum-Coppola Rubicon Rutherford, Napa ★ ★ ★

CHARDONNAY

The U.S. has fallen for Chardonnay in a big way. Since the wine made its first commercial appearance in the 1940s, the number of plantings of Chardonnay has exploded, and in 1994, Chardonnay finally usurped White Zinfandel as the most widely consumed American wine. Chardonnay has now become so ubiquitous that it has engendered a backlash. Some wine drinkers have proclaimed themselves part of the ABC—Anything But Chardonnay—movement.

Nonetheless, California's finest whites are indeed her Chardonnays. These wines have come a long way since the 1970s, when head-spinning alcohol and overwhelming oak were the norm. Now their styles range from refreshing and neutral to full, barrel-fermented wines with gobs of spicy French-oak and buttery tropical-fruit flavors. Most Chardonnays are almost totally dry, but many are so fruity that they *seem* sweet. The better wines show a sophistication that was unknown even a decade ago.

at the table

Because of the range in styles of California Chardonnay, it pairs with an equally diverse group of dishes. The lightest wines with delicate citrus and melon flavors can be served as aperitifs, alone or with hors d'oeuvres, and with mild fish and pasta. Medium-bodied wines with pineapple and tropical-fruit flavors provide good accompaniments for chicken, meaty fish like swordfish, lobster, risotto with mushrooms, and mild cheeses. The big, blockbuster Chardonnays with lots of smoky, toasty oak can stand up to robust food, such as smoked salmon or trout, grilled fish, wood-roasted chicken, and strong cheeses.

the bottom line   In the under $12 category, Australia, Chile, and the Languedoc-Roussillon give stiff competition to California Chardonnay and are generally better buys. Many good values, though, can be found in the $12 to $25 range. The most sought after Chardonnays will set you back at least $30, if you can find them.

what to buy CHARDONNAY

1996	1997	1998
★ ★ ★	★ ★ ★	★ ★ ★

1997 Chalone Vineyard Estate Bottled, Chalone   ★ ★ ★ ★ $$$
Chalone Chardonnay is one of the few original California classics that are still at the very top of the heap. It's the combination of concentrated, almost sweet tropical-fruit flavors, adamant acidity, and complex mineral nuances, all in perfect balance, that make it worth the price. It will age beautifully, too.

1997 Long Vineyards, Napa Valley   ★ ★ ★ ★ $$$
Pricey and hard to find but one of the best. Elegant and balanced, with superbly concentrated flavors of pear, green apple, and figs, this has the acidity to make it one of the few California Chardonnays that will age gracefully. Worth the splurge.

1997 Au Bon Climat Estate Bottled Le Bouge D'a Côté, Santa Maria Valley ★★★★ $$

Clear-as-a-bell aromas of tangy lemon, honey, and minerals that are followed by concentrated mineral, lemon, apple, and custard flavors driven by vibrant acidity. Smooth and harmonious, it's a dead ringer for a Premier Cru Puligny-Montrachet.

1997 Chalk Hill Estate Bottled, Chalk Hill ★★★ $$$

Aromas of tropical fruit, butter, and toasty, nutty, vanilla-scented oak. This is a big, full-bodied, buttery Chardonnay, packed with fruit flavors and slathered with spice from oak. Excellent acidity keeps it all in balance and gives it the ability to age well.

1996 Sonoma-Cutrer The Cutrer Vineyard, Russian River Valley ★★★ $$$

A superb wine from this Chardonnay specialist. It has apples and honey on the palate; oak is present but not overwhelming. Look for their also excellent, more moderately priced bottling from the Russian River Ranches.

1997 Testarossa, Chalone ★★★ $$$

This small winery makes excellent Chardonnays from half a dozen different vineyards, including this one from the Chalone appellation. It has a faint nose of fresh lemons and minerals followed by a lovely lemony flavor and a long finish.

1997 Clos Du Bois Calcaire, Alexander Valley ★★★ $$

Combines intense fruitiness with elegance. Green-apple and lemon flavors are highlighted by good acidity and balanced by new oak. This wine can benefit from bottle age but is delicious now.

1997 Freemark Abbey, Napa Valley ★★★ $$

Considerable new oak is apparent in the vanilla-scented aroma and the vanilla-laced citrus and pineapple flavors. This full-flavored, full-bodied wine has an admirably long finish. If the vineyard designation Carpy Ranch is on the label, the bottle holds an even more intense version.

1997 Robert Mondavi Winery, Napa Valley ★★★ $$

A reliable classic with full fruit flavors of apple, pear, and citrus graced with toasty oak. It has a rather sophisticated style: totally dry, with an almost European complexity.

1997 Monticello Napa Valley Estate, Napa Valley ★★★ $$

This classic Napa Valley Chardonnay has a bouquet of apples, pears, butter, and cream. It is full-bodied, with generous tropical-fruit flavors and a long harmonious finish.

1997 Mount Eden Vineyards MacGregor, Edna Valley ★★★ $$

California all the way—powerful, full-bodied, oaky, brimming with tropical-fruit flavors—but an extremely fine example of this sometimes over-the-top style.

1997 Cuvaison, Carneros ★★ $$

A pleasant vanilla and pineapple aroma belies a light, refreshing style, tart green-apple flavor, and a long fruity finish. An elegant Chardonnay with nice balance of acidity, fruitiness, and alcohol.

1997 Markham Vineyards, Napa Valley ★★ $$

This big, full-bodied wine has aromas and flavors of orange, lemon, and caramel with good balancing acidity. Barrel fermentation provides a creamy texture and oak flavors on the palate and finish.

1997 Rodney Strong Chalk Hill, Sonoma County ★★ $$

Aromas of toasty oak, fresh pineapples, and pears. This medium-bodied wine has delicious, concentrated pear and tropical-fruit flavors. Rodney Strong also makes a less expensive Sonoma bottling and a more expensive reserve. All are consistently good Chardonnays.

1997 Callaway Vineyard and Winery Calla-Lees, Temecula ★★ $

This boldly flavored, unoaked Chardonnay gains its fullness from time spent on the lees (yeast cells). An appealing wine for those who don't like lots of oak flavor, it's dominated instead by the flavor of fresh pineapple.

1997 Echelon, Central Coast ★★ $

Creamy, full-bodied, and fruity, this totally dry wine has flavors of tropical fruit and melon that are luscious. From Chalone Wine Estates.

1997 Gallo of Sonoma, Russian River Valley ★★ $

Smoky, apple, and vanilla aromas precede pineapple, butterscotch, and nutty flavors on the palate. It's full in body with good acidity and a creamy texture.

1997 Napa Ridge, North Coast ★★ $

Light and fruity, this simple Chardonnay is reliably good, readily available, and reasonably priced. Its attractive flavors run to pineapple, melon, and a little spice.

1996 Anapamu, Central Coast ★ $

Has a nutty, butterscotch nose. A refreshing and fruity wine, with a long, slightly tart finish. This simple but good, moderately priced Chardonnay is brought to you by the folks at Gallo.

1997 Estancia, Monterey County ★ $

Oak lovers rejoice. The aromas are of apples and pears. Refreshing acidity on the palate and a full, buttery finish. All at a great price.

SAUVIGNON BLANC

Sauvignon Blanc has been touted for years as the next Chardonnay but has yet to fulfill that prophesy. California Sauvignon Blanc is a grape in search of a style. Most producers in the state seem afraid of Sauvignon's aggressive character and either ripen the grapes to the point of low acidity or so overwhelm the wine with new oak as to make it virtually indistinguishable from Chardonnay. As citric, minerally Loire wines and pungent, herbal New Zealanders make inroads in the market, some California growers are responding with a brisker, less oaky style. Fumé Blanc, a name invented by Robert Mondavi as a marketing tool, is synonymous with Sauvignon Blanc but generally indicates a wine with a mellow, oaky style.

at the table

Sauvignon Blancs are versatile and food friendly. The lemon, grapefruit, and fresh herb flavors and palate-cleansing acidity of unoaked, cool-climate versions are a natural with cold shellfish, pasta in cream sauce, light chicken dishes, mild fish, and salads with chicken or seafood. When it comes to cheese, goat cheese is the one. Be more hesitant with oaky styles, pairing them with strong-flavored fish or chicken dishes and assertive cuisines such as Southwestern and Indian.

the bottom line You can find many good values in Sauvignon Blancs, which rarely cost as much as Chardonnays. But be careful. There are as many overoaked, overalcoholic, sweet, or just plain dull wines as there are good ones. Prices start as low as $7 and rarely exceed $20.

1997 Robert Mondavi Winery To-Kalon Vineyard Fumé Blanc Reserve, Napa Valley ★ ★ ★ $$$

Aromas of smoke and herbs waft on the nose, while a lovely counterpoint of citrus and vanilla titillates the palate. This is a full-bodied, creamy-textured Fumé Blanc that has both good acidity and length of finish.

1998 Cakebread Cellars, Napa Valley ★ ★ ★ $$

Brisk aromas of mint and melon. Vibrant, tart acidity brings out totally dry, balanced flavors of grapefruit and orange peel. Cakebread consistently makes one of California's best Sauvignon Blancs.

1997 Carmenet Reserve, Edna Valley ★ ★ ★ $$
This barrel-fermented Sauvignon Blanc has a nutty, toasty vanilla nose. It's full and oaky with excellent balancing acidity. Very Chardonnay-like, but very delicious.

1997 Caymus Vineyards, Napa Valley ★ ★ ★ $$
Toasty oak and pineapple aromas, with flavors of apple and butter with a hint of fresh herbs. Chardonnay grapes make up 10 percent of the grapes in this full-bodied wine. The antithesis of the refreshing, herbaceous style: a Sauvignon for Chardonnay fans.

1997 Frog's Leap, California ★ ★ ★ $$
One of the consistently fine California Sauvignon Blancs, made in the deliciously tart, Loire Valley style. Aromas of citrus and lemongrass lead to a lively flavor of concentrated citrus. The finish is long, again echoing nuances of citrus.

1998 Callaway Vineyard and Winery, Temecula ★ ★ $
This wine is refreshingly brisk, with pineapple and citrus flavors beautifully balanced by lively acidity. The long finish carries flavors of lemons and oranges.

1998 Clos Du Bois, Sonoma County ★ ★ $
A lightly herbaceous, mellow, and fruity style of Sauvignon Blanc that has lemon, mint, and subtle toasty-oak flavors, along with a moderate acidity.

1998 Markham Vineyards, Napa Valley ★ ★ $
The nose is lightly grassy. Dry and pleasantly tart, with flavors of grapefruit and fresh herbs, this is an easy-drinking, fruity style of Sauvignon Blanc, neither aggressively acidic nor overly herbaceous.

1998 R. H. Phillips Night Harvest, Dunnigan Hills ★ ★ $
Delightfully light and refreshing, this wine has a fruity, slightly nutty nose and lively grassy and citrus flavors. Add excellent balance among flavors, acidity, and alcohol, along with a nice tart finish, and you have a terrific value.

1997 Robert Mondavi Winery Fumé Blanc, Napa Valley ★ $$
Aromas of citrus peel and grass, with flavors of melon and lime. Tart and straightforward, this is an on-the-mark California Sauvignon Blanc from the man who invented the name Fumé Blanc.

VIOGNIER

If any white varietal is to be a challenger to Chardonnay, it will probably be Viognier (vee-oh-n'yay). The grape of Condrieu in the northern Rhône, Viognier has recently become fashionable in California, and some very fine examples are being made. The wines are full-bodied, with a peach flavor and a flamboyant honeysuckle aroma. They are best when consumed young before their perfumed aroma and fruity flavor begin to wane.

at the table

The power and exotic flavor of Viogniers can make them difficult at the table. You can pair them with slightly sweet ingredients, such as lobster, scallops, and soft-shell crabs. Better yet, contrast them with very simple fare, such as basic sautéed fish or veal and roasted chicken. Also consider Viognier for mild curries and other Indian dishes.

the bottom line

Right now there isn't much to go around, so Viogniers are relatively expensive. This year, expect to pay $15 to $30 for good examples. As more of the variety is planted, prices should drop.

1997 Calera Mt. Harlan, California ★★★ $$$

Fragrant floral and herbal aromas. This intense, full-bodied wine delivers flavors of peaches, apricots, and lemon drops and a long, fruity finish.

1997 Alban Vineyards, Central Coast ★★★ $$

From one of the best and most consistent producers of Viognier in California, this wine is powerful, with floral, peach, and butterscotch aromas and mouth-filling flavors of peaches, apricots, and spices. Atypically for Viognier, its acidity is sufficient to balance its full flavor.

1997 Joseph Phelps Vin du Mistral, California ★★ $$$

Exotic aromas of musk, peach, and apricot. Lushly full-bodied, this wine gushes with apricot and tropical-fruit flavors. With its first plantings in 1983, the Phelps winery was one of California's Viognier pioneers.

1998 Callaway Vineyard and Winery Estate Bottled, Temecula ★★ $$

Highly aromatic nose, with peach, spice, and floral notes. These repeat in the flavor of this full-bodied wine along with a taste of honey. Vivid acidity provides balance and good length of finish.

OTHER WHITE WINES

It's tough for a California winemaker to resist the lure of easy money to be made by producing Chardonnay. Luckily for us a few are passionate enough about other varieties, such as Pinot Blanc, Pinot Gris, Gewürztraminer, Marsanne, and Chenin Blanc, to grow them, too. Check these wines out; they're among California's hidden treasures.

THE BOTTOM LINE Unknown and unpopular means cheap, cheap, cheap; $7 to $15 will buy most of these wines.

1997 Caymus Vineyards Conundrum, California ★★★ $$
A blend of Chardonnay, Sauvignon Blanc, Sémillon, Viognier, and Muscat. Complex nose of spearmint, apricot, vanilla, orange, and tropical fruit. Full-bodied, packed with tropical-fruit flavors—fascinating.

1998 Byron Vineyard & Winery Pinot Blanc, Santa Maria Valley ★★ $$
Light pear and melon aromas. Dry and delicate, with flavors of lemon drops and pears, this is a lovely wine, perfect for food or for sipping on its own, perhaps as an aperitif.

1998 Jekel Vineyards Johannisberg Riesling, Monterey ★★ $
Juicy with peach, melon, and pineapple flavors. The slightly sweet style with good balancing acidity makes this a lovely aperitif.

1998 Callaway Vineyard and Winery Chenin Blanc, Temecula ★ $
A completely dry style of Chenin Blanc, unusual among California's myriad off-dry bottlings. A simple wine, with fruity pear and apricot flavors, it's an entirely pleasant aperitif.

CABERNET SAUVIGNON

California's greatest claim to fame is her powerful, distinctive, ageworthy Cabernet Sauvignons, especially those from the Napa Valley, which number among the greatest red wines in the world. The best have concentrated cassis, mint, and cedar flavors; powerful but velvety tannin; and good acidity. The wines are generally more refined than the rough, tannic monsters of a decade or two ago. The great Cabernet Sauvignons will improve with age, but today's winemakers strive to make them appealing in their youth as well. Simple, lighter styles abound for everyday consumption.

at the table

The top California Cabernet Sauvignons are big wines that need either full-flavored food to match them or simply prepared meats to show them off. Hearty stew, sausage, and steak au poivre fall into the first category; grilled, broiled, and roasted beef, lamb, duck, and venison, into the second. As these wines age, mellowing and developing complexity, you'll be better off pairing them with plain red meats and semisoft or aged cheeses. Light Cabs are fine with anything from burgers to burritos.

the bottom line

Hold on to your wallet! California winemakers seem to be competing with each other to win the ego prize for the highest priced Cabernet Sauvignon. If you must have the big names, get ready to pay $50 and up per bottle. But if you just want great wine, you don't have to worry. There are more than enough excellent wines between $15 and $35. It's getting difficult, though, to find good quality under $12.

what to buy CABERNET SAUVIGNON

1994	1995	1996	1997	1998
★★★★	★★★	★★★	★★★	★★★

1995 Caymus Vineyards, Napa Valley ★★★★ $$$$

If you love massive, deeply concentrated Cabernets with generous lashings of toasty, spicy new oak and bold cassis, plum, and chocolate flavors, this is your wine. Plenty of tannin, balanced by the wine's full flavor, makes this a bottling to keep. It will improve for years with proper cellaring.

1996 Laurel Glen, Sonoma Mountain ★★★★ $$$

Only pure cassis and light oak are evident in the nose of this extremely young and unevolved wine. It has restrained, but superbly concentrated, pure black-currant flavors, and huge tannin that augers well for the future. A great wine that will reward you well if you give it a lot more time.

1995 Clos Du Bois Winemaker Reserve, Alexander Valley ★★★ $$$$

Intense aromas of plum, blueberry, and cassis on the nose are followed by equally concentrated red- and black-fruit flavors on the palate. This is a full-bodied, brawny wine, powerfully tannic through to the finish, yet silky in texture.

1996 Cakebread Cellars, Napa Valley ★ ★ ★ $$$

The spicy aromas here constitute an effective prelude to blackberry, cherry, and cedar flavors. This is a big, full-throttle Cabernet with ample, but gentle tannin. Though still quite youthful and fully capable of age, it is delicious already.

1996 Frog's Leap, Napa Valley ★ ★ ★ $$$

An intriguing floral note rides over the aromas of cassis and toasty oak. This big, fruity wine has flavors of chocolate, coffee, and black cherry along with strong tannin and lively acid. Drink it now to enjoy its youthful fruitiness or savor its nuances as it develops with age.

1997 Whitehall Lane, Napa Valley ★ ★ ★ $$$

The wonderfully aromatic nose of this wine features cherries, cloves, cinnamon, and a cool note of mint. Robust, with flavors of chocolate, cherry, spice, and cassis, a gorgeous velvety texture, and a long, richly tannic finish. Delicious now, the wine will just become even better with time spent aging in the bottle.

1997 Honig, Napa Valley ★ ★ ★ $$

Medium bodied with lovely aromas and flavors of cassis, herbs, and mild vanilla and spice. A textbook Napa Valley Cabernet Sauvignon, and a real sleeper.

10 Outstanding Cabernet Sauvignons

The best California Cabernet Sauvignons can match any made in the world today. All of them on this list are top-tier, four-star wines. Also in the highest price range, they generally cost considerably more than $50. Not included here are those wines made in such small quantities as to be all but impossible to find.

1. Beringer Vineyards Private Reserve, Napa Valley
2. Caymus Vineyards Special Selection, Napa Valley
3. Diamond Creek Single Vineyards, Napa Valley
4. Robert Mondavi Winery Reserve, Napa Valley
5. Chateau Montelena Estate, Napa Valley
6. Joseph Phelps Backus Vineyard, Napa Valley
7. Ridge Vineyards Monte Bello, Santa Cruz
8. Shafer Vineyards Hillside Select, Napa Valley
9. Silver Oak Cellars, Napa Valley
10. Stag's Leap Wine Cellars Cask 23, Napa Valley

1996 Laurel Glen Counterpoint, Sonoma Mountain
★★★ $$

Gorgeous aromas of cassis and vanilla. Concentrated flavors and abundant, but velvety, tannin. This wine is made in a much more accessible style than Laurel Glen's Estate Cabernet Sauvignon. It can be drunk young with much pleasure or kept for 10 years or more.

1995 Beringer, Knights Valley
★★ $$

Currant and herb aromas with just a hint of vanilla and spice from oak. This wine is lusciously fruity, full-bodied, and delicious right now. It's reliably fine and widely available.

1996 Laurel Glen Quintana, North Coast
★★ $$

Made by Laurel Glen in their restrained, almost European style, this is an elegant Cabernet, with fine tannin and good length of finish. It has aromas and flavors of green peppercorns, strawberries, and blackberries.

1997 Liberty School, California
★★ $$

This second-tier wine from Caymus has light, fruity aromas, along with those of toasty oak and vanilla. Clear flavors of blueberries, currants, and black tea; good balance of flavor, tannin, and alcohol; and plenty of tannin in the finish make this a very good value.

1995 Gallo of Sonoma, Sonoma County
★★ $

An aromatic wine, with a fragrance of cherries and toasted oak. It's medium bodied, with cranberry, currant, black-cherry, and coffee flavors. There is strong tannin on the finish.

1997 Napa Ridge, Central Coast
★★ $

With mint and black-currant flavors and mild tannin, this one's easy to like. Napa Ridge is an affordably priced label from the major producer Beringer. The wines are consistently good values.

1996 Rodney Strong, Sonoma County
★ $$

This classic Cab has a spicy nose of cinnamon and cloves and flavors of black currants and cherries. Moderate tannin and a fruity finish make it a good everyday choice.

1996 Hawk Crest, California
★ $

Nice and fruity, mellow, and full-bodied, with an aroma and flavor of black-cherry jam. This second label of the excellent Stag's Leap Wine Cellars makes a fine house red.

MERLOT

A few years ago, wine lovers found that Merlot possesses the fruity mellowness they'd always wanted from Cabernet Sauvignon, and, ever since, Merlot has suffered from its own success. Attempts to satisfy the spiraling demand have led to overplanting and the use of inferior grapes, which have, in turn, resulted in many poor wines. The best producers have, of course, been making fine Merlots all along and now, as supply and demand come into better balance, things are looking up for Merlot lovers. Most of the better California Merlots are silky smooth, with luscious black-cherry, plum, and chocolate flavors. Some of the best wines are powerfully tannic and will benefit from bottle age.

at the table

Lighter tannin makes Merlot more flexible at the table than Cabernet Sauvignon. Roast chicken, veal, and pork, for instance, are often overwhelmed by Cabernet but are flattered by Merlot. Also good are lamb, steak, filet of beef, pâtés, and rich cheeses. Be aware, though, that the large-scale Merlots can be every bit as powerful as a big Cabernet and require equally robust cuisine. Pair especially light Merlots with simple things, such as hamburgers, sandwiches, and grilled chicken.

the bottom Line Merlot is the trickiest of California wines to buy. The scramble to increase production has given us oceans of thin, flawed, overpriced wines. However, in every price range, excellent Merlots can be found. Just stick to our suggestions or seek the advice of a trusted merchant. You'll find Merlots generally run $8 to $25 and top out around $50.

what to buy MERLOT

1995	1996	1997	1998
★★★	★★★	★★★	★★★

1996 Shafer Vineyards, Napa Valley ★★★★ $$$

Year after year, this is one of our favorite California Merlots. It's intense, with chocolate and spiced-plum flavors. Strong tannin and good concentration give the wine excellent aging potential, but it's the exquisite harmony of flavor, tannin, and alcohol content that makes it so special.

1997 Mietz, Sonoma County   ★★★★ $$

Opaque black color. The huge aroma of spiced plums fills a room. This is a concentrated Merlot with plum and chocolate flavors framed in velvety tannin. A top-notch high-end Merlot.

1996 Clos Du Bois, Alexander Valley   ★★★ $$

Intense fruit aromas of blueberries and plums. Luscious on the palate, it serves up concentrated dark-red fruit flavors, gentle tannin, and a silky texture.

1996 Freemark Abbey, Napa Valley   ★★★ $$

This lightly oaked Merlot has a spicy, fruity nose followed by raspberry, strawberry, and herb flavors. There's enough tannin and acidity to allow for improvement with age, but this wine's pretty tasty now.

1997 Ravenswood, Sonoma County   ★★★ $$

Classic California Merlot, full-bodied and redolent of chocolate, cherries, and plums. It has good acidity, velvety tannin, and a long, fruity finish.

1996 St. Francis Winery, Sonoma County   ★★★ $$

Aromas of dark chocolate and cherries; then concentrated spicy cedar, black cherry, and cassis flavors. Adroit use of American and French oak helps make this wine both complex and elegant.

1997 Markham Vineyards, Napa Valley   ★★ $$

This lush Merlot has full licorice and dark-chocolate aromas, along with vanilla notes from oak. Though the wine is totally dry, its black-cherry and chocolate flavors are so full that they give an impression of sweetness.

1997 R. H. Phillips Toasted Head, Dunnigan Hills   ★★ $$

Lots of attractive new oak in the smoky, toasty, cherry-scented nose. Smooth and sensuous, with intense plum and cherry flavors and full but mellow tannin, this wine is really easy to like.

PINOT NOIR

Great Pinot Noir has been the elusive goal for California winemakers since Hanzell Vineyards first made oak-aged Pinots in the 1950s. Calera, Chalone, and Robert Mondavi are other pioneers. The best areas for Pinot Noir are California's coolest: Santa Barbara, Sonoma's Russian River Valley, and Carneros, which straddles the chilly southern reaches of Sonoma and Napa. California Pinot Noirs are generally fruitier, smoother, and less earthy than Burgundies.

at the table

Pinot Noir is California's most versatile red because it is both light enough to partner foods traditionally associated with white wine and full and fruity enough for red meat. Grilled fish, roast chicken and duck, medallions of veal, hanger steak, game, and semisoft cheeses are only a few of the possible pairings. California Pinot Noir is the happy solution to a tableful of widely varied food orders. Pinot Noir even works with Chinese food.

the bottom line   California Pinot Noir isn't cheap, but, then again, Pinot Noir almost never is. However, these are some of the best Pinot Noirs outside Burgundy. Prices for good wines start at $15. You'll have to pay twice that for most of the better wines.

what to buy PINOT NOIR

1994	1995	1996	1997	1998
★★★★	★★★	★★	★★★	★★★

1996 Etude, Carneros ★★★ $$$
Lots of fresh fruit—raspberry and red cherry—and clove aromas. On the palate, the wine is fruity and concentrated, with all the elements in beautiful balance. Always one of California's finest Pinot Noirs.

1997 Byron Vineyard & Winery, Santa Maria Valley ★★★ $$
This is a fruit-bomb of a wine, with intense aromas of raspberry and quince, along with toast, and flavors of red and black berries with tangy woodsmoke. It is succulent and delicious.

1997 J Wine Company, Russian River Valley ★★★ $$
A lovely, spicy strawberry and raspberry nose. This wine features Pinot Noir's complex underbrush and mushroom flavors along with its delicate strawberry flavors. Understated and elegant.

1996 Sanford Winery, Santa Barbara County ★★★ $$
Renowned for Pinot Noirs, Sanford makes them bold and fruity, brimming with strawberry and blackberry flavors. Vibrant acidity, velvety tannin, and just the right amount of spicy oak make this wine delicious.

1997 Villa Mt. Eden Bien Nacido Vineyard Grand Reserve, Santa Maria Valley ★★★ $$
Beautifully perfumed fragrance of strawberries, cherries, and plums. On the palate, a note of black cherry joins the other fruit flavors along with excellent acidity and silky tannin.

1997 Foxen Sanford and Benedict Vineyard, Santa Ynez Valley ★ ★ $$$

Lovely aromas of light smoke, raspberries, and black cherries. Mellow tannin, good acidity, and mouth-filling body are perfectly balanced, suggesting the capacity for aging.

1997 Babcock Vineyard Mt. Carmel Vineyard, Santa Ynez Valley ★ ★ $$

Penetrating aromas and flavors of spice, red currants, and berries. This is one of California's bigger Pinot Noirs, with full body and strong tannin balanced by brisk acidity. The finish is long with nuances of smoke and cherries.

1996 Robert Mondavi Winery, Napa Valley ★ ★ $$

This is a light, elegantly styled Pinot Noir, with floral notes in the aroma, tart red-berry and currant flavors, full tannin, and mouth-watering acidity.

1997 Rodney Strong, Russian River Valley ★ ★ $$

Aromas and flavors of smoke, cranberries, and cherries. Elegant and light in style with excellent acidity and mild tannin. This wine is ready to drink now.

SYRAH

The great wines of France's northern Rhône Valley, Hermitage and Côte-Rôtie, are based on the Syrah grape. In the early 1970s, Joseph Phelps, noting the similarity between the northern Rhône's climate and that of Napa Valley, decided to plant some for himself. Many others followed, producing intense, full-bodied reds, packed with succulent cassis and blueberry flavors. As more and more excellent examples come onto the market, evidence is mounting that Syrah is one of California's finest reds, destined to become one of her most popular as well.

at the table

The dense, fruity style of California Syrah demands hearty, even rustic food—lamb or beef stew, chops, game, or roasted chicken with garlic. Some Syrahs have black- or green-pepper notes and complement peppery meat dishes, such as the classic steak au poivre. Vegetarians will enjoy Syrah with almost anything that includes mushrooms. As for cheese, the more flavorful the better; Syrah is the wine for that aged Alsace Munster.

the Bottom Line Most Syrah today is made in very limited quantities, and so prices are generally high. At between $20 to $30, the vast majority afford good value. A few quite agreeable wines can be found for as little as $12.

what to buy SYRAH

1995	1996	1997	1998
★★★	★★★★	★★★	★★★

1997 Foxen Morehouse Vineyard, Santa Ynez Valley ★★★★ $$$
This is one of the finest Syrahs to come from California. It has a gorgeous nose of spicy cassis and classic underlying hints of game. It is full in body with magnificently concentrated, pure flavors, restrained power, and elegance. It doesn't miss a beat from the irresistible aroma to the endless finish.

1997 Alban Vineyards Reva, Edna Valley ★★★ $$$
John Alban is a specialist in the Rhône varieties, and his Syrah is quite French. It has aromas of cassis, clove, pepper, and game and flavors of cassis and plums. This wine has a complexity and a fine balance of flavor, tannin, alcohol, and acidity that transcend most California Syrah.

1996 Edmunds St. John Durell Vineyard, California ★★★ $$$
Smoky aromas of black pepper and cassis with an edge of spices and Provençal herbs. Concentrated and spicy on the palate with a pleasing dry and long finish.

1997 Daniel Gehrs, Paso Robles ★★★ $$
On-the-money Syrah nose of black currant, game, and spice. Made in a full, fruity style, this wine includes toffee, spice, and vanilla flavors from oak and is absolutely delicious.

1996 Cline Cellars, Carneros ★★ $$
Inky dark with a smoky, oaky nose. This medium-bodied wine has concentrated flavors of blueberries, mocha, and cinnamon, with good balancing acidity and tannin.

1997 Qupé, Central Coast ★★ $$
Due to lots of experience with grape varieties from France's Rhône Valley, Qupé does Syrah right: lots of black pepper and olives on the nose and concentrated blueberry and plum flavors. The more expensive Bien Nacido Vineyard bottling is even finer, fuller bodied, and more complex.

1996 R. H. Phillips EXP, Dunnigan Hills ★ ★ $

Fruity and peppery, with vanilla flavor from oak and a velvety texture. This wine stands out for its crowd-pleasing style and moderate price.

ZINFANDEL

The popularity of the sweet blush wine called White Zinfandel has peaked, and real Zinfandel, deep red in color, full-blooded, spicy, and intense, is coming on strong. Some Zins are block-busters—high in alcohol and oozing concentrated, jammy blackberry flavor and massive tannin. Claret-style wines are lighter and more restrained. Zinfandel is the all-American wine; with rare exceptions, it is found only in California.

at the table

Big Zinfandels can stand up to full-flavored foods, such as strong cheeses, pasta with meat sauce, barbecued ribs, spicy sausage, Mexican cuisine, and chili. Lighter Zins are great with pizza, simple pastas, and tacos. Zinfandel is the ulti-mate Thanksgiving wine. Its spicy blackberry flavors and full body pair remarkably well with turkey, stuffing, and all the traditional trimmings.

the bottom line   Only in the last few years have Zinfandels broken the $20 mark, but today they are hot, and prices are rising quickly. Still, in the $15 to $25 range they are California's best red wine buys.

what to buy ZINFANDEL

1995	1996	1997	1998
★★★	★★★	★★★	★★★

1996 Sky Mt. Veeder, Napa Valley ★ ★ ★ ★ $$$

Herbal and floral notes in the aroma; complex, densely concentrated flavors of black currants and blueberry conserve; and graceful power and intensity. These attributes add up to a world-class wine. Sky pro-duces only Zinfandels and those only in small quantities. They are well worth seeking out.

1997 De Loach Vineyards Estate Bottled, Russian River Valley ★ ★ ★ $$

Spicy, almost meaty aromas, with dark berry and cassis flavors. Lively and full-bodied with mouthwatering acidity and a long finish, this wine is simply delicious.

1997 Frog's Leap, Napa Valley
★★★ $$

Smoky, herbaceous aromas; flavors of black currants and cloves; and a long, spicy finish. While many Zinfandels tend toward overly jammy fruit flavors or excessive alcohol, this elegant example shows admirable balance and restraint.

1996 Ridge Sonoma Station, Sonoma County
★★★ $$

Ridge is famous for its single-vineyard Lytton Springs, Geyserville, and Pagani Ranch Zinfandels. These massively tannic wines often need time to mellow. For earlier consumption, there is Sonoma Station with its luscious red-currant flavors, gentle tannin, and lively acidity.

1997 Storybook Mountain Mayacamas Range, Napa Valley
★★★ $$

Complex, spicy aromas and an inky intensity on the palate. Though thoroughly dry, its intense fruitiness seems almost sweet. This age-worthy Zin is already delicious now.

1997 Nalle, Dry Creek Valley
★★ $$

Highly aromatic blackberry and floral nose. The full, tart flavors of black fruits, spice, and tea are still youthful, hidden by the wine's tannin and acid, but will develop beautifully with two to three years of bottle age.

1997 Peachy Canyon Winery Bin 107, California
★★ $$

A spicy, light Zin with good balance of fruitiness, acidity, and alcohol. The lush flavors run to blackberry, clove, and tobacco, framed by moderate tannin. Long and fruity finish.

1997 Rabbit Ridge, Sonoma County
★★ $$

Aromas of blackberry jam, smoke, licorice, and a hint of prunes follow through nicely with similar flavors. Medium bodied and robust, with notes of cherry cough syrup and warming alcohol on the finish.

1997 Seghesio Family Vineyards, Sonoma County
★★ $$

Inky dark with berry and spice aromas and flavors of blackberries, cherries, and spices. This concentrated wine has a mouth-filling texture and a long, fruity finish. Also look for their Old Vines Zinfandel, another good value from this reliable producer.

1997 Ravenswood Vintners Blend, North Coast
★★ $

Excellent value from Zin master Joel Peterson. Mellow flavors of blueberry, clove, and cinnamon, with gentle tannin, make this a perfect everyday wine. Ravenswood's single-vineyard bottlings, including Old Hill Ranch, Dickerson Vineyard, Cooke Vineyard, and Monte Rosso are rare, expensive, and among the finest Zinfandels made.

ITALY IN CALIFORNIA

Italian grape varieties are hot in California, though not all of them are new. Barbera, for example, has been here since the gold rush, but until now it mostly disappeared into jugs and today's equivalent, the bag-in-box. Now many serious producers are taking an interest in Barbera and other Italian varieties. In 1995, the Robert Mondavi Winery introduced a line of California-grown Italian varietal wines. Randall Grahm of Bonny Doon Winery has been experimenting with Italian varieties since 1987, even daring to try his hand at Nebbiolo, a grape notorious for its refusal to produce good wines outside its native Piedmont. But the variety on everyone's lips is Sangiovese. Just don't expect Chianti; California versions have their own style, one well worth exploring. Some interesting whites are being made as well.

the bottom line Very few of these wines are available for less than $15, but with prices topping out at around $30, most offer at least fair value.

Red Wines from Italian Grapes

1994 M. Cosentino Il Tesoro Sangiovetto, Napa County ★★★ $$

Aromas of leather and coffee, with a touch of oak. Lush flavors of very ripe strawberries and a texture that has mellowed into silkiness with maturity make this deliciously ready to drink now. Notes of coffee echo in the finish.

1996 Atlas Peak Vineyards Sangiovese Reserve, Napa Valley ★★ $$$

Spicy, leather aromas, sweet fruit on the palate, and moderate tannin—this wine is unmistakably American. It's much fuller and fruitier than Italian versions and very easy to like.

1996 La Famiglia Di Robert Mondavi Sangiovese, California ★★ $$$

In contrast to the Atlas Peak (directly above), this wine leans more toward Italy in style. It has aromas of berries and herbs. On the palate, it is elegant, light bodied, and tannic, with underlying flavors of strawberries and cherries.

1997 Seghesio Family Vineyards Barbera, Mendocino County ★★ $$

Aroma of cherries. Nicely restrained vanilla notes add complexity to the refreshing berry flavors. Light, dusty tannin finish—lovely.

1997 Seghesio Family Vineyards Sangiovese, Alexander Valley ★★ $$

The house is one of the original proponents of Sangiovese in California. This wine has floral and woodsy aromas, with blueberry, spice, and mocha flavors; lively acidity; and a gently tannic finish.

1995 Martini & Prati Sangiovese, California ★★ $

This pleasant, straightforward, light and fruity red has a mild smoky, herbal aroma and strawberry on the palate. The wine is especially versatile with food and it's ready to drink now.

WHITE WINES FROM ITALIAN GRAPES
1997 La Famiglia Di Robert Mondavi Pinot Grigio, California ★★ $$

Attractive mineral and stone-fruit aromas precede refreshing flavors of lemons, peaches, and apricots. It's dry and tart, yet has considerable fullness on the palate.

1997 Wild Horse Malvasia Bianca, Monterey County ★★ $$

Lovely floral, orange and pear, and Muscat-like aromas. On the palate, it's luscious, with spicy notes added to the perfumey fruit flavors. A pleasing bitter note keeps the wine from becoming cloying.

1996 Martini & Prati Vino Grigio, California ★★ $

This delicate, delightfully refreshing white wine has a lightly lemony flavor and brisk acidity that make it an excellent aperitif or accompaniment to mild fish.

OTHER RED WINES

California is home to many less-known grapes that make for intriguing exploration by intrepid wine lovers. Cabernet Franc, Grenache, Mourvèdre, Petite Sirah, and Carignan, as varietal wines and various combinations as blends, all provide tasty respite from the ubiquitous Cabernet Sauvignon and Merlot.

the bottom Line There are excellent buys among these wines, with prices starting as low as $8. The sky's the limit for some special bottlings, but the top end is generally around $25.

1996 Jade Mountain Mourvèdre, California ★★★★ $$

Imposing aromas of smoked meat, black fruits, and a hint of iron. This full-bodied wine has authoritative plum, mulberry, and meat flavors that last long into the finish. The balance of flavor, tannin, and alcohol makes the wine's tremendous concentration and power harmonious.

tomorrow's Legends
to buy today

As we enter the new millennium, you may ask: What will be the legendary wines of the next century? Well, many of them haven't even been made yet, and we'll watch with delight as the vintages unfold. Here, however, is a mixed case of late-20th-century wines that are in the process of becoming legends in their own right.

Like the wines in the Wines of the Century list (see page 233), you will have to look to the auction market to find the great majority of these, but they are available. Don't be surprised if you have to mortgage the house to afford them!

1. 1985 Guigal La Turque, Côte-Rôtie
2. 1988 Krug Clos du Mesnil, Champagne
3. 1989 Huet Moelleux Cuvée Constance, Vouvray
4. 1990 Château d'Yquem, Sauternes
5. 1990 Domaine Compte Georges de Vogüé Vieilles Vignes, Musigny
6. 1991 Penfolds Grange, Barossa Valley
7. 1994 Fonseca Vintage Port
8. 1994 Ridge Cabernet Sauvignon Monte Bello, Santa Clara
9. 1995 Château Latour, Pauillac
10. 1996 Domaine Ramonet Le Montrachet
11. 1996 Weingut Robert Weil Kiedricher Gräfenberg Trockenbeerenauslese
12. 1997 Sassicaia, Bolgheri

1996 Bonny Doon Vineyard Le Cigare Volant, California ★★★ $$

Bonny Doon's signature wine is a blend of Rhône Valley grapes—Grenache, Syrah, Cinsaut, and Mourvèdre. Spicy, complex, and fruity, the wine is reminiscent of Châteauneuf-du-Pape, on which it is modeled.

1996 Foxen Cabernet Franc, Santa Maria Valley ★★★ $$

Attractive cassis nose, with nuances of barnyard and leather aromas. Bordeaux-like in its subtlety, this wine has a fruity flavor, excellent mild tannin, and a long, harmonious finish. Delicious.

1997 Daniel Gehrs Cabernet Franc, Santa Barbara County ★★★ $$

Aromas of chocolate, plums, and black currants. Uncommonly full and velvety for a Cabernet Franc, it resembles a classic Cabernet Sauvignon from the bottom of the Napa Valley rather than the mountains. One of, if not the best California Cabernet Francs we've ever tasted.

1997 Cosentino Winery Cabernet Franc, Napa Valley ★★ $$$

Cabernet Franc is a favorite of winemaker Mitch Cosentino. Here the aromatic nose mingles floral and cedary scents with those of cherries and cloves. The flavors include tart cherry and rhubarb. There's a bit of puckery tannin, but the fruit dominates on the long finish.

1997 Laurel Glen Vineyard REDS, California ★★ $

An easy to drink red made from a blend of Rhône grape varieties, with lots of cherry, a hint of black pepper, and a dash of spice.

PACIFIC NORTHWEST

Washington State and Oregon are often lumped together as the Pacific Northwest, but their vastly dissimilar climates make them two distinct growing regions. Their reputations are staked on different grapes, and thus different wines. Even their industries have contrasting structures, with the Washington scene dominated by one corporate behemoth, and Oregon's characterized by myriad small boutiques.

OREGON

Sandwiched between wine giants California and Washington State, Oregon has nonetheless carved out a niche based on world-class Pinot Noirs. Most of these are made by small independent-minded producers in the Willamette (will-AM-ette) Valley, where cool temperatures, sufficient rainfall, and volcanic soil create ideal conditions for this difficult grape.

Grapes and Styles

At their best, Oregon's Pinot Noirs are the finest outside Burgundy. Oregon also has the only major plantings in the U.S. of Pinot Gris, the state's fastest growing variety. Selecting the right Chardonnay clone to match the climate initially stymied producers; this grape is just now finding its footing. Oregon's wines are more delicate than California's, less earthy than Washington's.

ON THE LABEL

Wines from Oregon are labeled varietally as are most wines from the United States. (See page 16.)

PINOT GRIS

Oregon's best white grape is Pinot Gris, and many feel the variety holds promise as a challenger to the ubiquitous Chardonnay. Oregon's Pinot Gris wines are different from others around the world, falling stylistically somewhere between the tart, delicately flavored Pinot Grigios of Italy and the lush, powerful versions from Alsace. Oregon's are dry, medium-bodied wines with flavors of peaches, nuts, and marmalade. They are rarely oaked.

at the table

Dry, fruity Oregon Pinot Gris, with its zingy acidity, makes a spot-on choice for shellfish, both raw and cooked. Like Pinot Noir, Pinot Gris frequently accompanies grilled salmon in the Pacific Northwest. Pinot Gris can also be served with pork, ham, veal, and sweetbreads, as it is in Alsace, and delicately spiced Asian fish dishes. Semisoft cheeses and this style of Pinot Gris make good companions as well.

the bottom line This best and fastest-growing white wine of Oregon is also its best value. Many excellent bottles can be had for $15 or less.

1997 King Estate Reserve, Oregon ★★★ $$
A step up from the basic, nonreserve bottling, this wine is deliciously packed with fresh fruit-salad, peach, cantaloupe, and spice flavors. It has a full, silky texture and a long, fruity finish.

1997 Rex Hill Vineyards, Willamette Valley ★★★ $$
This is a serious wine with adamant mineral flavors vying with those of peach and melon for attention. Full-bodied, with excellent, refreshing acidity. Nice!

1997 Bethel Heights Vineyard, Willamette Valley ★★ $$
Bethel Heights has developed a well-deserved reputation for its Pinot Gris. Its style is fresh and light, with medium body and delicate pear and melon flavors.

1997 Chehalem Ridgecrest Reserve, Willamette Valley ★★ $$
A brisk style, with citrus and slightly mineral flavors. Somewhat hard to taste the flavors now, but the wine nonetheless shows potential for graceful development with short-term aging.

1997 The Eyrie Vineyards, Yamhill County ★★ $$
From the first and still most important producer of Pinot Gris in Oregon, this wine has lots of lemony and minty aromas. Tart on the palate, with flavors of apricot and cloves, it has a grapefruit flavor in the finish.

1997 King Estate, Oregon ★★ $
A light, refreshing, and charming wine, with delicate honeydew, pear, and lime flavors, snappy acidity, and a subtly flavored finish.

1997 Foris, Rogue Valley ★ $
Lively, simple, and refreshing, with cantaloupe and lemon flavors and a zesty finish. Drink this while it's still young.

OTHER WHITE WINES

The Chardonnays of Oregon are generally light bodied with snappy acidity and vivid fruit flavors, though some barrel-fermented versions have more body and complexity, along with spicy oak flavors. As a rule, the Rieslings and Gewürztraminers are dry compared to those of Washington State and are light, delicate, and floral. Refreshing Pinot Blanc is produced as well.

THE BOTTOM LINE Pinot Blancs, Rieslings, and Gewürztraminers all represent excellent value. Many Pinot Blancs sell for less than $10, Rieslings and Gewürztraminers for $2 to $3 more. Chardonnay is generally well priced, too, but the quality is spotty; the hits are worth the money; the misses are not.

1997 Adelsheim Chardonnay Reserve, Yamhill County ★★ $$
Spicy oak aroma and flavors of apples, lemons, pears, and vanilla. This wine is fairly full in body, with a nice long vanilla and lemon finish.

1997 Argyle Chardonnay, Willamette Valley ★★ $$
This noted sparkling-wine winery is getting noticed for its excellent Chardonnays. This one is creamy and mellow, with peach, pear, and vanilla flavors. The finish is long, fruity, and smooth.

1998 Sokol Blosser Riesling, Willamette Valley ★★ $
Lovely floral, talc, peach, and lime nose. This charming, slightly off-dry Riesling sings with peach and citrus flavors enlivened by excellent acidity.

1997 Willamette Valley Vineyards Chardonnay, Oregon ★ $$
Willamette Valley Vineyards is going against the tide with its light-bodied, oak-free Chardonnay, and we're glad. Scintillating flavors of pear, apple, and apricot.

1996 Amity Vineyards Pinot Blanc Helmick Vineyards, Willamette Valley ★ $
A light, slightly tart, and citrusy wine, with vibrant acidity and a pleasant, lemony finish. It makes a nice aperitif.

PINOT NOIR

For a long time, to borrow a phrase from Mark Twain, reports of Oregon's success with Pinot Noir were greatly exaggerated. The 1980s were disappointing as undercapitalized growers struggled with this finicky grape. Finally, with the 1991 vintage,

Oregon began to fulfill its promise. Today's Pinot Noirs have seductive black-cherry and raspberry aromas, vanilla accents from moderate use of new oak, and a silky texture. They are best drunk early to savor their deliciously youthful, fruity flavors, although some can age up to five years.

at the table

The Pinot Noirs of Oregon are good with a a range of foods. Pair lighter versions with grilled fish, such as salmon, fresh tuna, and swordfish, and hearty chicken dishes. Pâté and other charcuterie are naturals for the fuller styles of Pinot Noir, as are game, duck, and goose. Mushrooms love Pinot Noir: Try it with pasta and wild mushrooms or pork or veal in morel sauce. Soft, full cheeses, such as Camembert, will also be flattered by Pinot Noir.

the bottom Line Prices jumped with the popular, but atypical, 1994 vintage. Fans of that jammy style may feel subsequent Oregon Pinots are overpriced, but devotees of Oregon's delicate style will find many good buys between $15 and $25.

what to buy PINOT NOIR

1994	1995	1996	1997	1998
★★★	★★	★★★	★★	★★★

1997 Domaine Drouhin, Oregon ★★★★ $$$
Founded by Burgundy *négociant* Joseph Drouhin in 1988, DDO, as it is known to its fans, has quickly become one of Oregon's most prestigious wineries. This wine has smoky oak on the nose, with full, concentrated red-fruit flavors and herbaceous, spicy nuances. Though pleasurable now, this superb wine will improve dramatically with age.

1997 Archery Summit Premier Cuvée, Oregon ★★★ $$$
Raspberry, clove, and subtle oak-spice aromas. This polished wine offers seductive red-berry, cinnamon, and clove flavors and smooth tannin. Drink it now or wait three to five years.

1996 Erath Vineyards Pinot Noir Reserve, Willamette Valley ★★★ $$$
Here's an understated, elegant Pinot Noir, featuring dusty blackberry and cherry aromas and the same flavors accented by hints of anise and earth. On the finish there's, in addition, an uplifting note of menthol. This wine is great with food.

1997 Sokol Blosser Redland Winemaker's Reserve, Yamhill County ★★★ $$$

Susan Sokol Blosser is another of Oregon's Pinot pioneers. Her Redland Reserve has penetrating aromas and flavors of cedar, herbs, smoke, and berries. It has the elegance, concentration, ageablilty, and sheer succulence to place it among Oregon's elite Pinots.

1996 Ponzi, Willamette Valley ★★★ $$

Its outstanding reputation makes this wine hard to find, but worth searching out. This is a classic Oregon Pinot Noir, with delicate, spicy raspberry fruit flavors cast into high relief by snappy acidity.

1997 Elk Cove Vineyards, Willamette Valley ★★ $$

A light, delicate wine, silky on the palate, with flavors of cassis, berries, and a touch of herbs; moderate tannin; and good acidity.

1997 King Estate, Oregon ★★ $$

Aromas of currants and spice lead to similar flavors on the palate. This tasty Pinot Noir is light and delicate in style, with brisk acidity and moderate tannin.

1996 Panther Creek, Willamette Valley ★★ $$

This high-profile winery produces stylish, intensely fruity Pinot Noirs. This one has complex aromas and flavors of pepper, underbrush, and red berries; good body; and gentle tannin.

1997 Rex Hill Vineyards, Willamette Valley ★★ $$

An elegant Pinot Noir, highlighting aromas and flavors of red berries, cinnamon, and vanilla. Oak is pronounced, but not overwhelming. The reserve, at about twice the price, is one of Oregon's finest Pinot Noirs.

WASHINGTON
STATE

Grapes have been grown in the elevated desert valleys of the Columbia and Yakima Rivers for decades, but until the 1970s, they were destined for juice, jam, and eating. Now there are more than 100 wineries, many very small. Stimson Lane, owner of Chateau Ste. Michelle, Columbia Crest, and others, dominates the business with more than a third of the state's total output.

grapes and styles

Does climate affect style? Compare Washington State and Oregon. Washington is warmer and drier, so while Chardonnay struggles in Oregon, it is Washington's number one grape variety. Sémillon and Sauvignon Blanc, also abundant in Washington, are almost unknown in Oregon, where varieties, such as Pinot Gris, Riesling, and Gewürztraminer have a much easier time. Washington's top red is Merlot followed by Cabernet Sauvignon, two difficult varieties for Oregon. Most of what little Pinot Noir exists in Washington is grown near the Oregon border. Though Washington State wines are fuller than those of Oregon, they have less jammy fruit flavor than California's. A distinct earthy note is nearly always evident.

on the label

Like Oregon's, Washington State's wines are labeled by grape variety. (See page 16.)

CHARDONNAY

Washington State's Chardonnays can be excellent. Their earthy notes add satisfying complexity to their clear pear-and-apple fruitiness. Light in style, refreshing, gently oaked, if at all— they're some of the United States' best everyday Chardonnays. Fuller-bodied, more complex and spicy styles, fermented and aged in new oak are available, as well.

at the table

Light, citrusy Chardonnay can be served on its own as an aperitif or with omelets, mild fish, and shellfish. Heavier ones, with more intensely concentrated fruit flavors and spicy oak are matches for grilled chicken, pork, meaty fish, and pasta with cream sauce. The fullest, oakiest Chardonnays will overwhelm most food, but butter sauces, such as *beurre blanc*, and rich *triple crème* cheeses can handle them.

the bottom line For the best values, look to the lower end of Washington State Chardonnays, where many good wines can be had for around $12 or less.

1997 Chateau Ste. Michelle Cold Creek Vineyard, Columbia Valley ★★★ $$

Floral and oak notes on the nose. Packed with lush flavors of apple, pear, and vanilla, with sufficient acidity for good harmony. An altogether balanced, focused wine.

1997 Columbia Winery Otis Vineyard, Yakima Valley ★★★ $$

Lots of woodsmoke and vanilla-oak aromas, with spice and tart apple flavors. Full-bodied, with lovely fruit flavors in the finish.

1996 Columbia Winery Woodburne Cuvée, Columbia Valley ★★ $$

A very pretty nose of spicy oak and apples. Flavors of apple, citrus, and spice; excellent balance of acidity, fruitiness, and oak.

1997 L'Ecole No. 41, Washington State ★★ $$

Aromas of toast and peaches and flavors of pear, quince, and spice. Full-bodied and fruity, this wine has mellow acidity, mild tannin, and a good long finish.

1997 Kiona Vineyards, Columbia Valley ★★ $$

This is a full-bodied, high-alcohol style of Chardonnay, with pineapple, pear, and melon flavors and just enough balancing acidity.

1997 Hogue, Columbia Valley ★★ $

Has appealing, nicely balanced flavors of citrus, apple, and spice. This is a good value from a reliable producer.

1997 Waterbrook, Columbia Valley ★★ $

Now here's a lovely Chardonnay. It's medium bodied, with restrained tropical-fruit flavors, brisk acidity, and a hint of earth. An excellent wine with food.

1997 Covey Run, Washington State ★ $

Lemon and a little butterscotch on the nose lead to citrus and vanilla flavors on the palate. With a nice, easy-drinking style, this Chardonnay is simple and pleasant.

SÉMILLON & SAUVIGNON BLANC

The Sémillons from Washington State are lighter bodied and more acidic than the opulent, marmaladey Sémillons of Australia, leaning more to lemony, nutty, honeyed flavors and hints of ground mustard seed. Sauvignon Blancs are tart, light, and grassy. A great deal of Sémillon is bottled unblended, and it is probably Washington's best dry white wine. Sauvignon Blanc and Sémillon blends, made on the model of white Bordeaux, are also common and generally very good.

at the table

Washington's Sémillons and Sauvignon Blancs are some of the United States' most versatile wines at the table. Brisk Sauvignon Blanc partners successfully with salads, vegetables, mild fish, shellfish, and light chicken dishes. The fuller Sémillon is superb with oily fish, such as salmon and tuna, and is especially good with smoked fish of all kinds. The blends offer the best of both worlds: Sémillon's power provides the oomph to stand up to bold flavors, while the Sauvignon Blanc's acidity contrasts beautifully with creamy sauces.

the bottom line Washington State Sémillons and Sauvignon Blancs prove that avoiding Chardonnay's popularity premium opens the door to bargains galore. For $15 and much less, it's tough to do better.

1997 Chateau Ste. Michelle Sauvignon Blanc Horse Haven Vineyard, Columbia Valley ★★ $$
Herbs, citrus, and a little smoke on the nose are followed by lively lemon-lime flavors. Rather full in body with abundant, bracing acidity, this refreshing wine sports a finish with tangy fruitiness and good length.

1998 Barnard Griffin Sémillon, Columbia Valley ★★ $
From a small producer with an excellent track record, this is a full-bodied wine, with intense flavors of melon and honey bolstered by fruity acidity.

1998 Hogue Fumé Blanc, Columbia Valley ★★ $
This classic Washington State Sauvignon Blanc has lightly herbaceous, zesty aromas and the flavor of lemon. It's widely available and reliably good.

1997 Arbor Crest Wine Cellars Sauvignon Blanc, Columbia Valley ★ $
Both the Cameo Reserve and Bacchus Vineyard bottlings are refreshing and full of lively fruit flavors and balancing acidity. The Cameo is a bit spicier, the Bacchus, fuller bodied. Both are good values.

OTHER WHITE WINES

Gewürztraminer, Johannisberg Riesling, and Chenin Blanc, important in Oregon, also do well in Washington State. All three grapes are made into both dry and off-dry styles that typically are delicate and floral and retain true varietal character. The wines have excellent balance; even in the off-dry styles, brisk acidity offsets the sweetness.

THE BOTTOM LINE Many of these wines sell for as little as $6.99, making them incredible bargains.

1997 Hedges Fumé-Chardonnay, Columbia Valley ★ ★ $
Sauvignon Blanc and Chardonnay is an unusual blend (55 percent and 45 percent, respectively). Imagine mouth-filling grapefruit, pineapple, and citrus flavors, brisk acidity, and a full, viscous texture melded into a refreshing wine.

1997 Hogue Chenin Blanc, Columbia Valley ★ ★ $
Peaches and apples on the nose and similar flavors on the palate balanced by bracing acidity. Simple, delicious, and slightly sweet. A perfect aperitif or poolside quaffer.

1998 Washington Hills Sémillon-Chardonnay, Columbia Valley ★ ★ $
This blend is mellow and rather full on the palate, with flavors of peaches and pears. Drink it now.

1997 Columbia Winery Gewürztraminer, Columbia Valley ★ $
Flowery, citrus nose. A light-bodied, medium-sweet wine with delicate peach and floral flavors, pleasing acidity, and a lively finish.

1998 Columbia Winery Johannisberg Riesling Cellarmaster's Reserve, Columbia Valley ★ $
A charming, off-dry style of Johannisberg Riesling, slightly spritzy, with full peach and lemon flavors on the palate and enough acidity to balance the fruitiness. A good picnic wine.

1998 Covey Run Dry Riesling, Washington State ★ $
Light, fruity, and much drier than the Covey Run Riesling (follows). The wine is delicate, offering lemon and melon aromas with a hint of honey and pleasant peach and apricot flavors balanced by medium acidity.

1998 Covey Run Riesling, Washington State ★ $
Slightly tart, with lots of fruity flavors—apricot, grapefruit, and lemon peel. A gentle touch of sweetness makes it an excellent aperitif.

MERLOT &
CABERNET SAUVIGNON

Washington State Merlots and Cabernet Sauvignons are full and smooth, with succulent red-fruit flavors and distinct earthy tones. The best are powerful and concentrated though markedly less flamboyant than the jammier versions from California. In fact, the character of Washington Merlots and Cabs points more toward classic European wines, such as Bordeaux, than New World models. They're good drunk when young, and yet their excellent balance of acidity and tannin allows them to age gracefully.

at the table

Most Cabernet Sauvignons and Merlots can be served with roast pork, leg of lamb, braised beef, and hearty stews, especially those that include the complementary flavors of onions and mushrooms. Rich *double crème* and blue-veined cheeses are excellent, too. The full-bodied, high-alcohol Cabernets need full-flavored steak, goose, or venison.

the bottom line At $15 to $20, most Washington State Cabernet Sauvignons and Merlots are good buys. Single-vineyard and reserve wines cost a bit more but still give excellent quality for money. Value is less certain for many pricey boutique wines.

what to buy MERLOT & CABERNET SAUVIGNON

1994	1995	1996	1997	1998
★★★★	★★★	★★★	★★★	★★★

1995 Leonetti Cellar Cabernet Sauvignon, Columbia Valley ★★★★ $$$

A name to know in Washington State, but only a lucky few will ever taste the wines. This Cabernet Sauvignon, and the equally fine Merlot, are so highly regarded and made in such small quantities that finding them is difficult. The Cab is a benchmark: intensely flavored, powerful, and complex. If you see it, grab it.

1995 Columbia Winery Red Willow Vineyard Cabernet Sauvignon, Yakima Valley ★★★ $$$

Widely regarded as one of Washington State's most exciting Cabernet Sauvignons, this single-vineyard bottling has flavors that include blackberry, cinnamon, herbs, and cassis. Intense, tannic, and still quite youthful, it's full of promise for a long and graceful life.

1997 Woodward Canyon Canoe Ridge Vineyard Cabernet Sauvignon, Washington State ★★★ $$$

Powerful, with abundant tannin, and vivid black-currant flavor, this is a youthful, unevolved wine that needs time in the bottle to mellow.

1996 Canoe Ridge Vineyard Merlot, Columbia Valley ★★★ $$

This fine Merlot is chock-a-block with full-fruit flavors and generous, velvety tannin. The flavor and tannin are well enough balanced to drink the wine now or hold it several years. Canoe Ridge is a very highly regarded winery, owned by the Chalone Wine Group of California.

1996 Chateau Ste. Michelle Cabernet Sauvignon Canoe Ridge Estate Vineyard, Columbia Valley ★★★ $$

Spicy oak, currants, and a touch of herbs in the aroma. Concentrated flavors of currants, blueberries, and cinnamon, framed by gentle tannin, lead to a long, silky finish. Drink now or hold.

1996 Columbia Winery Milestone Red Willow Vineyard Merlot, Yakima Valley ★★★ $$

Columbia Winery (no relation to Columbia Crest) produces many of its finest wines from its wholly owned Milestone vineyard. This wine is lush, with intense chocolate and cherry flavors and mouth-filling texture. Densely concentrated and rich in tannin, it's a wine to keep.

1995 Columbia Winery Otis Vineyard Cabernet Sauvignon, Yakima Valley ★★★ $$

Earthy aromas, with notes of wood, tobacco, and mint and complex flavors of currants, licorice, blueberries, and smoke. Prominent tannin suggests a few years of cellaring, but there is enough gentle fruitiness to make it delicious right now.

1996 L'Ecole No. 41 Cabernet Sauvignon, Columbia Valley ★★ $$$

This lovely Cabernet has great body and distinct vanilla, toast, plum, and spice flavors. Good tannin and vivid acidity frame the flavors beautifully. Drink now or in a few years, when it will be even better.

1995 Cascade Ridge Merlot, Columbia Valley ★★ $$

Cassis and plum nose, then concentrated, luscious flavors of chocolate and dark berries. An admirable wine that finishes with good length.

1996 Chateau Ste. Michelle Merlot, Columbia Valley ★★ $$

Lots of oak on the nose and palate, giving lavish notes of vanilla and cloves, but there is enough intense blackberry flavor to balance the wood. The wine has moderate tannin and good length.

1996 Columbia Crest Merlot, Columbia Valley

★ ★ $$

This easy-to-like wine is the largest selling Merlot in the United States. Full plummy flavor, mild tannin, and a long, fruity finish make this one a crowd pleaser.

1997 Kiona Cabernet Sauvignon, Yakima Valley

★ $$

A light, fruity Cabernet Sauvignon with cherry and red-currant flavors on the palate along with just a little tannin. An easygoing wine for current drinking.

1996 Columbia Crest Cabernet Sauvignon, Columbia Valley

★ $

Pleasant berry-cherry aromas. Simple and fruity, with flavors of black cherry and spice. Some light tannin in the finish. This excellent value makes a good house wine. Drink now.

OTHER RED WINES

Washington State produces red blends as well as varietals from Syrah, Pinot Noir, and Cabernet Franc along with a number of other less-known grapes, such as Lemberger. In the hands of able vintners, all these wines can be quite good. Like the more popular varietals, they tend to be less overtly fruity than their California counterparts and have more earth nuances.

THE BOTTOM LINE As with Washington's white wines, exploring the less-known varietals means finding bargains. Prices can begin as low as $7, and they top out around $12.

1996 Col Solare, Columbia Valley

★ ★ ★ ★ $$$$

Italy's Piero Antinori and Chateau Ste. Michelle have collaborated to make Bordeaux-style blends. This vintage is a blend of 85 percent Cabernet Sauvignon and 15 percent Merlot, with lusciously intense berry, cherry, and dark-plum flavors; a silky texture; and a bonanza of velvety tannin. Delicious now, but should be utterly spectacular with time.

1996 Columbia Winery Cabernet Franc Red Willow Vineyard, Yakima Valley

★ ★ ★ $$

A beautifully aromatic wine with floral, coffee, and spice aromas and an intense black-cherry flavor on the palate and in the finish. With silky texture yet potent tannin and acidity, this is a wine to drink now or keep.

1996 Hedges Three Vineyards Red,
Columbia Valley ★ ★ ★ $$

Deep ruby purple with strong cassis, plum, herb, and briary aromas. A big wine, very tannic now, but there is ample concentrated fruitiness to assure graceful development over 5 to 10 years.

1996 Columbia Winery Syrah Red Willow Vineyard,
Yakima Valley ★ ★ $$$

Slightly herbaceous, with good cherry and strawberry flavors and a hint of black cherry in the finish. Syrahs from Washington State are wines to watch.

1998 Hedges Columbia Valley Red,
Washington State ★ ★ $

Lots of dark fruit, a hint of herbs, and a slightly gamy note on the nose. This Bordeaux-style wine is easy on the palate with cherry and cassis flavors and slightly elevated tannin in the long, smooth finish.

1997 Hogue Cabernet Sauvignon–Merlot,
Columbia Valley ★ ★ $

Aromas of cherries, cedar, and a hint of chocolate evolve into delicious dark-cherry flavors and a lush texture. The wine finishes with more cherries.

1997 Covey Run Cabernet-Merlot,
Washington State ★ $

Made from 50 percent Cabernet Sauvignon, 34 percent Merlot, and 16 percent Cabernet Franc. Light and fruity, this pleasant wine has flavors of red cherries, berries, and herbs. Simple, smooth, and tasty.

NEW YORK STATE

Only California and Washington State surpass New York State in U.S. wine production. Most of New York's wine is produced in the Finger Lakes region, where large lakes temper the severe climate, and the North Fork of Long Island, whose maritime influence and gravelly, Médoc-like soils make world-class wines possible.

grapes and styles

New York's best-kept secret is its Riesling from the Finger Lakes. In both bone-dry and sweet, late-harvest styles, they are among the country's finest wines. (For a discussion of the late-harvest type, see page 262.) Good sparkling wines made by the traditional method (see page 229) and brisk, steely Chardonnays are other specialties of the Finger Lakes. Long Island is home to Chardonnays, Sauvignon Blancs, Rieslings, Pinot Blancs, and Gewürztraminers that are fuller and have more fruit flavor than the whites of the Finger Lakes. However, it is red wines made from Cabernet Franc, Cabernet Sauvignon, and particularly Merlot that have established Long Island's reputation.

on the Label

New York State bottles are usually labeled by grape varieties, but some Long Island red blends bear fanciful proprietary names.

CHARDONNAY

The cool climate and shale soil in the Finger Lakes produce appley, Chablis-like Chardonnays with mineral-earthiness and good acidity. On Long Island, many of the Chardonnays are bar-

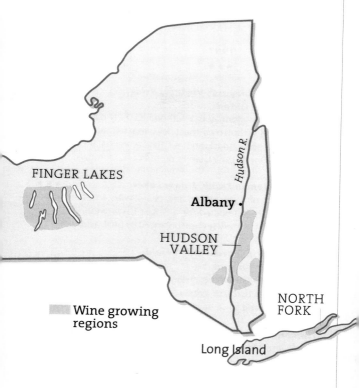

FINGER LAKES

Hudson R.

Albany .

HUDSON
VALLEY

NORTH
FORK

Wine growing
regions

Long Island

rel fermented and oak aged. They have more body and have aromas of spiced pears and buttered nuts, along with a hint of pineapple. Their style, with higher acidity, lower alcohol, lighter body, and clear fruit flavors, leans more toward the French than the Californian.

at the table

Unoaked Chardonnays from the Finger Lakes are a perfect match for delicate fish and for raw oysters and clams. Oak-matured wines, with their buttered-toast flavor, complement crab, lobster, and scallops. Try the oakier Chardonnays also with grilled swordfish, mako shark, roasted poultry, or small game birds. And fresh goat cheese or semisoft cheeses make a superb match.

the bottom line New York State's food-friendly Chardonnays are reasonably priced for their quality. Expect to pay between $8 and $20.

what to buy CHARDONNAY

1996	1997	1998
★★★	★★★	★★★

1997 Pellegrini Vineyards Vintners Pride, North Fork, Long Island ★★★ $$

Pellegrini's top Chardonnay is a full-bodied, fully oaked wine with complex aromas of buttered toast, lees, roasted nuts, and tropical fruit. Pineapple, spice, toast, and nut flavors are balanced nicely by snappy acidity. One of Long Island's premier Chardonnays.

1997 Dr. Konstantin Frank, Finger Lakes ★★★ $

Intense aromas of nuts, butter, and pears, with an ethereal floral note. Surprisingly full-bodied for a Finger Lakes wine, with stone-fruit flavors and a buttery texture balanced by brisk acidity.

1997 Gristina Vineyards Andy's Field, North Fork, Long Island ★★ $$

Aromas of toasty oak, apples, pears, and spices. Generously oaked, this mellow, silky-textured wine offers melon, stone-fruit, and pronounced vanilla and spice flavors emphasized by acidity.

1997 Millbrook Proprietor's Special Reserve, Hudson River ★★ $$

Lavish oak imparts an overlay of buttered nuts, nutmeg, and roasted coffee to the apple and pear aromas. On the palate, it's dry with vanilla, toast, nutmeg, and charred notes again trumping the tropical-fruit flavors. Good acidity gives it sparkle and a long finish.

1996 Lenz Winery Vineyard Selection, North Fork, Long Island ★★ $

Luscious apple and pear notes on the nose repeat on the palate along with cleansing lemony flavors and acidity. A good long finish completes this refreshing, lightly oaked, and very attractive package.

1998 Standing Stone Vineyards, Finger Lakes ★★ $

Toasted-bread and spiced pear aromas. This full-bodied Chardonnay offers concentrated, peach, pear, and toast flavors and a sensation of sweetness from alcohol atypically high for the Finger Lakes. It finishes with medium length and the snap of fruity acidity.

OTHER WHITE WINES

Rieslings from the Finger Lakes have excellent fruit concentration, admirable acidity, and a lovely mineral edge. Long Island Gewürztraminers can have the exotic spice and floral aromas of Alsace wines made from the same variety. Hybrid grapes are extensively used in New York State: Vignoles (Ravat) and Vidal make excellent late-harvest wines (see page 262), and the hardy Seyval Blanc is widely used for charming, off-dry quaffers.

THE BOTTOM LINE The white wines of New York State are generally cheap—between $7 and $12. Quality is uneven, as can be expected in a young industry searching for its own styles. Consistency will follow.

1998 Standing Stone Vineyard Gewürztraminer, Finger Lakes ★ ★ ★ ★ $

Exotic, penetrating aromas of rose water, litchi, apricot, and spice. The tremendous concentration, viscous texture, and apricot, floral, spice, and mineral flavors remind us of one of Zind-Humbrecht's Alsace gems. One of the best Gewürztraminers we've tasted from anywhere in the U.S. and, at this price, an out-and-out steal.

1997 Hermann J. Wiemer Johannisberg Riesling Reserve, Finger Lakes ★ ★ ★ $$

Intensely aromatic nose of marzipan, citrus, spring flowers, and mineral earthiness. A dry wine that demonstrates the amazing concentration, the depth of flavor, and the electric acidity possible from the noble Riesling grape. This is a keeper; it will evolve well.

1998 Dr. Konstantin Frank Rkatsiteli, Finger Lakes ★ ★ $$

Rkatsiteli is thought to be the third most widely planted grape in the world, but it is virtually unknown outside Russia. Dr. Frank's unique wine has an intriguing aroma of musk, minerals, and perfumed face powder. It's dry and refreshing, finishing with delicious nuances of cantaloupe and ginger. A fabulous food wine.

1998 Paumanok Riesling, North Fork, Long Island ★ ★ $$

Inviting fragrance and flavor of peaches and wild-flower honey. Off-dry, with a spicy, slightly drying finish.

1997 Hunt County Vineyards Viva Vignoles, Finger Lakes ★ ★ $

Intense, heady aromas of apricot and muskmelon. Off-dry and full-bodied, with enough acidity to save it from becoming cloying. This great warm-weather sipper showcases the potential of this hybrid.

1995 Lenz Winery Estate Bottled Gewürztraminer, North Fork, Long Island ★ ★ $

Exotically perfumed, yet delicate nose of orange blossoms, apricots, and gingerbread. This is dry, in an Alsace style, with a viscous texture, good flavor concentration, and enough acidity to keep it lively. It finishes long and spicy.

1997 Palmer Vineyards Estate Pinot Blanc, North Fork, Long Island ★ ★ $

Aromas of apples, almonds, honeydew melon, and a touch of vanilla from the oak. Lovely, clear melon and nut flavors, vivacious acidity, and a long finish. Palmer's best wine.

RED WINES

In New York State, only Long Island is warm enough to grow red grape varieties with the consistent success necessary to produce high-quality red wines. Merlot, with its medium body and earthy plum and cherry flavors, is receiving the most attention now and right at the moment is the best, but in good vintages, Cabernet Sauvignon can be its equal. Cabernet Franc may in fact be the grape best suited to the environment. Long Island vintners fashion Cabernet Franc into medium-bodied reds in a Loire Valley style. Merlot, Cabernet Sauvignon, and Cabernet Franc are all varieties used in Bordeaux-like blends, complementing one another and giving the wines complexity.

at the table

Merlot's fruit flavors make it the perfect accompaniment to grilled vegetables, tuna or salmon steaks, roast pork, and Long Island duckling with a fruit sauce. Cabernet Franc's herbal nuances pair well with cheeses like Gouda and Havarti, *salade niçoise*, turkey, and rare beef. Cabernet Sauvignon and Bordeaux-like blends, fuller in body and more tannic than the other two, need well-seasoned beef or lamb, stews made with wine, or hard aged cheeses.

the bottom line

As the vines get older and both vineyard management and winemaking techniques improve, quality is jumping. At $12 to $25, the better reds are now competitive with wines from other areas in both price and quality.

what to buy RED WINES

1994	1995	1996	1997	1998
★★★	★★★★	★★★	★★★	★★★★

1995 Lenz Winery Estate Bottled Merlot, North Fork, Long Island ★ ★ ★ $$$

Classic Merlot fragrance of plum, raspberry, black pepper, and chocolate. We're happy just to smell it. The flavors are classic, too, and backed up with velvety tannin, brilliant acidity, and a subtle, lingering, toasty-oak and vanilla finish. Aroma will develop even more with more age.

1995 Paumanok Estate Bottled Assemblage, North Fork, Long Island   ★ ★ ★ $$$

A blend of Cabernet Sauvignon, Cabernet Franc, and Merlot that reminds us of a classified-growth Médoc. It has complex aromas of chocolate, black currants, black cherries, and plums as well as spice, vanilla, and earth notes. Abundant tannin and solid acidity create the balance necessary for a long, graceful bottle maturation.

1994 Bedell Cellars Cupola, North Fork, Long Island   ★ ★ ★ $$

A complex Bordeaux-style blend of Cabernet Sauvignon, Cabernet Franc, and Merlot made from grapes grown in a drought year. It has intoxicating black-currant, plum, black-raspberry, smoke, and pumpkin-pie spice aromas and densely concentrated, complex flavors that finish on a strong tannic note of chocolate. Further bottle aging is warranted; it will be worth the wait.

1997 Knapp Estate Grown Pinot Noir, Cayuga Lake   ★ ★ $$

Fragrant plum, spice, and vanilla nose. Succulent sweet and tart red-plum flavors are nicely framed by pleasantly gentle tannin and brisk acidity in this light-bodied, charming wine.

1997 Macari Vineyards Cabernet Franc, North Fork, Long Island   ★ ★ $$

Typical aromas of good Cabernet Franc: herbs, black raspberry, and a note of ash. This refined wine has a sense of latent power from its strong tannin, concentrated berry flavors, and thrusting acidity. A wine from a promising new winery.

1995 Ternhaven Cellars Cabernet Sauvignon, North Fork, Long Island   ★ ★ $$

Spicy plum and black-currant aromas. An elegantly styled Cab with interesting herbal and blackberry flavors, along with medium body, moderate tannin, and good acidity. Long, definite finish.

SOUTH AFRICA

Here's an opportunity to drink good wine and support an emerging democracy at the same time! Apartheid kept South Africa isolated, but when sanctions were lifted in 1991, it enthusiastically rejoined the international market. The country's first exports were dismal. However, a continuing shift from government-controlled, bulk-wine production to small cooperatives and independently owned wine estates has resulted in soaring quality and some superb wines. This is an exciting time for the South African wine industry, which is experimenting freely with grape varieties and winemaking techniques. It will only get better.

grapes and styles

The international varietals—Chardonnay, Sauvignon Blanc, and Riesling for whites; Cabernet Sauvignon, Merlot, and Syrah, which the South Africans call Shiraz, for reds—are among South Africa's best wines. Steen (Chenin Blanc) is by far the most widely produced white. It comes in dry and off-dry styles. The earthy, mulberry-flavored Pinotage, a cross of Pinot Noir and Cinsaut, is unique to South Africa. Stylistically, South Africa's wines tilt toward the European, with more subtlety and *terroir* (see page 17) influence and better balance, than many others from the New World.

Wine growing regions

SWARTLAND

PAARL

Cape Town

STELLENBOSCH

on the Label

Wine of Origin (WO) is similar to the French Appellation d'Origine Contrôllée (see page 18). Look to the main growing areas, Paarl and Stellenbosch, for fine Chardonnay, Sauvignon Blanc, Cabernet Sauvignon, Merlot, and Pinotage and to the district of Swartland for value. Varietal labeling is the rule.

WHITE WINES

Dry or off-dry, Steen is a lovely quaffing wine. Chardonnays and Rieslings are good and improving. Sauvignon Blancs are particularly fine, sometimes rivaling those of New Zealand.

at the table

Steen's hint of melon makes it perfect as an aperitif. Chardonnay is best with butter and cream sauces, roast chicken, scallops, and lobster. Riesling is excellent with Thai and other Asian cuisines. Sauvignon Blancs from Stellenbosch can be powerful, pairing well with fried fish and salmon. Enjoy all these wines when they're young.

the bottom Line Prices range from $7 for Steens to around $18 for the better Chardonnays. Great value.

1998 Buitenverwachting Sauvignon Blanc, Constantia ★★★ $$

Muted grassy, lemony nose and surprisingly good acidity. A big Sauvignon Blanc with lime and mineral flavors and a long, zesty finish.

1997 Mulderbosch Chardonnay, Stellenbosch ★★★ $$

Charry, smoky vanilla oak dominates the nose but is well-balanced with lively, lemony apple, pear, and pineapple flavors on the palate. Good acidity keeps this oaky wine tasting fruity and refreshing.

1997 Brampton Sauvignon Blanc, Stellenbosch ★★ $$

A subdued nose hints at spice, lemon, and minerals. Medium bodied; lovely acidity balances mellow flavors of lemon, pineapple, and peach.

1998 Delaire Chardonnay, Stellenbosch ★★ $$

Toasty oak, mineral, caramel, toffee, and tropical-fruit aromas. Low acidity—count on early, but very tasty, drinking.

1997 Hamilton Russell Vineyards Chardonnay, Walker Bay ★★ $$

Lots of toasted oak in the aroma, flavor, and finish. Happily, there is ample tropical fruitiness and zesty acidity to handle the oak.

1998 Boschendal Sauvignon Blanc, Paarl ★★ $

Lemon-lime and honey nose. This refreshing, medium-bodied Chardonnay has well-concentrated lemon-lime and melon flavors tinged with grassy herbal overtones.

1997 L'Avenir White Table Wine, Stellenbosch ★ $

Some earthy Chenin Blanc in the nose. Off-dry but well-balanced, with a tangy finish; a slight chemical note late in the finish may bother some, but this wine is delightful for its lime-zest flavor.

1997 Bloupunt Unwooded Chardonnay, Montagu ★ $

This is a mellow Chardonnay with a short finish, but there are lots of attractive pear and vanilla flavors before then.

1998 Cape Indaba Sauvignon Blanc, Robertson ★ $

Pungent lemon-lime and pineapple nose. Gentle acidity makes it easy to enjoy the delicious, slightly nutty, lemon-lime flavor.

RED WINES

Pinotage is South Africa's most interesting red, but it's still searching for an identity. Styles range from simple, Beaujolais-like wines to tannic, earthy heavyweights. Currently, South

Africa is doing better with its Cabernet Sauvignon, Merlot, and Shiraz, all of which can be excellent.

at the table

Lightweight Pinotage is a delightful, fruity red, perfect for , sandwiches, salads, and mild cheeses. Fuller Pinotage favors mushrooms, wild rice, roasted vegetables, and game birds. Serve the peppery Shiraz with barbecue and grilled meats. The Cabernets and Merlots do best with beef and aged cheese.

the bottom line Quality has improved faster than prices, which range from $7 to $30—relatively good values.

1996 Rustenberg, Stellenbosch ★★★★ $$$
Cassis, blackberry, cherry, and rich-soil aromas. Full-bodied and intense; ample tannin. The cherry and plum flavors are kept lively by the acidity.

1995 Meerlust Merlot, Stellenbosch ★★★★ $$
Aromas of plums, cassis, and cherries dusted with cocoa. Medium-full body, concentrated flavors, silky tannin, and a long, chocolaty finish.

1995 Thelema Cabernet Sauvignon, Stellenbosch ★★★ $$$
Mint, eucalyptus, pepper, and smoked-meat nose. Flavors of chocolate, cherry, and earth balanced by lots of new-oak notes of spice and toast.

1996 Backsberg Cabernet Sauvignon, Paarl ★★ $$
Plum, mint, cassis, and roasted-meat aromas. Medium bodied with a solid streak of gamy flavor and a good bitter-cherry finish.

1997 Brampton Cabernet Sauvignon–Merlot, Stellenbosch ★★ $$
Aromas of plum, cassis, and oak. Fruity and medium bodied. Just enough oak and tannin to set off the sour-cherry and plum flavors.

1995 Cathedral Cellar Cabernet Sauvignon, Paarl ★★ $$
Gobs of toasty American oak and black-fruit aromas. Bold blackberry and blueberry flavors with bitter chocolate in the finish.

1998 Swartland Merlot, Swartland ★★ $
Cherry, blackberry, raspberry, and plum flavors that just don't quit—a fruit bowl of a wine and no oak to mess it up.

1997 KWV Cabernet Sauvignon, Paarl ★ $
Full-bodied and packed with jammy fruit flavors. A simple, one-dimensional style, but, at this price, why not just relax and enjoy it?

AUSTRALIA

The wine industry in Australia has developed rapidly since the late 1960s. Aided by advances in the technology of viticulture and vinification, Australia has earned the adulation of wine lovers everywhere for its fruity, flavor-packed wines at terrific prices. In the 1990s, the world discovered the complex, concentrated wines from Australia's myriad small estates. Today's Australia satisfies the everyday drinker and connoisseur alike.

GRAPES AND STYLES

Most Australian wines feature our familiar and cherished grapes: Chardonnay, Sauvignon Blanc, Riesling, and Sémillon for whites; Cabernet Sauvignon, Merlot, and Pinot Noir, for reds. Australia's number one red variety, however, is Shiraz, the Syrah of the northern Rhône. Less frequently seen are Grenache, Mourvèdre, Marsanne, and Roussanne, which usually appear in blends. As a rule, Australian wines offer bold fruit flavor, lush texture, and early drinkability.

ON THE LABEL

Like the United States and other New World countries, Australia labels its wines by variety. The better-known wine regions are in the cooler southern reaches of the continent, within the states of South Australia, New South Wales, and Victoria. All three are commonly lumped together into the huge region noted on bottles as South Eastern Australia. On the western coast of Australia, the Margaret River district is gaining a reputation for distinctive, cool-climate wines.

CHARDONNAY

Many Australian Chardonnays are evolving away from overemphasis on fruitiness and overpowering use of oak to

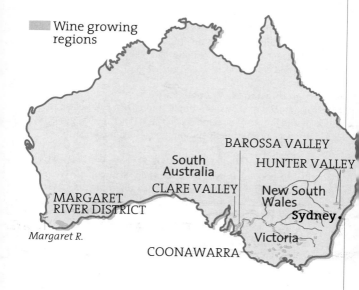

Wine growing regions

BAROSSA VALLEY

South Australia

HUNTER VALLEY

CLARE VALLEY

MARGARET RIVER DISTRICT

New South Wales

Sydney.

Margaret R.

Victoria

COONAWARRA

a more restrained style. The result is moderately toasty, pleasantly fruity wines, the flavors of which include pineapple, melon, and coconut. The wines are generally at their best when young. We are fans of the hot new trend toward so-called unwooded Chardonnays. These lively wines let the clear flavors from ripe Chardonnay grapes come through completely free of the taste imparted by oak.

at the table

The fullest Australian Chardonnays have a lush fruitiness that can seem almost sweet. This can be a plus alongside the slight sweetness of shellfish, such as lobster, shrimp, crab, and scallops. Chicken, especially with fruit in its sauce or accompaniment, also works well. The oakiest Chardonnays, too aggressively flavored for many dishes, can be successfully tamed by prosciutto, smoked trout, grilled chicken, and grilled fish steaks.

the bottom line   Australian Chardonnays are great values. In the $10 to $15 range, most U.S. Chardonnays can't match the quality and sheer pleasure these wines provide. Higher-end wines may lack the complexity of American and European offerings but compare very favorably in price.

1996 Petaluma Piccadilly Valley, South Australia ★★★ $$$
This elegant Chardonnay shows welcome restraint. The lightly oaked citrus and spice flavors are intensely concentrated, but bracing acidity keeps the wine refreshing. Has a long finish with flavors of peaches and orange peel.

1998 Hugo Unwooded, McLaren Vale ★★★ $$
Penetrating nose of pineapple, apple, and citrus. Full-bodied, with concentrated flavors of pineapple, papaya, and mango. Tangy acidity carries the flavors effortlessly through the refreshing finish.

1997 Chateau Reynella, McLaren Vale ★★★ $$
Made in the popular full-blown oaky style with copious vanilla, clove, and cinnamon aromas mingling with those of tropical fruit. The wine is full, yet refreshing, with balancing acidity that also drives the palate-cleansing, citric finish.

1997 Scotchman's Hill Geelong, Victoria ★★★ $$
Scotchman's Hill is a recent arrival in the U.S., and the wines are impressive. This elegant 1997 Chardonnay has mouth-filling pear, vanilla, and honey flavors; a smooth texture; brisk acidity; and a long, lemony finish.

1998 David Wynn Unwooded, South Eastern Australia ★★★ $$
The tropical-fruit flavors of Chardonnay grapes grown in a warm climate are highlighted here due to the complete lack of oak. Medium bodied, with a briskly acidic, palate-cleansing finish, this wine is a natural with food.

1997 Peter Lehmann, Barossa ★★ $$
Restrained use of oak allows the flavors of apples, figs, and cloves to take center stage. This appealing wine has a creamy texture and a good fruity finish.

1998 Carramar Estate, South Eastern Australia ★★ $
Made in a straightforward, light, fruit-driven style. The wine has pear, apple, and mango flavors nicely balanced with snappy acidity. A medium-length finish.

1998 Hardys Nottage Hill, South Eastern Australia ★★ $
Light and charming, this smooth, medium-bodied Chardonnay offers pineapple and lemon flavors that last nicely through the finish.

1998 Mc Guigan Brothers Bin 7000, South Eastern Australia ★★ $
Another classic Australian crowd pleaser, this medium-bodied Chardonnay features clear, smooth pineapple and other tropical-fruit flavors. Refreshing.

1998 Rosemount Estate Diamond Label, South Eastern Australia ★ ★ $

Each year this prestigious winery releases a dizzying number of wines, including many fine Chardonnays. The Diamond Label is the most widely distributed and least expensive. It is dry, full of citrus and pineapple flavor, and quite intense on the palate, particularly for a modestly priced wine. Also look for Rosemount's famous Hunter Valley Show Reserve Chardonnay.

1997 Seaview, McLaren Vale ★ ★ $

Flavors of apple, coconut, and pears, along with a hint of spice, and a refreshing acidity. A modest but good Chardonnay.

1998 Tyrrell's Long Flat, South Eastern Australia ★ ★ $

A simple and direct Chardonnay, with clear flavors of pear and lemon and a pleasant, fruity finish.

1998 Oxford Landing, South Eastern Australia ★ $

Oxford Landing's light Chardonnay has apple, pineapple, toffee, and butterscotch flavors. A hint of earth on the finish gives a bit of welcome grown-up complexity.

OTHER WHITE WINES

Sémillon, (pronounced SEM-uh-lahn in Australia) is a specialty of the Hunter Valley where it produces broad, full-bodied wines with intense nutty marmalade flavors. Though rarely oaked, with age they develop flavors you'd swear are from wood. Good Sémillon is made in other regions as well. Look to the Clare Valley for distinctive lemon-lime and peach Rieslings. They are now becoming readily available. Australia also makes good Sauvignon Blanc and the unique Sémillon-Chardonnay blend.

THE BOTTOM LINE Expect to spend between $9 and $25 for Australian white wines.

1998 Brokenwood Sémillon, Hunter Valley ★ ★ ★ $ $

Here's a terrific example of the unwooded Hunter Valley style of Sémillon. Right now the nose is faintly nutty and herbaceous, and little except satiny texture and bracing acidity show up on the palate. With age, the wine will develop the glorious fruit, honey, and buttered-toast flavors that made these wines famous.

1998 Grosset Polish Hill Riesling, Clare Valley ★★★ $$

Intensely minerally and chalky on the nose, with hints of lime, spring blossoms, and passion fruit. This dry wine's steely passion-fruit and lime flavors last on the long finish, which also has a hint of toastiness. One of Australia's finer Rieslings, it will age beautifully for up to 10 years. Try to give it at least five.

1996 Petaluma Riesling, Clare Valley ★★★ $$

Though Aussies revere their Clare Valley Rieslings, they have yet to be embraced by Yanks. You may have to search a bit, but this prize is worth the effort. The wine has a perfumed lime, lemon, and melon nose and flavors of peaches and melons, along with the acidity to enhance them.

1998 Shaw and Smith Sauvignon Blanc, Adelaide Hills ★★★ $$

A delectable Sauvignon Blanc that combines Australia's smooth fruitiness with the electric acidity typical of New Zealand. It has lovely aromas and beautifully balanced flavors of malt, herbs, citrus, and gooseberries that persist through the long, succulent finish.

1997 Leeuwin Estate Rhine Riesling, Margaret River ★★ $$

A dry and understated Riesling with peach, apricot, and melon flavors enlivened by balancing citric acidity.

1998 Taltarni Sauvignon Blanc, Victoria ★★ $$

This zesty crowd pleaser emphasizes the tropical, melony side of Sauvignon Blanc, downplaying its typical herbaceousness. Vigorous acidity keeps it lively through the long finish.

1998 Lindemans Bin 77 Sémillon-Chardonnay, South Eastern Australia ★★ $

Mellow and lush with flavors of pear, lemon drops, and cantaloupe and just enough mild acidity to perk up the fruit flavors and make the finish last.

1998 Penfolds Koonunga Hill Sémillon-Chardonnay, South East Australia ★★ $

With 70 percent Sémillon and 30 percent Chardonnay, Sémillon clearly dominates, providing pineapple and peach flavors in this light, appealing wine. The Chardonnay contributes citric notes and brisk acidity.

1997 Tyrrell's Old Winery Sémillon, Hunter Valley ★★ $

Offers effusive aromas of spices, herbs, and tropical fruits and the flavor of pineapple. Light and lively with a lingering, spicy finish. You can drink this young.

CABERNET SAUVIGNON

Australia is a treasure trove of, on the one hand, easy-to-drink, everyday Cabernet Sauvignons with gobs of jammy fruit flavors and little or no tannin and, on the other hand, world-class wines displaying big, bold black-currant flavors, mouth-filling texture, and generous spicy oak. South Australia's cool Coonawarra region, with its famous terra rosa (red soil), makes some of the most complex Cabs in the country. In general, Australian Cabernet Sauvignons are a bit lighter than the powerhouses of the Napa Valley and are not even Australia's biggest red wines; that title goes to Shiraz (see page 202).

at the table

Serve the simpler Cabernet Sauvignons with simple food, like hamburgers. The bigger wines, just like those of California, need hearty food: roast beef, aged steak, or robust stews. Vegetarians take heart. These flavorful reds are delicious with such varied dishes as pasta with cheese or mushroom sauce, risotto with Parmigiano-Reggiano, strong and hard aged cheeses, and even with the notoriously difficult to match bittersweet chocolate!

the bottom line Extraordinary value. The best Cabernet Sauvignons don't quite match up to California's superstars, but in the $10 to $20 range, you generally get much more wine for your money.

what to buy CABERNET SAUVIGNON

1994	1995	1996	1997	1998
★★★★	★★★	★★★★	★★★	★★★

1996 Parker Estate Terra Rossa First Growth, Coonawara
★★★★ $$$$

A youthful blockbuster Cabernet Sauvignon blend from a relatively new winery. The abundant tannin is prominent now, but a core of concentrated currant and eucalyptus flavors lies in wait. Good, brisk acidity imparts zest and adds to the long, powerfully tannic finish.

1996 Wolf Blass Presidents Selection, South Australia
★★★ $$

Fine balance between the mellow tannin and the black-currant and black-cherry flavors. The wine is good now but will continue to develop for several more years.

1997 Wynns Estate, Coonawarra ★ ★ ★ $$

A good example of an archetypal Australian Cabernet Sauvignon—medium bodied, with generous, clear black-cherry, cassis, mint, and eucalyptus flavors and a mildly tannic finish.

1995 Rosemount Show Reserve, Coonawara ★ ★ $$

On the nose, aromas of smoke and plums. This is a full Cabernet Sauvignon, packed with berry, plum, and cassis flavors slathered with generous helpings of vanilla and spice from new oak. Gentle tannin and acid.

1996 Sandalford, Mount Barker–Margaret River ★ ★ $$

Oak dominates the nose of this wine, but it has ample fruit flavor to handle the wood. This is a big, full-bodied Cabernet, spicy and complex, with penetrating, tart black-currant flavor. A wine that will improve with age.

SHIRAZ

Australia has taken the Syrah grape of France's northern Rhône Valley and made it uniquely its own. Most Shirazes are mellow, fruity, and ready to drink upon release. With smooth, spicy blackberry flavors and modest prices, Shiraz makes the perfect house wine. More complex, ageworthy Shirazes, with pungent peppery notes, intense fruity flavors, and powerful tannin, are among the greatest reds in the world. Many of these top-drawer Shirazes, including the coveted Penfolds Grange, are made in South Australia's Barossa Valley.

at the table

Light, fruity Shiraz makes the perfect barbecue wine. Serve it with grilled hamburgers and with barbecued chicken, pork, and ribs. The lighter Shiraz also complements turkey and flavorful cheeses. The more serious, peppery Shiraz with its berry flavors, will match lamb stew, steak au poivre, charred filet of beef, roasted goose, duck, and any blue-veined cheese beautifully.

the bottom line Australian Shirazes are unique wines that represent awesome value. From under $10 quaffers to over $40 for some of the blockbuster cellar treasures, you generally get a lot more quality than you pay for. A few top-end wines like Penfolds Grange, however, are priced stratispherically, more as collectibles than beverages.

WHAT TO BUY SHIRAZ

1994	1995	1996	1997	1998
★★★★	★★★	★★★★	★★★	★★★

1997 Cape Mentelle, Margaret River   ★★★★ $$
This high-profile Western Australian winery was started by the founder of New Zealand's Cloudy Bay. It produces small quantities of intense, robust, complex Shiraz with dark-fruit flavors, some herbal notes, and abundant tannin. The wine is made in a style more like that of the northern Rhône than of Australia.

1996 Stanley Brothers John Hancock,
Barossa   ★★★★ $$
Intense blackberry, earth, and cocoa-powder aromas on the nose. This serious Shiraz sports superbly concentrated, berry, spice, and chocolate flavors; thrusting acidity; massive tannin; and a persistent finish. Despite all these potent constituents, the wine is remarkably balanced and elegant.

1995 Hardys Eileen Hardy, South Australia   ★★★ $$$$
A typically full-bodied Shiraz, from one of Australia's largest and most reliable producers. The nose is all cedar and blueberries, and a slight vegetal character enhances the flavor. It has a strongly tannic and spicy finish.

1996 Jim Barry McCrae Wood, Clare Valley   ★★★ $$$
Pleasing aromas of mint, eucalyptus, coffee, and plums mingle in the nose of this rather idiosyncratic Shiraz. On the palate, it is concentrated, medium bodied, and elegant. Mint and plum flavors repeat the nose on the finish.

1996 St. Hallett Old Block, Barossa   ★★★ $$$
Old vines produce an intense style of Shiraz, with concentrated flavors. This one tastes of plums, black cherries, chocolate, and cloves. Though only medium bodied, its clear flavors and lusty tannin promise good future development.

1997 Hugo, McLaren Vale   ★★★ $$
Impressive, inky ruby color. Intense aromas of blackberry jam and toffee precede an extraordinarily, almost painfully intense, blackberry-jam flavor.

1996 Peter Lehmann, Barossa   ★★ $$
This wine is wonderfully intense on the palate, with the flavor combination of licorice and blackberry. A fine, mellow wine that's ready to drink now.

1996 Sandalford Mount Barker, Margaret River ★★ $$

Aromatic nose of blackberries, woodsmoke, and herbs. Great blackberry, cinnamon, vanilla, and herb flavors, lively acidity, and mild tannin.

1997 Yalumba, Barossa ★★ $$

Clear floral and oak aromas; spice, blueberry, and coffee flavors. Some tannin in the finish, along with nuances of cloves and black cherries. Clean.

OTHER RED WINES

In Australia's unique Shiraz–Cabernet Sauvignon blends (the grape with the highest percentage in the blend must be named first), Shiraz plays the role that Merlot does in Bordeaux. The fruitiness of Shiraz fleshes out Cabernet's natural austerity. Grenache and Mourvèdre show up as fruit-filled varietals or in blends. Some very fruity Pinot Noir and Merlot is produced as well.

the bottom line Australia's other red wines generally cost between $10 and $20, although some are priced higher.

1996 Penfolds Cabernet Sauvignon–Shiraz Bin 389, South Australia ★★★ $$$

Many Australian wineries use bin numbers to distinguish different bottlings. Bin 389 is one of Penfolds' best, packed with dark-plum, cassis, herb, chocolate, and earth flavors. Full-bodied, with a full complement of tannin. Drink now or hold.

1995 Frankland Estate Olmo's Reward, Western Australia ★★★ $$

An elegant blend of the five red Bordeaux grapes. This wine has Bordeaux-like aromas and flavors of black currant and cedar with some herbaceous notes. Because the tannin is gentle, you can drink the wine now, but it will age gracefully for a decade or more.

1997 Wynn's Cabernet-Shiraz-Merlot, South Australia ★★★ $$

Blackberry and plum aromas are accented by lots of toast and cinnamon and a whiff of the barnyard. Refreshing acid highlights the Shiraz-influenced fruit flavors. Snappy acidity remains on the finish, with a slightly gamy note.

1998 Jenke Merlot, Barossa ★★ $$

Spicy, woody aromas join those of plums. This smooth, medium-bodied wine has cherry and chocolate flavors and a long, spicy finish.

1996 Lindemans Merlot Reserve, South Australia ★★ $$

Made in a fruity, easy-drinking style with generous vanilla and spice aromas from oak. Full, plummy flavor, and mild tannin. Drink this silky-textured wine young.

1998 Rosemount Estate Grenache-Shiraz, South Eastern Australia ★ $

A smooth, cheerful quaffing red chock-full of jammy berry flavors. It's readily available and moderately priced.

CAN WINEMAKERS fly?

Because the seasons down under are the reverse of those up north, Australian "flying winemakers" can consult in the off-season, spreading Aussie expertise and technology to the rest of the world. They're particularly helpful in areas that have an abundance of inexpensive grapes and labor but lack the technical know-how to exploit their resources. Vintners such as Hugh Ryman and Jacques Lurton are justifiably famous not only for their delicious, inexpensive Australian wines but also for their impact on wines throughout the Northern Hemisphere, including southern France, Italy, Iberia, and Eastern Europe.

NEW ZEALAND

The cool, damp climate and fertile volcanic soils of New Zealand produce extraordinarily penetrating wines. Their vibrant fruit flavors combined with mouthwatering acidity never fail to excite. As any Kiwi will tell you, their wine is like no other in the world.

grapes and styles

Sauvignon Blanc put New Zealand on the map, but Chardonnay is the country's most widely grown grape, and it makes some very fine wine, indeed. Riesling and Pinot Noir are coming on strong. New Zealand rarely produces good wines from Cabernet Sauvignon or Merlot, both of which struggle in the cool climate.

on the label

Virtually all New Zealand wines are varietally labeled. The best white wines come from Marlborough, on the northern tip of the South Island. Awatere Valley, sometimes seen on the label, is a subdistrict of Marlborough. Look to Martinborough and Central Otago for Pinot Noirs.

SAUVIGNON BLANC

New Zealand Sauvignon Blanc's signature aromas of gooseberry, citrus, herbs, asparagus, and malt are both thrilling and unmistakable. The grassy, sometimes vegetal flavors combined with high acidity may be an acquired taste, but to devoted fans, these wines are some of the most exciting in the world. Cloudy Bay, the first superstar, is now one among many excellent producers.

Auckland

Wine growing
regions

North
Island

MARTINBOROUGH

MARLBOROUGH

South
Island

CENTRAL OTAGO

at the table

Light-bodied and citric, New Zealand Sauvignon Blancs are an excellent match for shellfish, grilled vegetables, gazpacho, and freshwater fish. Asparagus and artichokes clash with most wines but actually complement these Sauvignon Blancs because of their similar vegetal character. Salads, another tough match, are a natural; if the salad includes goat cheese, even better.

the bottom line New Zealand's Sauvignon Blancs are terrific bargains, with some excellent wines starting below $10 and the best wines topping out around $20. Not only is the style unique, but today's New Zealand Sauvignon Blancs may just be the best money can buy.

1998 Cloudy Bay, Marlborough ★ ★ ★ ★ $$
The wine that put New Zealand on the map. Now difficult to find but worth the search. An explosive nose of lemon-lime, grapefruit, and fresh-cut grass. On the palate, a thrilling interplay of smooth fruitiness, lush texture, and rapierlike acidity leading to an almost endless finish.

1998 Nautilus Estate, Marlborough ★ ★ ★ ★ $$
Pungent aromas of lime and asparagus and a hint of malt are irresistible. The wine is dry, with citrus fruits, especially lime, and a streak of mineral that together cut a refreshing swath across the palate. This is an exceptionally fine example of a Sauvignon Blanc in the Marlborough style.

1998 Babich, Marlborough ★ ★ ★ $
Aromas of lemons and cut hay. Citrus and mint flavors enhanced by zingy acidity make this a delicious and refreshing wine. Year in and year out, one of New Zealand's best values in Sauvignon Blanc.

1998 Selaks Premium Selection, Marlborough ★ ★ ★ $
Lemon, lime, passion fruit, and gooseberry aromas. This full-bodied Sauvignon has a lovely mélange of lemon, passion-fruit, and grassy asparagus flavors. Excellent.

1999 Stoneleigh, Marlborough ★ ★ ★ $
Herbs, asparagus, and green banana accent citrus and minerals in the nose of this aggressively herbaceous wine. On the palate, tarragon, green-peppercorn, and citrus flavors are buttressed by palate-cleansing acidity. A delicious example of this style.

1998 Vavasour Dashwood, Marlborough ★ ★ $$
Full citrus aromas, with notes of asparagus and malt. A fairly low-acid, fruity style Sauvignon Blanc with excellent flavors that trail off a bit in the finish.

1997 Wairu River, Marlborough ★ ★ $$
The aggressive green-bean and asparagus nose may be an acquired taste, but it screams New Zealand. Flavors of lemon peel, grass, and herbs married to ample acidity complete this archetypal picture.

1998 Longridge, Hawkes Bay ★ ★ $
Serves up green-apple aromas and snappy citrus flavors. Drink it now to revel in its youthful exuberance.

CHARDONNAY

New Zealand's Chardonnays, like her Sauvignon Blancs, tend toward the light bodied, citric, and unoaked. Use of oak barrels is on the rise, however, and now many fuller, oaky Chardonnays can be found. You can take your choice.

at the table

Use the light, acidic, unoaked Chardonnays as you might a Chablis. Pair them with mild fish, shellfish, salads, and light chicken dishes. The oaked versions are unusual in that unlike most oaky Chardonnays, they have penetrating acidity that allows them to counterbalance rich food. Cream and butter sauces, pork, choucroute garnie, and charcuterie are all creative choices.

the bottom line   Unlike her unique Sauvignon Blancs, New Zealand's Chardonnays present fewer compelling reasons to buy them. At $10 to $20, prices are fair, not bargains.

1996 Te Mata Estate Elston, Hawkes Bay ★★★ $$$
An impressively full and fruity Chardonnay from one of the most prestigious wineries in New Zealand. Look also for their very fine Cape Crest Sauvignon Blanc and their surprisingly assertive Syrah.

1996 Babich Iron Gate, Hawkes Bay ★★ $$
A light Chardonnay with the fragrance of orchard fruit and the flavor of Granny Smith apples. It has a fine balance of flavor and vibrant, palate-cleansing acidity.

1998 Kim Crawford Unoaked, Marlborough ★★ $$
Citrus and pineapple aromas hit you first. The pleasant, mellow, full-bodied style of this Chardonnay is one that anyone tired of oak will admire for its clear fruit flavors.

1996 Mills Reef Winery, Hawkes Bay ★★ $$
This full, barrel-fermented wine offers a nose of tropical fruit and toasty oak and lots of lush melon and peach flavors. It has a long, fruity finish.

1998 Nobilo Fall Harvest, Gisborne ★★ $
A straightforward, simple Chardonnay, featuring pear and tart apple flavors. It has medium body and a refreshingly zesty finish.

RIESLING

New Zealand's cool climate, with its long, dry autumns, creates Rieslings that fall somewhere between those of Germany and Alsace in style. They have both delicacy and power, and a blossomy, talcum-powder character all their own. Riesling represents only about 4 percent of New Zealand's total harvest, making them difficult to find, but worth the search.

the Bottom Line   Most New Zealand Rieslings are fairly priced at about $9 to $14. The trick is finding them.

1998 De Redcliffe Rhine, Marlborough   ★ ★ ★ $$
Strong mineral, lime-peel, and gooseberry nose with hints of earth and peaches. On the palate, the wine is dry with high acidity and the flavor of Rose's lime juice augmented with minerals and blossoms. A long, minerally finish. Will improve with age.

1998 Saint Claire, Marlborough   ★ ★ $$
Blossomy aromas. This slightly off-dry Riesling tastes of citrus, with a floral flavor reminiscent of lavender lozenges in the finish. Good!

1998 Villa Maria Private Bin, Marlborough   ★ ★ $
A dry wine featuring full, intense apple and pear flavors and insistent acidity.

PINOT NOIR

It is our belief that, while New Zealand is now known for its pungent Sauvignon Blancs, in 20 years the country's reputation will rest solidly on Pinot Noirs. This grape likes cool climates; Martinborough on the North Island and Central Otago on the South are ideal. Pinot Noir is relatively new here, but already there are some beautiful wines with aromas of raspberries, blackberries, and herbs that would please a died-in-the-wool Burgundy lover.

at the table

Pinot Noir is a most adaptable wine, and New Zealand versions, with their characteristic high acidity, are even more flexible than most. Serve them with duck in fruit sauce and veal, chicken, or pork with mushrooms. Grilled salmon is an exceptionally good partner. Most New Zealand Pinots pair well with light meats, but some particularly full versions acquit themselves well with lamb or mixed grills.

THE BOTTOM LINE   The one sour note with New Zealand Pinots is their price. At $20 to $30 and up, they are expensive when compared to other New World Pinot Noirs.

1996 Rippon Vineyard, Central Otago ★★★★ $$$

What a nose: full of complex red and black fruits, Asian and Indian spices, and fresh-chopped herbs. This seductive wine has tremendously concentrated berry and spice flavors that keep unfolding to the kaleidoscopic finish. It reminds us of a great Vosne-Romanée.

1997 Martinborough Vineyards, Martinborough ★★★ $$$

Somewhat exotic Pinot Noir, with intense dark-berry and spicy oak flavors, good acidity, and solid tannin. Fine now, but has the potential for excellent development with bottle age. If the Rippon above is Vosne-Romanée, this is Pommard.

1997 Te Kairanga, Martinborough ★★ $$

An elegant style of Pinot Noir. Aromas and flavors of blackberries and cloves. Medium bodied and fairly tannic, with good balance of flavor, tannin, acidity, and alcohol content. It will improve with some time in the bottle.

SOUTH AMERICA

Winemaking has flourished in South America for more than a century, but until recently there was little reason to export. Home demand more than exceeded supply. Beginning in the 1980s, huge foreign investments inspired by cheap labor and even cheaper land led to an explosion of good, soundly made, and attractively priced wines. Now the U.S. imports more wine from Chile than from any other country except France and Italy. And South America in general is a place to watch.

ARGENTINA

In the past, even though Argentina ranks fifth in the world for sheer volume of wine production, few bottles left the country. As local consumption has declined and demands for capital have become more pressing, Argentina has entered the export market and is now making a concerted effort to introduce her wines to the world.

grapes and styles

Cabernet Sauvignons are the best Argentine wines, but for its sheer personality as well as curiosity value, Malbec is where it's at. The world's largest plantings of Malbec are in Argentina,

Wine growing regions

CHILE

ARGENTINA

Andes Mts.

CASABLANCA

Santiago

SAN JUAN

MAIPO

RAPEL
COLCHAGUA

MENDOZA

Buenos Aires

CURICÓ
MAULE

and in its warm, dry climate this otherwise ordinary grape produces surprisingly good wines—full-bodied and fruity with enough tannin to allow development for a decade or more. Also keep an eye out for up-and-coming, ageworthy Syrahs, very good Merlots, fruity Pinot Noirs, and the singular Torrontés, an aromatic, fruity, white.

on the Label

One of Argentina's quirks is that red wines are aged longer before release than in other areas of the world. Don't be surprised if a 1995 or even 1994 is actually the current vintage. Mendoza and San Juan are the two main growing areas. Cafayate is excellent for the white Torrontés. Along with the rest of the New World, Argentina employs varietal labeling.

WHITE WINES

Argentina's white wines lag far behind her reds, but are improving. The majority are thin, a result of sky-high yields, and a few oxidized throwbacks to the bad old days still exist. The Chardonnays tend to be overoaked. For now you're better off sticking to the reds. Of course, there *are* exceptions; some decent Chardonnays and Sauvignon Blancs can be found. Argentina's most interesting white is Torrontés, which tastes like a cross between Muscat and Gewürztraminer.

at the table

Most of the whites should be enjoyed young. They make excellent aperitifs, especially Torrontés. Sauvignon Blancs, unoaked Chardonnays, and Torrontés pair nicely with salads, mild fish, light chicken dishes, and other simple summer fare. Oakier Chardonnays can handle stronger flavors.

the bottom Line   Argentina's Chardonnays and Sauvignon Blancs have a way to go before we feel comfortable recommending them as good value. Torrontés, on the other hand, is unique and cheap—$6 to $9. Try it!

1997 Catena Agrelo Vineyard Chardonnay, Mendoza ★★★ $$

Inviting aromas of lees, toasty oak, orange peel, and tropical fruit. This delicious Chardonnay stands out among most Argentine whites for its full body, well-concentrated tropical-fruit flavors, lush texture, and unusual complexity.

1997 Navarro Correas Chardonnay, Mendoza ★★ $$

This barrel-fermented Chardonnay is made in a California style but escapes being just another oaky Chardonnay by its refreshing mandarin-orange-flavored finish.

1998 Trapiche Chardonnay, Mendoza ★★ $

Lovely lemon-candy, cream, tropical-fruit, and earth nose. Features pear, apple, and tropical-fruit flavors on the palate. Some invigorating spritz lends liveliness, and there's a note of caramel in the finish.

RED WINES

Established by Italian, French, and Spanish immigrants in the late 19th century, Argentina's red-wine industry has deep European roots. The wines are not as fruity as most New World ones, though a growing number of modern-style Cabernet Sauvignons, Merlots, and Pinot Noirs emphasize clear berry flavors.

at the table

The sturdy, earthy quality of Argentine reds brings to mind comfort food rather than haute cuisine. An Argentine Cabernet Sauvignon or Malbec will enhance pot roast, meat loaf, hamburgers, or braised short ribs. Merlots pair very well with roasted vegetables, grilled poultry or game birds, and lamb. Try the modern-style Pinot Noirs and Syrahs with ham sandwiches, sausages, and charcuterie.

the bottom line

Good value, particularly with the better wines. Most are under $15; they rarely exceed $20.

what to buy RED WINES

1994	1995	1996	1997	1998
★★★	★★★★	★★★★	★★★	★★★

1994 Navarro Correas Malbec, Mendoza ★★ $$

In contrast to the Weinert Malbec below, this wine is elegant, with aromas and flavors of plums and dried violets.

1994 Weinert Malbec, Mendoza ★★ $$

Earthy nose hinting at toasted grains. A full wine, with slightly rough tannin, plum and prune flavors, and a touch of chocolate.

1997 Balbi Malbec-Syrah, Mendoza ★★ $

A vibrant blend with a nice nose of raspberries and blueberries. Berry flavors echo on the palate and in the full-bodied finish.

1996 Correas Cabernet Sauvignon, Maipu ★ ★ $
Correas is a second, lower-priced line of wines from Navarro (see page 215). This light crowd pleaser has simple, full fruit flavors and a refreshingly minty aroma. Just drink it.

1995 Humberto Canale Malbec, Rio Negro ★ ★ $
For four generations, Humberto Canale has produced elegant wines. Its Malbec is mellow and delicious, full of succulent Bing cherry flavor. A great alternative to Merlot.

1996 Temporada Syrah, Mendoza ★ ★ $
From the Vista Alba winery in Mendoza, this Syrah is made in a light, easygoing style—inviting, mellow, with just enough spice to let you know it's really Syrah. Also be on the lookout for the winery's premium line called Altos De Temporada. The Malbec is particularly fine.

1997 Terra Rosa Cabernet Sauvignon, Mendoza ★ ★ $
A full-bodied wine to drink now, with lots of flavor (cherry and plum) and tannin. Only a slightly bitter nip in the finish costs it a third star. Though aged, bottled, and sold by California's Laurel Glen winery, this Cab is made in and labeled Mendoza.

1997 Balbi Malbec, Mendoza ★ $$
Beautiful, vibrant ruby-purple color. Not as earthy as Malbec often is, this boasts clear blueberry flavor with a nice spicy note reminiscent of Syrah. Its keen acidity demands food.

1991 Humberto Canale Cabernet Sauvignon, Rio Negro ★ $
Age gives this Cabernet Sauvignon more elegance and mature, developed flavors than the vintages usually available. The finish still has a tannic bite.

1996 Correas Syrah, Maipu ★ $
A light, simple, easy-drinking Syrah with a dark-purple color, lively black-pepper aroma, and flavors of spice and blueberries.

CHILE

Chile's fertile soil, abundant sunshine, and endless supply of snowmelt from the Andes make grape growing almost too easy. Chilean wines burst onto the U.S. scene in the early

1980s with aggressively priced, well-made varietals, but growers, flush with their early success, could not resist over cropping—and quality plummeted. Chile quickly recovered, though, and the wines are now reliable and rapidly improving. Spain's Miguel Torres, the United State's Robert Mondavi, Bordeaux's Lafite Rothschild, and others have recognized Chile's enormous potential and established wineries there. Chile is just getting started.

grapes and styles

Look to Chile for familiar varietals: Sauvignon Blanc and Chardonnay for the whites; Cabernet Sauvignon and Merlot for reds. Whites are well made in the modern style but can be a bit thin; the reds are much more interesting.

on the Label

Chile's winegrowing regions surround the capital, Santiago, in the vast Central Valley. Important subregions you will see on the label include Curicó, Maipo, Maule, Colchagua, and Casablanca. Chile labels its wines according to grape varieties.

WHITE WINES

Today's Chilean reds wines are a far cry from the flavorless, watery bottlings of the early 1990s. Refreshingly zippy Sauvignon Blancs and deliciously full, fruity Chardonnays are now the rule.

at the table

Chile's white wines are best when they are youthful and vibrant. The light-bodied Sauvignon Blanc makes an excellent aperitif or accompaniment to light fish, shellfish, and salads. Chardonnay is better paired with richer fish and chicken dishes.

the bottom line   Chilean whites are extraordinary values with the vast majority selling for $10 or less.

1996 Errazuriz Wild Ferment Chardonnay, Casablanca Valley
★ ★ ★ $$

Fermented with wild yeasts, this is one of Chile's top Chardonnays. It's a big wine—oaky, yes—but with loads of tropical-fruit flavor to stand up to the oakiness and a marvelous grown-up leesy quality. It finishes with strong fruit flavors and spicy oak.

1998 Casa Lapostolle Sauvignon Blanc, Maule Valley ★ ★ ★ $

Michel Rolland, the great Bordeaux enologist, makes the excellent wines here. This medium-bodied wine has lovely aromas of melon, spring flowers, fresh-cut herbs, and honey. Drink it young to savor its buoyant fruitiness.

1998 Chicureo Sauvignon Blanc, Maule Valley ★ ★ $

Chicureo is a grape grower of long-standing in southern Chile's lata Valley, and he's now bottling his own wines. In the aromas and flavors of this wine, he achieves a wonderful synthesis of Sauvignon Blanc's grassiness with sweet honeysuckle and clover. The wine is delicate and floral, yet fruity and tangy at the same time. A real success.

1998 Santa Rita 120 Sauvignon Blanc, Lontué Valley ★ ★ $

Attractive, varietally correct pineapple and grass aromas. The pineapple carries through to the palate and is joined by sprightly citrus.

1998 Undurraga Chardonnay, Maipo Valley ★ ★ $

This is a mellow, easy-to-drink Chardonnay with inviting lemony aromas and pear and apple flavors.

1998 Los Vascos Chardonnay, Colchagua Valley ★ ★ $

The aromas and flavors of this surprisingly good wine are alive with vibrant lemon and lovely honeysuckle. On the palate, their vitality easily stands up to the toasty vanilla from oak.

1998 Concha y Toro Sauvignon Blanc–Sémillon, Maipo Valley ★ $

A pungent, aggressive, grassy Sauvignon Blanc nose leads to assertive citrus and herb flavors, nicely balanced by the gentle fruitiness of the Sémillon. Wonderful value!

1998 Concha y Toro Sunrise Chardonnay, Valle Central ★ $

A simple, straightforward Chardonnay that offers a lot of flavor for an amazingly low price! Perfect for an everyday house Chardonnay.

RED WINES

Chile's reds range from mellow, earthy, traditional styles to fruit-driven, international-style Cabernet Sauvignons and Merlots. High-end Cabernets, such as M from Montes and Don Melchor from Concha y Toro, the country's largest winery, are proving that Chile can produce world-class wines as well as excellent values.

at the table

Enjoy the full, fruity reds of Chile with simple, straightfor-ward hamburgers or roast chicken. Earthier styles lend themselves to full, long-simmered flavors, like those of pot roast or beef stew, and to dishes with mushrooms. The top Cabernet Sauvignons, like great Cabs from anywhere, should be served with plain grilled steaks or chops without any extraneous flavors to interfere with those of the wine.

the Bottom Line

Like the Chilean whites, the reds are among today's greatest values in wine. Surprisingly good wines are almost always priced under $10. Some luxu-ry *cuvées*, whose high prices are meant primarily to create splashy publicity, may be excellent wines but are certainly dubious values.

1997 Carmen Cabernet Sauvignon Reserva, Maipo Valley
★ ★ $$

This is a sturdy, powerful, and full-bodied Cabernet Sauvignon. It's densely packed with bursting berry, plum, and bacon-fat flavors, and the tannin in the finish is nice and gentle, which makes this Cab especially easy to savor.

1996 Caliterra Cabernet Sauvignon, Maipo Valley
★ ★ $

An inviting cherry aroma is the first draw. Then this pleasant, medium-bodied wine offers simple blue-fruit flavors and light tan-nin. It's made to drink now.

CARMENèRE CONFUSION

In the early 19th century, having contributed greatly to the growing reputation of Bordeaux, Carmenère was brought to Chile from the Médoc. Sadly, phylloxera almost totally erased it from Bordeaux, leaving only Chile with healthy, productive vineyards. The problem is, the grape looks just like Merlot, and most growers thought it was. So Carmenère was never recognized as a varietal, and most of it was bottled as, or blended with, Merlot. Only a few wineries have been visionary enough to produce a varietal Carmenère and label it as such. This unique Chilean wine is smooth and chocolaty, with mild tannin and a lovely cinnamon spiciness. It's special. Look for more to come!

1997 Canepa Cabernet Sauvignon, Rapel Valley ★★ $

Invigorating aromas of mint and eucalyptus with underlying cassis and chocolate. A lively Cabernet with deliciously concentrated cassis flavor, medium body, and perfect, light tannin. The distinct flavor of a chocolate mint patty on the finish. Yum!

1996 Chicureo Cabernet Sauvignon Reserva, Maule Valley ★★ $

A California-style Cabernet loaded with fruit flavors of cherries and plums, along with vanilla and spice flavors from oak. Mellow and very easy to take.

keep your eye on URUGUAY and BRAZIL

Uruguay is a hidden gem. California winemaker Paul Hobbs recently mused, "I wonder if Uruguay will forever be one of the best-kept wine secrets in the world?" To other Old World varieties given new leases on life in South America, such as Argentina's Malbec and Chile's Carmenère, Uruguay adds Tannat. Though it's dense and astringent when grown in the Madiran appellation of southwest France, Tannat comes alive with fruitiness in Uruguay. While retaining their signature brawniness, the wines are resplendent with flavors of violets and smoky bacon. It's only a matter of time before these treasures, along with Uruguay's Nebbiolos and Barberas, appear in our markets.

Some of Brazil's low-end wines (such as those from the Marcus James winery) have already been exported, but the untapped potential at all levels is huge. Moët & Chandon thinks so, too. They're already producing sparkling wine in Brazil.

1997 Mont Gras Cabernet Sauvignon, Colchagua Valley ★★ $

Zesty aromas of cherries and raspberries. A pleasant, straight-forward, medium-bodied Cabernet with simple, unpretentious cherry and herb flavors. Drink up!

1997 Montes Cabernet Sauvignon, Curicó Valley ★★ $

This wine has the typical Cabernet Sauvignon black-currant and cedar aromas and flavors. Excellent concentration and intensity for this price.

1995 Santa Carolina Merlot Reserva, Maule Valley
★ ★ $

Aromas of plum, chocolate, and tobacco. On the palate, the wine is medium bodied, with smooth plum and chocolate flavors and a hint of earthiness on the finish. A lovely Merlot.

1997 Concha y Toro Marqués de Casa Merlot, Rapel Valley
★ $$

An earthy, tasty Merlot that you can drink now. It's chock-full of simple, full fruit flavors and has a dusting of cocoa-powder flavor on the finish.

1997 Concha y Toro Trio Merlot, Maipo-Peumo Valley
★ $

A simple but good, easy-drinking wine that is notable for its pleasant dried-cherry flavor.

1997 Pionero Merlot, Valle Central
★ $

Founded in 1996 by Concha y Toro winemaker Pablo Morande, Pionero is one of Chile's newest wineries. Morande developed Concha y Toro's lauded Cabernet Sauvignon, Don Melchor, but at Pionero, he is focusing on value. This distinctive little wine tastes of blue fruits, especially elderberry, making it far more interesting than many of the cherry fruit cocktails available in this price range.

CHAMPAGNE & OTHER SPARKLING WINES

Sparkling wines are *so* misunderstood. Everyone loves preprandial Champagne for a holiday or other celebration, but when was the last time you reached for a bottle to drink with a meal, even a somewhat special one? We thought so. Don't get us wrong; we enjoy sparklers before dinner on a special occasion as much as the next person. But we also think these wines are among the most food-friendly in the world. And many of them are inexpensive enough to uncork at cocktail time any night of the week.

at the table

Champagne and other sparkling wines are remarkably adaptable at the table. The high acidity of most bubbly wines cuts right through rich foods and refreshes the palate; and so sparklers make perfect foils for cream sauce, hollandaise or béarnaise, or *beurre blanc*. Full styles pair remarkably well with eggs and cream soups. On the other hand, the delicate flavor and moderate alcohol level of these wines make them an ideal complement to today's lighter cooking. Classic matches for Champagne include oysters and caviar, but try a sparkling wine to enliven more prosaic dishes, such as salads, roasted vegetables, sushi, both lean and oily fish, or chicken. And, of course, sparkling wines make the ultimate aperitif.

CHampaGNe

Although Champagne is a sparkling wine, not all sparkling wines are Champagne. To be called Champagne (in the European Union, at least), a wine must come from France's cool northern Champagne region and be made in the strictly controlled method known as the *méthode champenoise*. Champagne's complex toasty flavors, subtlety, delicacy, and ageability make it the model for sparkling wines the world over.

Grapes and Styles

Three grapes are used to make Champagne: Chardonnay, which contributes finesse, Pinot Noir, body, and Pinot Meunier, fruitiness. Wines made entirely from Chardonnay are called Blanc de Blancs, while the rarely encountered Blanc de Noirs are produced from Pinot Noir or Pinot Meunier or both. Rosés can be made by leaving the juice in contact with the skins long enough to extract some pigment (the standard method). In addition, Champagne is the only region in the European Union where rosés may legally be made by combining red and white grapes, their juice, or by blending red and white wine at any stage in the winemaking process. A *prestige cuvée*, such as Dom Pérignon from Moët & Chandon or Cristal from Roederer, is a Champagne house's finest wine, made from its best grapes, aged longer than its other wines, and sold in upscale packaging.

NONVINTAGE AND VINTAGE

The Champagne region is so cool that its wine industry could not survive if it were restricted to vintage bottlings; in most years, the wines would be too thin to be saleable. Over the centuries, the Champenois have turned this challenge to their advantage. Some wine is saved in better years and then blended with wines from lesser harvests, enabling the producers to achieve consistent house styles and strong brand identities. These nonvintage (NV) wines make up the vast bulk of a Champagne house's total production, and its reputation depends on them. Three or four years per decade, however, the harvest is good enough to produce wines made exclusively from that year's grapes. Vintage Champagnes are not necessarily better than nonvintage, but they do reflect the unique characteristics of their year.

on the Label

The most important information on a Champagne label is the producer's name, as each has a distinct house style. The words *brut, extra dry, sec, demi-sec,* and *doux* indicate ascending levels of sweetness; the most commonly drunk Champagnes are bruts, which, though they have a slight residual sweetness, taste very dry indeed. If a wine is a particular style, such as Blanc de Blancs, that will also be indicated on the label, as well as the year, of course, on vintage bottles.

the bottom line   There's no way around it: Champagne's time-consuming, labor-intensive production methods make it expensive. With the expected increase in millennial demand, prices will go nowhere but up. Expect to pay $25 to $40 for nonvintage Champagnes, $50 to $80 for vintage Champagnes, and $75 to well over $100 for *prestige cuvées*. For some less expensive sparkling wines, see page 227 and following.

what to buy   VINTAGE CHAMPAGNE

Vintage ratings follow, but note that nonvintage Champagnes can be bought with confidence year in and year out.

1985	1986	1987	1988	1989	1990
★★★	★★	NV	★★★★	★★★	★★★★

1991	1992	1993	1994	1995	
★	★★	★★	★★	★★★	

NV Alfred Gratien Brut Classique   ★★★★ $$$$
Subtle nose of toast, apple, pear, and orange. Full bodied, with concentrated, tangy lemony orange flavor, lively acidity, and a long finish. An unusual Champagne style in that it emphasizes fruit. Excellent.

1995 Pierre Peters Brut   ★★★★ $$$$
Floral, minerally, chalky nose with tremendous pear and apple aromas. This wine has concentrated, intense leesy, minerally flavors that evolve into an insistent mineral finish. A superb and unique Champagne from a small estate.

1990 Pol Roger Brut   ★★★★ $$$$
A primarily apple nose with delicate lemon and toast notes. Full and forceful for a Pol Roger, it has lemon, toffee, and toast flavors, full body, and a superbly penetrating, dry finish. It's not quite ready but will become a fabulous Champagne.

1993 Taittinger Comtes de Champagne
Blanc de Blancs   ★ ★ ★ ★ $$$$

Gorgeous nose is rich with scents of toast and chalk along with hints of orange peel. Elegant, with chalky flavors. Tremendous concentration and an endless finish suggest a long life.

NV Bollinger Special Cuvée   ★ ★ ★ ★ $$$

The toasty, lemony, gingerbread nose has a strong leesy character and subtle hints of spice from oak. Classic Bollinger: Full-bodied and powerful, yet dry and brisk. Great stuff.

1993 Deutz Brut   ★ ★ ★ ★ $$$

Toasty, biscuity nose. Deutz's medium-bodied Champagne is forceful in its flavors, but they're impeccably balanced and harmonious.

CHAMPAGNE SHORTAGE?

At the end of the first quarter of 1999, Champagne orders were up 50 percent over the year before, and at the same time the remaining stocks of Champagne were half of what they should be, according to Jean-Louis Carbonnier, director of the Champagne Wines Information Bureau. A few houses are already showing signs of running out. But don't worry. There will be plenty of Champagne for celebrating the millennium as long as you're not hung up on a particular brand.

1993 Roederer Brut Rosé   ★ ★ ★ ★ $$$

A wonderful nose of strawberries and toffee and lovely, delicate red-fruit flavors—a beautiful rosé.

NV Heidsieck Monopole Diamant Bleu
Blanc de Blancs   ★ ★ ★ $$$$

In Champagne's cool climate, Chardonnay makes brisk, lemony, light-bodied wines. This archetypal one will improve with a year or two.

NV Vranken Demoiselle Blanc de Blancs Cuvée 2000 ★ ★ ★ $$$$

Hints of lemon cream grace the nose. Lively, with good acidity and mineral flavors. Fruity rather than toasty. Long finish.

NV Deutz Brut Classic   ★ ★ ★ $$$

Deutz is doing everything right. This is a simply lovely brut with excellent balance of fruity, minerally, and leesy elements. Here's a nonvintage Champagne that will age beautifully.

small growers
enter the market

The most exciting recent development in Champagne has been the appearance of wines from small growers, such as Montaudon, Pierre Peters, Pierre Gimmonet, and Gaston Chiquet. These idiosyncratic bottlings are to those from the grand houses what single malts are to blended Scotch: distinctive, sometimes flamboyant, alternatives to the big names' more measured styles. Their quality has so far been quite high; however, small growers are just that: Their wines can be difficult to find.

NV Pierre Gimmonet et Fils Premier Cru
Blanc de Blancs   ★★★ $$$
Huge toasty, biscuity aromas. Lemon and complex mineral flavors, formidable acidity, a long minerally finish—a classic Blanc de Blancs. Give it a year or two to let the fruit flavors develop and the acidity mellow.

NV A. R. Lenoble Brut Reserve   ★★★ $$$
Yeasty nut and caramel nose. Complex nut, caramel, toast, and pear flavors. This is a mellow style that apparently has lots of older reserve wines in the blend. Drink now.

1995 Montaudon Blanc de Blancs   ★★★ $$$
Pear and apple flavors, refreshing acidity, and a long finish combine to make this a lovely Blanc de Blancs in a full, fruity style.

NV Bruno Paillard Première Cuvée   ★★★ $$$
Has a nice minerally nose. The lemony citrusy flavors are vibrant, making this an excellent aperitif wine.

NV Piper-Heidsieck Brut   ★★★ $$$
Lovely nose of ginger, spice, and toast is followed by vibrant full fruit flavors. A long finish completes the experience.

1992 Taittinger Brut   ★★★ $$$
A delicate nose with toasty, smoky, lemony nuances. Pear and lively citric flavors, and a long finish. An elegant, medium-bodied style.

1988 Champagne de Saint Gall Cuvée Orpale
Blanc de Blancs   ★★ $$$
Beautiful nose of toasted bread. A Champagne packed with citrus and toast flavors. Huge, lemony acidity is dominant now, showing the wine's youth. Typical of the 1988s, it still needs some time to mellow.

NV Pommery Brut Royal Apanage ★★ $$$
Notes of mushroom and truffle on the nose. This is made in a light, brisk, elegant style, dry and delicate. It is the perfect aperitif.

NV Nicolas Feuillatte Brut Premier Cru ★★ $$
Classic spicy, toasty nose with chalky, lemony flavors. The good apple and pear flavors have a hint of ginger and nutmeg.

cava

Spain's high-quality, low-priced sparkler made by the same method as Champagne, Cava comes mostly from the Penedès region, where three local white grapes, Parellada, Xarel-lo, and Macabeo, are used. Some Cavas now incorporate Chardonnay as well. Cava's compelling value makes it one of the most popular sparkling wines in the United States.

THE BOTTOM LINE Codorníu and Freixenet have proved Cava can deliver good quality for a pauper's price. Only a few top Cavas exceed $15 and many fine choices are $10 or less.

NV Segura Viudas Brut Aria ★★★ $$
Herbal nose with hints of minerals. Lively acidity and the concentrated flavors of herbs last through the long, smooth lime-accented finish. Not a fruit-driven wine, but rather one of harmony and grace.

NV Vallformosa ★★★ $$
Mellow and much fruitier than most Cavas. The delightful *mousse* and long, fruity finish make this an excellent alternative to much more expensive sparklers.

NV Paul Cheneau Blanc de Blancs ★★ $
Elegant, harmonious flavors of pear, apple, and nutmeg; there is none of the burned-toast taste often found in Cavas. Perfect *mousse*. A sophisticated wine for the price.

NV Freixenet Brut Carta Nevada ★★ $
Aromas of pears, apples, and lemons. Delightfully light lemon, mint, and pear flavors and a long finish. A lovely, surprisingly delicate wine.

NV Freixenet Brut Cordon Negro ★ ★ $

Classic Cava nose scents of burned toast along with pear and earth. Fuller in both body and flavor than the Carta Nevada above, this tastes of nectarines and pears. The finish is smooth as silk.

NV Mont Marçal Brut Reserva ★ $

Mont Marçal makes a dry Cava that's fairly neutral in flavor but quite refreshing due to good acidity.

NV Segura Viudas Brut Reserva ★ $

Faint but intriguing aromas of poached pears and lime zest. Full-bodied. Rather neutral flavors with some earthiness on the finish.

sparkling wines from italy

Italy has two important types of sparkling wine. The refreshing and generally high-quality Prosecco is produced from grapes of the same name in the Veneto. At home, Italians down it without ceremony from tumblers. From Piedmont come Asti and Moscato d'Asti, charming, moderately sweet, gently sparkling wines made from the Muscat grape. Their very low alcohol content (5 to 7 percent) and succulent fruitiness make these wines wonderful aperitifs, and a dessert of biscotti and Moscato is a treat that shouldn't be missed.

the bottom line Due to their relative obscurity, both Astis and Proseccos are real bargains. Astis run $12 to $16, Proseccos, $12 to $20.

1998 Vietti Cascinetta Moscato d'Asti, Piedmont ★ ★ ★ ★ $$

A playful eruption of perfume, flowers, peaches, and crushed-grape aromas is just the beginning. The combination of delicate flavors and refreshing acidity is ravishing.

1992 Ca'del Bosco Cuvée
Annamaria Clemente Franciacorta, Lombardy ★ ★ ★ $$$$

This Champagne taste-alike has a yeasty nose of toffee and toasted almonds, and nutty, toasted-brioche flavors. It's full-bodied for an Italian sparkler, with excellent concentration and a pleasing note of earth on the finish.

1998 La Morandina Moscato d'Asti, Piedmont ★ ★ ★ $$

A lovely, delicate Moscato featuring spring-flower aromas and full peach and grape flavors—so refreshing.

1998 Paolo Saracco Moscato d'Asti, Piedmont ★ ★ ★ $$

Here's a fuller-bodied, lower-acid style of Moscato than that of the delicate Vietti and Morandina described here. This offers a mouthful of succulent, grapey flavor.

NV Toffoli Prosecco di Conegliano, Veneto ★ ★ ★ $$

This delicious discovery has aromas and flavors that are dead ringers for ripe Anjou pears. It has a creamy *mousse* and a finish that hints at caramel and currants.

NV Nino Franco Prosecco Rustico, Veneto ★ ★ $

Has an apple and peach nose. The light, fairly neutral flavors are brisk and refreshing. On the finish, some peachy flavor follows up on the aroma.

SPARKLING WINES from the UNITED states

American sparkling wines are made in many states, including Washington, New York, and of all places, New Mexico. The Finger Lakes region in New York produces some admirable bubblies. The great majority, however, are from California, where the warm climate is a challenge. The wines tend to be fruity and full-bodied but low in acidity. Planting grapes in the coolest regions, such as Carneros and the Anderson and Green Valleys, retains their vital acidity. Many of Champagne's big houses such as Moët & Chandon and Taittinger have set up

California operations, helping the once inferior quality of local sparkling wines to soar in the last decade. A few of this state's sparklers now rival Champagne's elegance and complexity.

THE BOTTOM LINE Quality U.S. sparklers run the gamut from inexpensive wines beginning around $12 on up to *prestige cuvées* that sell for $60 or more. The best value is generally found in the $15 to $30 range.

1995 J Wine Company Vintage Brut, Sonoma County ★★★ $$$

The nose offers faint banana, peach, and lemon aromas. This assertive, full-bodied, creamy-textured sparkler has flavors of lemon, earth, toast, and peaches. Its finish is elegantly long and refreshing.

1990 Acacia Brut, Carneros ★★★ $$

Big aromas of apple juice, lemon custard, and minerals. A full-bodied, vigorous, and powerful bubbly with superb flavor concentration, creamy texture, and impressive palate impact. It has wonderful mineral complexity.

1994 Domaine Carneros Brut, Napa Valley ★★★ $$

Toasty aroma, with lemon and pear notes. Creamy on the palate, with lemon and apricot flavors and a hint of minerals. The Champagne house Taittinger owns the winery, and it shows in this wine made in an elegant, French-influenced style.

1994 Iron Horse Classic Vintage Brut, Green Valley ★★★ $$

Made from grapes grown in the coolest area of Sonoma, Iron Horse's sparkling wines are bracing, yet have superb flavor concentration and persistence. This one, with its lime, mineral, toast, and lees aromas and flavors is no exception. Always one of California's finest.

NV Roederer Estate Brut, Anderson Valley ★★★ $$

One of California's finest sparklers, this is made by Louis Roederer of Champagne fame. It could easily be mistaken for good Champagne. Creamy *mousse*. Classic toasty, yeasty nose and an intense nutty flavor. A finish of impressive length.

NV Gloria Ferrer Brut, Sonoma County ★★ $$

Has aromas of toast and apples, along with a refreshing strawberry note. This is a robust sparkler, with excellent acidity and a nice fruity finish.

NV Gruet Blanc de Blancs, New Mexico ★★ $$
Straightforward appley nose. On the palate, it's snappy lemon, with a delightfully creamy *mousse* and a long delicately fruity finish.

1995 Lamoreaux Landing Brut, Finger Lakes ★★ $$
Sophisticated lemon and lightly yeasty nose. Dry and refreshing with lemon, pear, and lees flavors and an elegant finish. It shows just how good New York bubbly can be.

NV Pacific Echo Brut Rosé, Mendocino County ★★ $$
Many people feel that Mendocino's cool Anderson Valley is America's most promising region for quality sparkling wine. This one has lovely briskness and finesse, with delicate strawberry flavors, hints of mineral, and a long, elegant finish.

OTHER SPARKLING WINES

Every winemaking country in the world, as well as every region of France, produces sparkling wine, not just the Champagne region. Within France, Appellation Contrôlée sparkling wines must be made by the same exacting and traditional method as that used in Champagne, though they will reflect their own *terroir* (see page 17) as well as the grape variety from which they are made. Look, for instance, for Crémant d'Alsace with its almost creamy flavor, the earthy Blanquette de Limoux from Languedoc, and the excellent Chenin Blanc–based sparklers from Saumur and Vouvray in the Loire Valley. The country also produces a raft of value-oriented bubblies that have no Appellation Contrôlée and therefore are entitled to specify simply *France* on their labels.

Sekt is Germany's sparkling wine. The least expensive can be made by any method, and even with grapes from outside Germany. The best, however, are made from Riesling by the traditional Champenois method. Australia is another great source of inexpensive fruity, as well as sophisticated, top-end sparkling wines. We're sure to see more of the country's unique sparkling Shiraz soon. And New Zealand's cool climate may offer the most promise of all the New World countries for high-quality sparkling wines.

the bottom line With so many wines, prices range widely, but generally start around $8 and top out around $30 (for the best German Sekts). Those between $10 and $20 offer superb alternatives to expensive Champagne.

1996 Reichsrat von Buhl Riesling Sekt, Germany ★★★★ $$$
Has a lovely, deep lemon color. Exciting toasted-brioche and nut aromas from spending two years on the lees complement peach and citrus scents from the grapes. This brilliant sparkler is fruity and full, with superbly refreshing acidity.

1994 Green Point Brut Sparkling Wine,
South Eastern Australia ★★★ $$$
Alluring aromas of lemon peel and fresh-baked bread. Lemon, lime, and apple flavors and a winsome lemony finish. The winery is owned by Moët & Chandon.

NV Lucien Albrecht Cremant d'Alsace, Alsace ★★ $$
Vanilla and spice nose. Low acidity and lots of vanilla, butter, and banana flavors. Some toffee and light peach emerge on the finish. Drink this now.

NV Cabrière Pierre Jourdan Belle Rosé, South Africa ★★ $$
Slightly candied raspberry and cherry aromas. The flavors, again, seem almost candied. This rosé sports a nice creamy *mousse*. A very appealing wine.

NV Champalou Sparkling Vouvray, Loire Valley ★★ $$
The appealing nose is of wildflowers and honey. This elegant wine features delicate floral, honey, and peach flavors, gentle acidity, and a smooth, fruity finish.

NV Domaine Collin Blanquette de Limoux Cuvée Prestige,
Languedoc-Roussillon ★★ $$
Light citrusy nose. This is a full-bodied, robust sparkler, with fairly neutral, but very concentrated, earthy, minerally, nonfruity flavors. It cries out for food.

NV Charles de Fère Brut Reserve, France ★ $
An aroma of vanilla custard with hints of pine resin. Surprisingly sophisticated for its price, with a creamy *mousse*, light toffee, nut, and yeast flavors, and a refreshing finish.

WINES OF THE CENTURY — THE LEGENDS

Remembering and comparing great wines is, albeit something of a fool's errand, a gloriously hedonistic exercise. So many great wines have been made over the last 100 years that to pick a dozen, or even a dozen dozen, is almost comical, but not entirely without its usefulness: Many of these wines still turn up at auctions today. Each has been selected because of its superb quality and its almost mythical status in the eyes of collectors and critics alike.

1. 1921 Château d'Yquem, Sauternes
2. 1931 Quinta do Noval Nacional Vintage Port
3. 1945 Domaine de la Romanée-Conti La Tâche
4. 1947 Château Cheval Blanc, St-Émilion
5. 1947 Huet Vouvray Moelleux Le Haut-Lieu
6. 1959 Verwaltung der Staatsweingüter Rauenthaler Baiken Trokenbeerenauslese
7. 1961 Paul Jaboulet Aîné La Chapelle, Hermitage
8. 1961 Moët & Chandon Cuvée Dom Pérignon, Champagne
9. 1966 Domaine de la Romanée-Conti Montrachet
10. 1968 Beaulieu Vineyard Cabernet Sauvignon Georges de Latour Private Réserve, Napa Valley
11. 1971 Penfolds Grange Hermitage, Barossa Valley
12. 1985 Tenuta San Guido Sassicaia, Vino da Tavola di Toscano

FORTIFIED
WINES

Americans are rediscovering the unique pleasures of fortified wines. In the 1970s and 1980s, a shift to eating and drinking styles that were believed to be healthier turned people against the high alcohol and powerful, weighty flavors of these wines. Also, the quality of two fortified wines, Sherry and Madeira, plunged, and a whole generation knew them only as cooking wines. Today, standards are improving dramatically, and all fortified wines are on the comeback trail.

To make fortified wines, vintners add alcohol, usually grape spirits. This stabilizes the wines and prevents them from spoiling, a traditional problem in hot climates. Though the modern use of refrigeration in vinification obviates the need for fortification, enough people love these wines that their continuation seems assured.

SHERRY

Sherry is produced from grapes grown in the chalky soil and dry, torrid climate of Jerez, at the very southern tip of Spain. What distinguishes Sherry (and other Sherry-type wines) from Port (and other Port types) is that fortification takes place *after* the wines ferment to complete dryness. Thus Sherries have none of the fresh, grapiness of Port. In its place, are less fruity, more developed flavors, which are further enhanced by maturation in the lengthy aging and blending system known as the solera.

The solera is the heart of the process of making Sherry. In each solera, wines are stored in tiers of barrels, with each layer, or *criadera*, containing wine at a particular stage of aging. At bottling, wine is drawn from the barrels of the oldest *criadera*, which are then refilled by those from the next oldest *criadera*. In turn, these barrels are refilled from the next *criadera* back, and so on, with the youngest *criadera* topped up with fresh wine. Each Sherry style made by a particular producer has its own solera, which guarantees its uniformity and consistency. Some complex soleras may have 25 *criaderas* or more, and every Solera contains, albeit in ever diminishing amounts, some of its original wine.

grapes and styles

Sherries are nonvintage wines. They're blended from many years, and each brand, like Scotch whisky or Champagne, has its own well-defined house character. The two major styles of Sherry, Fino and Oloroso, are made from the otherwise undistinguished Palomino grape. Pedro Ximénez (PX) and Moscatel grapes are each made into small amounts of motor-oil thick, extremely sweet dessert wine (variations of Oloroso). The musts (juices) of these varieties are also used for sweetening and coloring the Palomino-based wines.

● **Finos** mature under the influence of a yeast called flor that grows on the surface of the wine. Flor protects the wine from oxygen, keeping it pale, and digests glycerine, making the sherry light bodied. Flor also imparts a unique yeasty, floral aroma and flavor. The Fino family includes Manzanilla, Fino itself, and true Amontillado.

● **Olorosos** mature without flor and so gain none of its flavor and aroma. Through contact with oxygen, however, they darken to rich amber shades and pick up flavors of nuts, figs, and tobacco. The Olorosos include sweetened versions and the unique Palo Cortado (see next page).

on the Label

Sherries are, for the most part, labeled by their styles, though some like Dry Sack (a fairly dry Amontillado) are marketed under brand names. Look also for an indication of sweetness such as *medium* or *medium dry*. The designation *cream Sherry* means the wine will be very sweet. The following are the most commonly encountered styles:

● **Fino** The lightest bodied and palest of the Sherries. When you can get it fresh (often a problem because of the shortness of its shelf life), it has penetrating aromas of almonds, green apples, and flor.

● **Manzanilla** Finos that have been aged, not in Jerez, but near the sea in Sanlúcar de Barrameda, where conditions promote ideal growth of flor. This makes Manzanillas the most delicate wines in the Fino family. They are as brisk and refreshing as a salty sea breeze.

● **Amontillado** A true Amontillado is a Fino that has been allowed to age further without its flor, that is, in contact with oxygen. The combination of flor- *and* oxygen-induced characteristics makes Amontillados especially complex.

● **Oloroso** Amber in color, with rich flavors and aromas of nuts, dates, figs, and sweet pipe tobacco. These are usually sweet to very sweet, but many of the best are bone-dry.

● **Palo Cortado** Rarely encountered and potentially the best of all Sherries. Essentially Olorosos that, for one reason or another, develop a bit of flor. They are like Amontillados, but even more complex and intensely flavored.

at the table

In Spain, Finos and Manzanillas are served with the appetizer tidbits known as tapas. Manzanillas are also exceptional with oysters, whose briny liquor mirrors the sea-kissed tang of Sanlúcar's ocean air. Amontillados and Olorosos are well matched with roasted hazelnuts, walnuts or almonds, fresh figs, sautéed mushrooms in garlic and olive oil, olives, and sheep's milk cheeses. Sweet cream Sherries are best reserved for solo sipping, while the treacly Pedro Ximénez is perfect with espresso and with creamy desserts, such as English trifle. The Spanish pour it over vanilla ice cream.

the bottom Line Given the labor-intensive nature of its production and the huge cost of carrying decades of stocks, Sherry has to be the greatest bargain in wine, bar none. Good Sherries can be had for as little as $10 per bottle. Some old and rare bottlings do rise to $50 and more, but their complexity almost always justifies the price.

FINOS

Pedro Domecq La Ina Very Pale Dry ★★★ $$

Enticing nose of marzipan, flowers, and just-baked bread. This Fino is silky in texture with mouthwatering acidity and beautifully balanced flavors that perfectly mirror the aromas.

Gonzalez Byass Tio Pepe Muy Seco ★★★ $

The penetrating flor nose has a sweet, lemon-drop quality with nuances of mint. This delicious wine is, nevertheless, bone-dry. It's surprisingly full, with lemon and yeast flavors and a bit of alcohol heat on the finish.

Osborne Pale Dry ★★ $

Herb, raw-almond, and bread-dough nose. Medium weight with a creamy texture. Delicate chamomile flavor and brisk acidity extend through the finish.

MANZANILLAS

Hidalgo La Gitana ★★★★ $

The finest Manzanilla on the U.S. market. Pungent, penetrating aromas of almonds, flor, lemon, apples, and sea salt. Almost impossibly bracing, with yeasty, lemony, nutty flor flavors and a long, dry finish.

Emilio Lustau Almacenista Pasada
Cuevas Jurado ★★★ $$

Almacenistas are small family producers whose wines are usually very fine. This aged Manzanilla has an intense aroma of bread dough and toasted nuts, similar flavors, and mild balancing acidity. The wine finishes with good length.

Hijos de Rainera Pérez Marín La Guita ★★★ $

Brisk, salty, floral aromas. A good aperitif and also a food-friendly wine. Delicate and fragrant. It has flavors of lemon peel, nuts, and yeast along with floral accents. A classic Manzanilla: refreshing and very fine.

AMONTILLADOS

Pedro Domecq 51-1a Very Rare ★★★★ $$$$

Pale walnut-brown with flecks of amber. Intense, concentrated nose of vanilla, butterscotch, and toasted almonds. Full-bodied and dry, with a deeply satisfying flavor, excellent balancing acidity, and a long, complex, nutty, smoky aftertaste.

Hidalgo Dry Napoleon ★★★ $$

This beautifully dry and tremendously complex Amontillado has enticing notes of flor mingling with aromas of warm nuts and toffee. It's vigorous on the palate, with complex flavors of nuts, smoke, toffee, and raisins. A long finish.

Olorosos
Osborne Bailen Dry   ★ ★ ★ $$
Walnut, vanilla, and butterscotch aromas leap from the glass. Off-dry with intensely concentrated toasted-walnut, toffee, date, and woodsmoke flavors. High acidity nicely balances the sweetness. New on the U.S. market and therefore a bit hard to find. Worth the search.

Sweet Sherries
Pedro Domecq Venerable Very Rare
Pedro Ximenez   ★ ★ ★ ★ $$$$
Enveloping aromas of raisins, figs, molasses, and toffee. This luscious wine has flavors of dates, orange peel, molasses, and figs, with a note of pine tar and a sumptuous, velvety texture. It has surprisingly brisk balancing acidity and finishes on a climactic note of coffee. Pure hedonism!

Emilio Lustau Moscatel Superior Emilin   ★ ★ ★ $$
Moscatel (Muscat) is the rarest of the three Sherry grapes. This wine has an impenetrable teak-brown color and aromas and flavors of burned sugar, tea, and golden raisins. It's unctuous and satisfying with a satin texture and a long, lingering finish. Rare, exotic, and wonderful.

Toro Albalá Don Pedro Ximénez,
Montilla-Moriles   ★ ★ ★ $$
Montillas are not fortified; it's so hot in Montilla they achieve their high alcohol naturally. Nonetheless, they are so similar to Sherries, we include this one here. Intense smells of golden raisins, butterscotch, and floral honey spring from this splendidly aromatic wine. Though it is treacly thick and incredibly sweet, it is polished, harmonious, and sophisticated.

Emilio Lustau Solara Reserva Rare Cream   ★ ★ $$$
Has a deep tawny-brown color. Molasses and toasted-nut aromas. Medium sweet and full-bodied with a creamy texture and raisiny fruit flavors. Good acidity keeps it balanced and helps the finish last and last.

Osborne Cream   ★ ★ $
There's a rather intense nose of dried-apricot, fig, and date aromas here. This Sherry is sweet, but good balancing acidity keeps it from being cloying. It has a medium-long finish with an aftertaste of burned sugar.

port

To make Port, the classic fortified wine of Portugal's arid and rocky Douro river valley, pure grape spirits are added at the point when the fermenting grape juice reaches about 6 percent alcohol. This kills the yeasts and creates a full-bodied and grapey wine with high alcohol (about 18 to 20 percent), robust tannin, and considerable sweetness. Interest in Port has been exploding of late, ignited in part by the cigar craze.

grapes and styles

Ports are blended wines, made from as many as 41 different, mostly obscure, grape varieties. The most important are the Tinta Roriz (Tempranillo), Touriga Nacional, and Touriga Francesca. Various combinations of aging and blending techniques are used to create the individual styles described below.

on the Label

The following are the major styles of port, unfortunately not always specified on the label:

● **Ruby Port** Basic red port. Youthful and vigorous, with peppery, grapey, mulberry flavors. Bottled after two to three years of cask aging.

● **White Port** Port's, in our opinion rather poor, answer to Fino Sherry.

● **Tawny Port** If there is no indication of age, it's basic Tawny Port, which is made by blending Ruby and White Port.

● **Vintage Character Port** Essentially a better Ruby, usually given four to six years of maturation before bottling.

● **Tawny Port with an Indication of Age** Cask-aged for many years, these are the real deal. They're blends of several lots that are of various origins and ages; the age shown on the label is an average. These wines are truly tawny in color and have very complex flavors that include figs, tea, orange peel, smoke, and caramel.

● **Vintage Port** These flagship wines of the Port trade represent only 2 percent of the total production, but a Port house's reputation depends on them. They are made of the finest grapes from the best vineyards and from single, exceptional vintages. Bottled after only two to three years in wood, they need extensive bottle age before they're ready to drink.

● **Late-Bottled Vintage (LBV)** Ports of a single vintage of lesser quality than those declared for Vintage Ports (see page 239). Given four to six years of maturation in wood before bottling, LBVs are ready to drink upon purchase.

Many Ruby and Vintage Character (a term you'll only occasionally see on a label) Ports are sold instead under proprietary names, such as Fonseca's Bin 27 or Graham's Six Grapes. Ignore such terms as *fine old* and *rare*. They have no meaning. Vintage Ports will show the year of harvest and Late-Bottled Vintages will show both the vintage and the year of bottling.

at the table

Simple, fruity Ruby Ports and basic Tawnies pair well with plum and berry compotes and tarts, steamed puddings, coffee or chocolate confections, and vanilla custard. The more complex Tawny Ports with an indication of age want toasted nuts, caramel, toffee, and dried prunes or figs to complement their flavors. These same suggestions also work with aged Vintage Ports, but the classic partners for these magnificent wines are salty, creamy-textured Stilton and just-shelled or toasted walnuts.

the bottom line Renewed interest in Vintage Port has put significant upward pressure on prices. Expect to pay $40 to $80 per bottle for current vintages; $10 to $20 will buy most basic Rubies and Tawnies. Late-Bottled Vintages cost $20 to $30. Tawny Ports with an indication of age range from $20 for 10-year-old to more than $100 for the over-40-year-old Ports. At around $40, the better 20-year Tawnies are excellent values.

what to buy VINTAGE PORT

1982	1983	1984	1985
★★★	★★★	NA	★★★★
1986	**1987**	**1988**	**1989**
NA	NA	NA	NA
1990	**1991**	**1992**	**1993**
NA	★★★	★★★	NA
1994	**1995**	**1996**	**1997**
★★★★	★★★	★★★	★★★

RUBY PORTS

Quinta do Infantado Ruby ★★ $

This medium-dry Ruby has a fine, restrained nose of cherries and plums. Its flavor of purple plums melts into those of figs and raisins in the finish. Mellow.

TAWNY PORTS

Dow's Boardroom Premium Tawny ★ $$

Caramel, cinnamon, and fig aromas. Spicy flavors dominate in this full-bodied Port. Only mildly tannic, the finish has some alcoholic heat.

VINTAGE CHARACTER PORTS

Smith Woodhouse Lodge Reserve ★★★ $$

Can you imagine drinking chocolate-covered cherries? This satisfying wine might just fulfill the fantasy, making a perfect dessert all by itself. The acidity of this Port is in perfect balance with its sweetness and fruitiness.

Graham's Six Grapes ★★ $$

Vibrant ruby color and straightforward plum, cherry, pepper, and alcohol nose. This sweet, full-bodied wine delivers vigorous cherry, prune, and plum flavors, gentle tannin, and a long, spicy finish that's warm from the alcohol.

TAWNY PORTS WITH AN INDICATION OF AGE

Taylor 20 Year Old Special Reserve Tawny ★★★★ $$$

Complex aromas of nuts, underbrush, roasted mulberries, marmalade, and toasted orange peel. Mellow and only medium sweet, this gorgeous wine manages remarkable harmony of its many flavors. Smooth tannin and mild balancing acidity. About as good as Tawny gets.

Ferreira Duque de Bragança 20 Year Old Tawny ★★★ $$$

In general, this house produces fairly sweet Ports, and this 20-year-old Tawny is no exception. The heady scent of dried roses and the flavors of pear and dried peach are in perfect harmony.

Fonseca 10 Year Old Tawny ★★★ $$$

Glowing peach color and exuberant brown-sugar, butterscotch, citrus-peel, and toasted-nut aromas. Full-bodied and velvety smooth with flavors of buttered nuts, dates, peaches, and mandarin oranges, all balanced by refreshing acidity. Deliciously complex.

Rozès 10 Year Old Tawny ★★ $$$

Rozès is a small Port house owned by the Louis Vuitton-Moët-Hennessy group and most known for its Ruby Port. Its Tawny boasts coffee aromas and rather sweet caramel flavors, which develop nuances of figs in the finish.

Vintage Ports

1997 Graham's ★★★★ $$$$
Brilliant purple black in hue. Huge, gushing aromas of fresh mulberry and ground black pepper. Typically sweet and thick in Graham's style, with a tidal wave of succulent fruit flavor that currently hides a ramrod of tannin. This dense, formidable wine finishes with a pleasing nip of alcohol and reminds us of the terrific 1992 Graham's.

1994 Churchill's ★★★ $$$
Started in 1981 by Johnny Graham, of the eponymous Port house (see above), Churchill's produces Ports that represent impressive value. This wine is a sweet, chocolate-cherry parfait that with time should develop complexity and refinement.

1995 Osborne ★★★ $$$
Since their first release in 1967, Osborne's Ports have been vying for recognition. This recent release has notes of menthol and eucalyptus enlivening the aromas of blackberries and blueberries as well as the densely concentrated berry and fig flavors. Good, strong tannin on the finish.

1996 Quinta de la Rosa ★★★ $$$
After decades of selling off their wines to other producers, Quinta de la Rosa bottled its first estate wine in 1988 and has been improving ever since. This 1996 has a complex, herbal, plum, cherry, and black-currant aroma. Medium-to-full bodied, it's packed with black-cherry, cassis, and walnut flavors and includes a long, tannic finish with notes of chocolate and smoke.

1982 Smith Woodhouse Madalena ★★★ $$$
Toffee, coffee, dates, and smoke on the nose and complex flavor combining dried red fruits, figs, bacon fat, dried violets, and earth. This densely textured, yet elegant wine features good tannin and a long, chocolate-flavored finish.

1995 Ramos-Pinto ★★ $$$
Since 1983, Ramos-Pinto has made a concerted effort to produce drier Ports. This dark, plummy Port is a good example. Its tart raspberry and blueberry fruit flavors give it liveliness. A bit less alcohol would have brought the wine into better overall balance and perhaps won it another star.

1995 Sousa ★★ $$
Black-currant, blackberry, and chocolate aromas are followed by similar flavors and notes of coffee and spice on the finish. Full-bodied. Very reasonably priced

Late-Bottled Vintage Ports

1994 Quinta do Crasto ★ ★ ★ ★ $$

Magical aromas of black cherries, dried violets, anise, vanilla, and sizzling bacon pour from the glass. Flavors of red fruits, bacon fat, spices, and nuts, augmented by delicate acidity, last through the smooth finish. The tannin is strong but velvety, and the currently searing alcohol will mellow with age. This company only started bottling Ports recently. They're worth seeking out.

1986 Smith Woodhouse ★ ★ $$$

Aromas of dates, figs, and spicy potpourri. Full-bodied, with a satiny texture and enough acidity to prevent heaviness. Fully developed flavors of mulberries, black pepper, figs, dates, and raisins are perfectly framed by velvety tannin.

1992 Dow's ★ ★ $$

Dow is among the venerable Port houses, having made top-tier wines for over a century. Though the firm is known for its dry style, this offering has a mulberry nose with a hint of char and amiable cherry and plum flavors. Mild tannin.

australian muscat & port

Australians affectionately call all their sweet wines stickies. They range from botrytis affected Sauvignon-Sémillon blends modeled on Sauternes to the spectacular Liqueur Muscats and Ports produced in Victoria. The Ports and Muscats are fortified wines, and these treacly sweet, complex Aussie specialties are among the greatest of the world's sweet treasures.

Muscats

Benjamin Museum Reserve Muscat ★ ★ ★ ★ $$

Nose of spices, dates, raisins, and licorice. This medium-bodied, mellow wine is spicy and complex, sporting flavors of smoke, anise, cinnamon, pepper, and dates. Just a slight nip of alcohol in the long and satisfying finish.

Chambers Rosewood Vineyards Rutherglen Muscat ★ ★ ★ $$
Clear aromas of orange peel, fresh grapes, figs, and raisins. Incredibly viscous and sweet with lively fig, orange, and grape flavors. The sweetness is balanced by the alcohol, rather than by acidity, adding a touch of heat to the fruity finish.

PORTS

Yalumba Galway Pipe Tawny Port   ★ ★ ★ ★ $$
Full, complex bouquet of toffee, tea, orange peel, fig, and smoke, with hints of the oxidized character typical of Tawnies. This luxurious wine delivers harmonious, concentrated roasted-nut, smoke, spice, and molasses flavors perfectly balanced by unobtrusive alcohol. A long and delicious finish.

McGuigan's Personal Reserve Tawny Port   ★ ★ ★ $$
Aromas of caramel, figs, dates, chocolate, alcohol, and the usual oxidized character of Tawny Ports. Silky texture. Wonderful acidity balances the sweetness and enhances the chocolate and raisin flavors. A lively note of orange peel on the finish.

Wyndham Estates George Wyndham Old Tawny Port ★ ★ ★ $$
Spicy whiskey-barrel, orange-peel, toffee, cooked-berry, nut, and subtle oxidized aromas and flavors. The port is medium bodied with a fruity character.

madeira

As our founding fathers hammered out the guidelines for a new nation, they were probably drinking Madeira, our most popular wine at the time. The long, hot sea voyages from the Portuguese island cooked the Madeira, creating its unique burned, tangy character. Today that character is induced in steam-heated chambers called *estufas*. Most Madeiras are made in the Sherry style, sweetened and fortified after fermentation to between 18 and 22 percent alcohol. After waning for a long period, worldwide interest in fine Madeira is once again on the rise.

grapes and styles

The four major styles of Madeira—Sercial, Verdelho, Bual, and Malmsey—are named for the grape from which each is made.

Madeiras range from the very dry and very tart Sercial (translation: dog strangler) to the sweet, caramel and fig flavored Malmsey. For most of this century. however, these grape varieties have been on the decline, and the wines have been made mostly from Tinta Negra Mole, which, though vastly inferior in quality, can approximate the styles of its betters. When Portugal joined the European Union in 1986, the country was required to conform to rules requiring that wines contain at least 85 percent of any variety named on the bottle. Tinta Negra Mole is now relegated to generic Madeiras usually called Rainwater. Regardless of style, all Madeiras have a singed, tangy flavor and mouthwatering acidity.

ON THE LABEL

Be warned: If one of the four major fine-grape varieties, Sercial, Verdelho, Bual, or Malmsey, does not appear on the bottle's label, no matter how fancy the name given to the Madeira, it is made from Tinta Negra Mole. Some of these can be rather good. The vast majority of Madeiras are nonvintage, but the label will have an indication of approximate age: 5, 10, 15, or 20 years. The rare vintage wines will, of course, indicate the date of the grape harvest and occasionally, you will find a vineyard shown as well.

at the table

Sercials and Verdelhos make excellent aperitifs. With their slight sweetness, but very dry finishes, they tango well with salty appetizers, such as olives, hard cheeses, salted nuts, and a variety of smoked fish and meat. Soups, normally a challenge for wine, are accentuated and enlivened by the electric acidity of these wines. Experiment with potages of fish, shellfish, poultry, and vegetables. The full Buals and Malmseys are delicious partners for desserts based on nuts, caramel (crème caramel is fabulous), and raisins and other dried fruits.

THE BOTTOM LINE Madeira is one of winedom's greatest bargains, with prices beginning as low as around $13. Varietal Madeiras start at about $20 for 5-year-old wines and rise to $45 and more for 15-year-olds. As few as five years ago, century-old (and older) Madeira was readily available for as low as $50. Now these bottles are rare and cost $200 to $500.

TINTA NEGRA MOLES
Colombo Old Reserve 10 Year Old Sweet ★★★ $$
Aromas of burned sugar, spices, and dates. Sweet, with beautiful balancing acidity and a silky texture. Long, smoky finish.

Broadbent Fine Rich ★★ $$
Matured three years in cask, this wine has a beautiful medium amber color. An enticing nose of toffee, butterscotch and spice cake introduces full-bodied and concentrated crème brulée–like flavors of burned sugar and vanilla custard. It finishes slightly tart with the flavors of dried Turkish apricots.

Leacock's Rainwater Medium Dry ★★ $$
Aromas of burned sugar, spirits, dried figs, and dates. This wine has medium body and mouth-puckering acidity. Sweet, harmonious fig and date flavors.

SERCIALS
Henriques & Henriques 10 Year Old ★★ $$$
Spiritous nose of dates, smoke, ash, and lime zest. Very dry, with date and raisin flavors enlivened by a note of citrus and a hint of licorice. Quite full-bodied for a Sercial.

BUALS
Cossart Gordon 15 Year Old ★★★ $$$$
Intriguing aromas of sugar-coated buttered nuts, caramel, and dates on the nose, and a whiff of banana. This full-bodied Madeira is medium sweet with complex, concentrated flavors and characteristically high, palate-cleansing acidity. There's a pleasant smoky tang on the long finish.

Cossart Gordon 5 Year Old ★★ $$
This full wine has straightforward aromas of toasted walnuts and caramel. The typically brisk acidity gives tanginess to its medium-length finish.

MALMSEYS
Broadbent 10 Year Old Rich ★★★ $$$
Medium colored with the satisfying aromas of butterscotch, spicy fruitcake, and vanilla on the nose. Full, smooth, and sweet with a long aftertaste of smoke and spice. Mouthwatering acidity keeps it from becoming cloying.

Blandy's 5 Year Old ★★ $$
A nose of caramel, dried figs, and apricots. This wine is medium sweet, with tangy flavors of dried apricots and toffee and a sustained finish.

VIN DOUX NATUREL

Vins Doux Naturels are a specialty of southern France, where the alchemist who perfected the technique for making them, called *mutage*, was granted a patent from the king in 1299. Four hundred years later, this process of adding spirits to stop the fermentation of the wine began to be used to create another wonderful fortified wine—Port.

GRAPES AND STYLES

The intensely perfumed Muscat grape is used for white Vins Doux Naturels, whose immediate gush of fresh fruit and spring flowers makes them among the most beguiling of sweet wines. The red Vins Doux Naturels are based on Grenache, ideal for its ability to ripen to high sugar levels and for its spicy, roasted-raspberry character. Vins Doux Naturels have been compared to Port, but, while they share Port's fruitiness and roasted character, they have a lower alcohol content (15 to 16 percent) and far milder tannin. Most Vins Doux Naturels are ready for drinking upon release.

ON THE LABEL

Look for the appellations Muscat de Beaumes-de-Venise, Muscat de St-Jean de Minervois, and the Muscats de Lunel, Frontignan, and Rivesaltes for white wines; Banyuls, Maury, and Rasteau for reds. Like Vintage Port, some wines are from a single year and carry that date on the bottle. Others, like Tawnies with an indication of age, are blends of many years and show instead an average age. The term *rancio* indicates a particularly full and tangy, intentionally oxidized style.

at the table

The white Muscats are fine matches for strawberry shortcake; strong, well-aged cheeses; and any desserts based on orange flavors. The Grenache-based reds, with their intense, spicy blackberry flavors, are scrumptious with English summer pudding, cake or pie made with plums, and berries of any kind. In the winter, fruit poached in port or dried-fruit desserts are superb partners as well. Hard cheeses harmonize well with these wines. It is often said that Banyuls is the one wine that truly works with chocolate.

the Bottom Line With prices starting at around $15 for current vintages, these wines are cheap relative to their quality. Older vintages and rare bottlings can easily cost $50 to $80.

what to Buy VIN DOUX NATUREL

1994	1995	1996	1997	1998
★★★	★★★	★★★	★★	★★★★

White Vins Doux Naturels

1993 Mas Cristine, Rivesaltes   ★★★ $$
Deep orange. The wonderfully complex bouquet includes aromas of tea, caramel, bergamot, fennel, quince, dried apricots, and spices. Earthy, spicy, rum-soaked fruitcake flavors. The finish sports a lively rumlike whiff of alcohol and a taste of cloves.

1997 Paul Jaboulet Aîné,
Muscat de Beaumes-de-Venise   ★★★ $$
Aromas of fresh green grapes, flowers, musk, and pears, all seasoned with a surprising hint of ground pepper. Intensely sweet and thick, even syrupy, this is a young wine that needs a year or two to mellow. The long, spicy finish hides the high alcohol content well.

1997 Domaine Joliette, Muscat de Rivesaltes   ★★★ $
Delicate floral, muskmelon, spice, fresh-grape, and peach aromas. This is lovely and delicate with light flavors of cinnamon, nutmeg, and peach and a nice little nip of alcohol on the finish

NV Val d'Orbieu, Muscat de St-Jean de Minervois   ★★ $
Aromas of apricot, peach, honey, mushroom, and damp earth. Full-bodied, thick, and very sweet, this somewhat rustic wine makes up in sheer flavor what it lacks in finesse.

Red Vins Doux Naturels

NV Mas Amiel 15 Year Old, Maury   ★★★★ $$$
Gorgeous brick color. Complex, developed nose of figs, raisins, spice, licorice, minerals, toffee, carob, and smoked meat. Exhilarating acidity balances the full flavors and enhances the superlong, supremely satisfying finish. Extraordinary wine.

1991 Domaine du Traginer, Banyuls   ★★★★ $$$
An awesome nose of prunes, coffee, chocolate, caramel, and candy cane along with the aged, oxidative aroma called *rancio*. The flavors of orange peel, mulberry, chocolate, and prunes mimic those of a top-notch Tawny Port. With excellent tannin and a sweet, satisfying, long, long finish, this wine is nothing short of spectacular.

1997 Mas Amiel, Maury ★★★★ $$

Gorgeous nose: pepper, roasted mulberries, game, sandalwood, bitter chocolate, cherries, and black plums. The alcohol exquisitely balances the sweetness and mouth-coating thickness. Chocolate and plum finish. Superb!

1996 Les Clos de Paulilles, Banyuls ★★★ $$

A note of mint freshens the mulberry, coffee, and toffee aromas. On the palate, the wine is full and smooth, with flavors of plum, orange peel, tea, spice, and caramel that call to mind plum pudding or mincemeat. Elegance comes from the perfect balance of fruit flavors, sweetness, and alcohol. Long finish.

1996 Domaine de la Casa Blanca, Banyuls ★★ $$

Resembles a Ruby Port, with cherry, plum, and chocolate aromas, full mulberry flavors, medium body, and good concentration. Some heat from alcohol on the finish.

DESSERT WINES

Sauternes, Tokay, Vin Santo—for centuries these fabled wines have slaked the thirst of kings, presidents, and popes, but in the 1970s and 1980s, as the fashion pendulum swung to dry wines, these classics fell from favor. Now, we're learning once again that dessert wines are among the greatest, rarest, and most complex of vinous treats. They're intensely sweet. The key to their excellence is high acidity, which balances the sugar in a dazzling and sophisticated duet. The best sweet wines are surprisingly refreshing, never cloying.

At the risk of loss to rot, hungry animals, and frost, grapes are left on the vine long after the normal harvest to concentrate their flavor and sweetness. Drying (as in Strohwein), freezing (Eiswein), and, most commonly, the action of botrytis lead to further concentration. Harvesting must be done by hand. Selection is strict, yields miniscule. It naturally follows that prices can be high. Among the best sources of excellent dessert wines are the Sauternes and the Loire Valley regions in France and virtually all of Germany. Alsace and a handful of other regions make superb wines in smaller quantities.

Botrytis cinerea

Many of the finest dessert wines would not exist without the help of a lowly fungus called *Botrytis cinerea* (bo-TREYE-tiss sin-eh-RAY-ah). Affectionately known as *noble rot*, it attacks ripe grapes in the fall, causing their water to evaporate, which shrivels the grapes and concentrates the sugar, acid, glycerin, and flavor into a syruplike nectar. Along the way, botrytis adds its own incredibly luscious nuances of honey, nuts, caramel, apricots, and earth.

Making botrytis wines is a gambler's game, one that can be played, unfortunately, in relatively few winemaking areas of the world. To develop, the *Botrytis cinerea* requires cool, moist mornings followed by warm, dry afternoons, conditions that, even in the most favored spots, occur only about five times in a decade. During these special years, botrytis spreads randomly, and so the grapes must be hand harvested, one by one as they're ready, in multiple, labor-intensive passes through the vineyard. Late-season rains can, and often do, turn noble botrytis into bilious black rot, ruining the entire crop. Luckily, though, in this game of chance, the sporting vintner wins in the long run more frequently than the Las Vegas bettor.

Grape and Styles

In theory, dessert wines can be made from any grape, but for most such wines, the variety must be high enough in acidity to balance the sweetness, and, particularly in cool climates, the grape is preferably one that is susceptible to botrytis. The Riesling grape is ideal. It is used for virtually all of Germany's incredibly delicious dessert wines as well as for many New World, Austrian, and Alsace bottlings. Gewürztraminer, Pinot Gris, and Muscat are also used to make dessert wines in Alsace, and Chenin Blanc is the choice for the fabulous sweet wines of the Loire Valley.

Often, however, to achieve proper balance, a blend of grapes is necessary. The most common blend is the Sémillon and Sauvignon Blanc combination used in Sauternes and other similar wines. The gentle Sémillon adds body and fruitiness while the Sauvignon Blanc contributes abundant acidity. For Tokay wines, Furmint and Hárslevelü grapes fill the same roles, respectively. In Tuscany, vintners craft piquant, nonbotrytised Vin Santos from a blend of the Malvasia and the Trebbiano varieties.

at the table

Sauternes and Roquefort form a classic partnership. The sweet fruity flavors in the wine contrast beautifully with the salty tang of the cheese. Sauternes also pairs nicely with cream- and custard-based desserts, such as crème brûlée. Dried fruit, berries, and nuts all work well, too. Only the sweetest of Loire wines are true dessert wines; most are better drunk as aperitifs or as accompaniments to first courses. Foie gras is a perfect match for any sweet wine. Incredibly fresh acidity makes German Beerenausleses and Eisweins terrific palate refreshers and great accompaniments to tart, fresh berries or fruit salads. Strawberry shortcake and fruit tarts are superb as well. Vin Santos are best suited to simple biscotti. The key to serving these wines is to make sure the dessert is not sweeter than the wine. And, despite the name *dessert* wines, the truly great ones are perhaps best savored on their own after, or instead of, dessert.

france

France is home to some of the world's greatest dessert wines. Sauternes is renowned and is the benchmark for many similarly styled wines from both nearby regions and other countries. Of lesser fame, but certainly not lesser quality, are the superb, unoaked late-harvest wines from the Loire Valley and Alsace. In addition, France turns out a bevy of intriguing sweet fortified wines known as Vins Doux Naturels (see page 247).

THE SAUTERNES AREA

Bordeaux's most famous dessert wine, Sauternes (so-tairn) is a model for sweet wines around the world. Its richly fruity flavors include apricot, pineapple, and orange peel augmented by crème brûlée, vanilla, toffee, and spice from aging in new-oak barrels. Botrytis adds an overlay of honey. Sauternes is a sweet and opulent wine, exotic, powerful, high in alcohol (14 to 15 percent), full bodied, and complex.

The Sauternes growing area, about a 45-minute drive south of the city of Bordeaux, consists of five *communes*, Sauternes, Bommes, Preignac, Fargues, and Barsac. All are entitled to the name Sauternes, though Barsac may be bottled under its own name. Facing Sauternes across the Garonne River are Cadillac, Loupiac, and Ste-Croix-du-Mont. Along with Cérons to Barsac's north, these outlying areas produce lighter, simpler, less-expensive wines in the same style as Sauternes.

the bottom line Most Sauternes will cost $40 and up per full bottle, but expect to pay $200 or more for the famed Château d'Yquem. Of course, a half-bottle is often all you need. Cadillac and the other lesser wines sell for between $10 and $25; however, only the very best offer good value.

what to buy SAUTERNES AREA

1988	1989	1990	1991	1992
★★★★	★★★★	★★★★	★	★

1993	1994	1995	1996	1997
★	★★	★★★	★★★	★★★

1997 Château Rieussec, Sauternes ★★★★ $$$$
About 90 percent Sémillon. Nose of toasty oak, coconut, orange, dried apricot, peach, honey, and flowers. This full-bodied, sweet blockbuster offers intensely concentrated flavors of apricots, peaches, and nuts topped by a long, honeyed finish.

1997 Château Climens, Barsac ★★★★ $$$
Entirely Sémillon. Always one of our favorite Sauternes for its ravishing elegance, this vintage serves up intoxicating aromas of tropical and citrus fruits, butterscotch, minerals, and flowers. Medium-to-full bodied, its brilliantly vivid acidity highlights the clear, concentrated flavors and ensures a long and graceful development.

1997 Château Lafaurie-Peyraguey, Sauternes ★★★ $$$$
This oaky, mellow Sauternes offers copious aromas and flavors of spices from the oak, along with tropical fruits, honey, and apricots. There's a lot of botrytis as well, contributing to the wine's unctuous texture. The finish is long, with a note of earthy nuttiness.

1997 Château Suduiraut, Sauternes ★★★ $$$$
Enveloping aromas of apricot, butterscotch, honey, and coconut are followed by flavors of honeyed peaches and nuts. This is a

powerful wine but still elegant. Vibrant acidity balances its sugar, leaving an impression of only moderate sweetness.

1996 Château Bastor-Lamontagne, Sauternes ★★★ $$$

A light, lemony, elegant style that emphasizes spice and toast flavors. The oak flavors don't overwhelm; this wine is almost Loire-like in its liveliness. Little or no botrytis.

1995 Château Clos l'Abeilley, Sauternes ★★ $$

Attractive nose of butter, apricot, and vanilla. Not a complex wine, but it has a satisfyingly thick texture and full flavors of earthy apricot and oak spice. A long finish.

LOIRE VALLEY CHENIN BLANC

The Loire Valley produces an exquisite array of sweet wines from botrytis-affected Chenin Blanc. Their unusually complex flavors include quince, flowers, peaches, apricots, honey, beeswax, spices, and herbs. The wines' blazing acidity gives them tremendous longevity and can hide a surprising amount of sweetness. Like the sweet wines of Germany, their moderate alcohol levels and absence of oak give their flavors a clarity and delicacy that rarely fail to enchant.

COTEAUX DU LAYON The Anjou district's Layon Valley is a fine source of medium-weight, moderately sweet wines, especially those given the right to use Coteaux du Layon along with the village name on their labels. This means the wine comes from one of seven villages—Beaulieu, Faye, Rablay, Rochefort, St-Lambert, Chaume, or St-Aubin. In good years, Villages wines can rival Bonnezeaux and Quarts de Chaume (below).

QUARTS DE CHAUME and **BONNEZEAUX** These two tiny subregions within the tenderloin of the Coteaux du Layon produce luscious, elegant, and intense dessert wines that rank right along with the best from Sauternes and Germany.

VOUVRAY and **MONTLOUIS** Facing each other across the Loire to the east of Tours, these appellations produce delicious, fruity, and floral dessert wines in sunny years. Vouvray wines are the fuller and more concentrated of the two.

ON THE LABEL
Demi-sec (half-dry) indicates a wine of moderate sweetness. *Moelleux* (literally *mellow*) means a full-bodied, concentrated wine that can be medium to toothache sweet.

THE BOTTOM LINE Due to their relative obscurity, most of these wines cost a fraction of the price of Sauternes and other famous dessert wines. Coteaux du Layons and Montlouis range from $12 to $25, with a few of the best wines pushing $40. Quarts de Chaume, Bonnezeaux, and Vouvrays run a bit more. All represent top values.

WHAT TO BUY LOIRE VALLEY CHENIN BLANC

1989	1990	1991	1992	1993
★★★★	★★★★	o	★	★★★

1994	1995	1996	1997	1998
★	★★★★	★★★★	★★★	★★★

1997 Château Pierre-Bise, Coteaux du Layon-Chaume ★★★★ $$$
A ravishingly lovely nose of honey, peaches, nuts, and spices brightened by citrus and floral aromas. This refreshing, vivacious wine has marvelous intensity combined with remarkable elegance. A very class act.

1997 Château Pierre-Bise, Coteaux du Layon-Rochefort ★★★★ $$$
This wine is much fuller than the Chaume above, with much more botrytis and mineral deepening the flavors. Apricot and mushroom are added to the honey, spice, citrus, and floral flavors. A huge streak of mineral on the amazingly long finish.

1997 Domaine des Baumard, Coteaux du Layon ★★★★ $$
An astonishing wine from its gorgeous gold color to its incredible finish. The nose is awesome: fresh apricot nectar, white raisin, caramel, honey, blood orange, and beeswax. The apricot, spice, mineral, apple, peach, honey, and barley-sugar flavors are equally remarkable. Amazingly delicious now, this will age gracefully for 20 years or more.

1996 Château de Fesles, Bonnezeaux ★★★ $$$$
Apricot, mushroom, quince, and linden-flower nose and tangy blood-orange flavor tinged with Indian spices. This lively, elegant wine avoids the Bonnezeaux tendency toward too-low acidity and seems only medium sweet.

1989 Marc Brédif Vin Moelleux Nectar, Vouvray   ★★ $$$
Initially thick and a bit ponderous with waxy peach, quince, and floral notes, but surprising acidity comes to the rescue, keeping things lively.

1996 Domaine René Renou Les Melleresses, Bonnezeaux ★★ $$$
Peach, tangy singed-orange-peel, caramel, and mineral aromas and flavors with mushroomy botrytis notes. Sweet, thick, and tasty.

ALSACE

Alsace produces two types of sweet wines. One is labeled Vendange Tardive, literally *late harvest*. These wines have balanced, concentrated depth of flavor and can be either dry or medium sweet. Since the labels don't specify, it's tough to know which level of sweetness a given wine will deliver. The other type, Sélection de Grains Nobles, can be almost overwhelming in the extravagant intensity of its sweetness and aroma. This type is made from late-harvested, individually selected, botrytised Riesling, Pinot Gris, Muscat, or Gewürztraminer grapes and compares in price to German dessert wines.

1997 Hugel Gewürztraminer SGN   ★★★★ $$$$
Almost overpowering fragrance of spiced apricots, peaches, honey, and roses. This full-bodied wine is smooth, mouth-filling, and intensely sweet, with spicy, honeyed tropical-fruit flavors well balanced by surprisingly vivid acidity for this variety. A long, spicy finish. We feel Gewürztraminer is Hugel's best variety.

**1997 Domaine Weinbach Riesling
Schlossberg SGN**   ★★★★ $$$$
The classic Riesling nose—clear, incredibly intense peaches, citrus, apricots, flowers, and ineffable minerality. This will be a great Sélection de Grains Nobles someday, but today it's all latent power, turbocharged acidity, and embryonic flavors. The finish is almost endless. Don't spend the money on this future superstar unless you have a good place to age it.

**1997 Zind-Humbrecht Tokay Pinot Gris
Clos Jebsal SGN**   ★★★★ $$$$
Enthralling botrytis-affected aromas of apricot, peach, honey, and minerally earth repeat in a starburst of *terroir*-inflected flavors. A textbook example of the exquisite balance of unctuous sweetness and blazing acidity that makes great sweet wines great. The alcohol is in perfect balance with the other elements, unlike some prior vintages of this wine.

1997 Domaine Paul Blanck Gewürztraminer
Furstentum VT ★ ★ ★ ★ $$$

Pungent aromas of litchi, rose, tropical fruit, gunflint, and apricots and amazingly concentrated flavors of tropical fruit and Indian spices. It's moderately sweet and perfectly balanced with good acidity. A long, spicy finish.

GERMANY

Germany's greatest vinous treasures are her exquisite sweet wines. Scintillating acidity, luscious sweetness, low alcohol, and vivid fruit flavors that haven't been obscured by oak make the wines intensely succulent and astonishingly light at the same time. Thanks to their acidity, they can age almost forever. These rarities can only be produced from grapes grown in great vineyards and only in years when the notoriously fickle late-season weather conditions are just right. Not surprisingly, German dessert wines don't come cheap.

GRAPES AND STYLES

Beerenauslese wines are made from very late-harvested botrytis-affected grapes. They are luscious and quite sweet. When the grapes have been shriveled to raisins by botrytis, they are then used for the even more intense, unctuous, and sweet Trockenbeerenauslese. Botrytis adds flavor notes of honey, nuts, caramel, and earth. Eiswein differs significantly from Beerenauslese and Trockenbeerenauslese in that the grapes are not affected by botrytis. Instead, the grapes are allowed to remain on the vine until winter temperatures freeze them. When they are pressed, the frozen water is left behind, so that the juice is a concentrated syrup that provides much purer than usual fruit flavors and piercing acidity. The best wines of all three types are made from Riesling, though top-notch examples can also be found produced from Gewürztraminer, Scheurebe, and Silvaner. Many poor examples use undistinguished grapes, such as Ortega, Optima, and Huxelrebe, whose only claims to fame are that they ripen easily in any soil and they're cheap.

ON THE LABEL
For a detailed discussion of the German label, refer to page 128.

THE BOTTOM LINE Quality and rarity conspire to make prices high. Good examples start at around $50 for a full bottle, but top producers' gems can easily cost $100 or more for a *half*-bottle. And the wines can be difficult to find. Now you know what to bring back from a trip to Germany.

WHAT TO BUY GERMAN DESSERT WINES

1990	1991	1992	1993	1994
★★★★	★	★★	★★★	★★★★

1995	1996	1997	1998
★★★★	★★★★	★★★	★★

1998 Reichsgraf von Kesselstatt Kaseler Nies'chen Riesling Eiswein, Ruwer ★★★★ $$$$
Aromas of orange, peach, banana, and honey. Apricot, peach, spice, and honeyed botrytis flavors. A huge wine, the considerable sweetness of which is perfectly balanced by acidity. Long, impressive finish.

1998 Josef Leitz Rüdesheimer Klosterberg Riesling Eiswein, Rheingau ★★★★ $$$$
Fascinating, complex nose of pineapple, papaya, spearmint, pepper and other spices, and minerals. Superb Golden Delicious–apple, banana, yellow-plum, and lees flavors that build to a high-impact finish. One of the finest Eisweins of the vintage.

1998 Robert Weil Kiedricher Grafenberg Riesling BA, Rheingau ★★★★ $$$$
The subtle nose of peach and tangerine is currently dominated by lavender, mineral, and floral notes. This medium-weight, astonishingly elegant wine delivers lots of classic peach, berry, honey, and red-fruit flavors. It has moderate acidity to enhance them and a beautifully long finish.

1998 Schloss Saarstein Serriger Schloss Saarsteiner Riesling Eiswein, Saar ★★★ $$$$
Spicy, herbal nose highlightling light pineapple, lemon, lavender, floral, and pepper aromas. This wine stands out in a vintage of gentle Eisweins due to its revved-up acidity and lovely lemony, peachy, and lightly slately flavors. Delicate, yet piercing, it's a magnificent Eiswein.

1998 Gunter Wittmann Westhofener Steingrube Albalonga BA, Rheinhessen
★ ★ ★ $$

Albalonga is the grape here, a cross of Riesling and Sylvaner. The wine has a nose of honeysuckle, nuts, earth, and muted fruit and the flavor of honey-lemon drops. Smooth, with a medium-length, fruity finish.

RISKY EISWEIN

On Christmas morning in 1996, vintner Martin Kerpen rose at 4:00 in the morning and gathered his family and friends. A freeze the night before meant that this was the day to pick and press the grapes for his Eiswein. The group stamped and puffed their way up the steep Wehlener Sonnenuhr Vineyard to the small patch of super-ripe Riesling that Herr Kerpen had left unpicked. What they saw broke their hearts. Not a vine was standing, and the ground looked as if earthmovers had worked overtime. Kerpen knew instantly what had happened: A herd of wild boars, attracted by the sweet scent, had feasted overnight on the exquisite grapes he had hoped to turn into a few bottles of precious, and profitable, nectar.

OTHER COUNTRIES

AUSTRIA

Within Austria's Burgenland region, the shallow Neusiedler See and also the lake's surrounding marshy low country provide the perfect humid environment for botrytis to form virtually every year. This unusual certainty allows the vintners of the area to produce superb Eisweins, Beerenausleses, and Trockenbeerenausleses, as well as dried-grape Strohweins, on a consistent basis—and all at relatively inexpensive prices. The grapes of the area are Riesling, Weissburgunder, Chardonnay, and Scheurebe. For a discussion of what to expect on Austrian wine labels, please refer to page 143.

1995 Alois Kracher TBA #12 Grande Cuvée ★★★★ $$$$

Big botrytis here. Nuts, figs, fruitcake, marmalade, apricot, and spices mingle in the complex aromas. Mouth-filling texture. The concentrated spiced-apricot and almond flavors are balanced by vivid acidity and a strong mineral contrast. This is an incredible dessert wine.

1995 Weingut Familie Nigl Grüner Veltliner TBA ★★★★ $$$

This spectacular Trockenbeerenauslese boasts a captivating fragrance of caramel, white raisins, and butter. The flavors are of honey and spices with a minty note. Massively concentrated, yet elegantly harmonious, with crystal-clear flavors and superb acidity deftly balancing the considerable sweetness.

1997 Heidi Schrock Ausbruch ★★★ $$$$

Only 400 liters of this incredible wine were made, but it's eminently worth the search. It has explosive flavors and aromas of orange peel, apricot, and mushroom. A blend of many varieties, this powerfully sweet, full-bodied wine has just enough acidity to keep it from seeming syrupy.

1997 Alois Kracher Cuvée Beerenauslese ★★★ $$$

Peach, lemon, lime, orange peel, and flowers grace the nose. A lively style emphasizing fruit flavors with light botrytis. Medium weight and moderately sweet. Elegant and tasty.

HUNGARY

The great sweet wines from the Tokaji (toe-kai) region of Hungary, frequently referred to as Tokay, were once among the most sought after in the world, but years of Communist neglect diminished both Tokaji's stocks and its good name. Since 1989, new companies have been reviving the old traditions and starting new ones. The early results are very encouraging, with about a dozen Tokaji wineries represented in the United States. Tokaji wines are labeled in ascending levels of sweetness, from three to six *puttonyos* culminating in the nectarlike *Essencia*. Prices are commensurate with sweetness, starting at around $15 for three *puttonyos* and rising to $75 for six. Essencia starts around $65.

1993 Disznoko Tokaji Aszu 6 Puttonyos ★★★★ $$$

Lots of botrytis in this wine adds honey and earthy mushroom nuances to the complex apricot, toasted orange peel, toffee, lemon, and spice aromas. This wine is supersweet, but it is exquisitely balanced by thrilling lemony acidity. A long finish of dried apricots, toasted nuts, and caramel. Utterly ravishing.

1993 *Château Pajzos Tokai Aszu 5 Puttonyos*　　★ ★ ★ $$$

Deep, golden-orange color. Classic Tokay nose of nuts, honey, dried apricots, mint, and spice with a characteristic oxidized component. The wine is full-bodied and sweet, with caramel, dark wildflower-honey, and dried-apricot flavors. Cleansing acidity keeps the finish vibrant.

1993 *Oremus Tokaji Aszu 5 Puttonyos*　　★ ★ $$$

The nice, smoky aromas here include toasted almonds, dried apricots, and faint notes of oxidation. The wine is sweet and full with perfect balancing acidity. The tangy singed-orange-peel flavor lingers, joined on the long finish by the slightly bitter notes of citrus pith and walnut skins.

1993 *Disznoko Tokaji Aszu 4 Puttonyos*　　★ ★ $$

Golden-orange color. Honey, caramel, orange-peel nose with only a whiff of oxidation. Medium sweetness and good acidity make the wine seem almost light. Concentrated finish with a burned-orange-peel flavor.

ITALY

A specialty of Tuscany, Vin Santo is made from Malvasia and Trebbiano grapes dried indoors during the winter. It is aged in small (50 liter) casks for six years. The casks are not topped up as the liquid evaporates, so the wines become oxidized. The resulting dry and medium-sweet wines are medium bodied with the nut, fig, and fruitcake flavors of oxidation. Italy also crafts a fabulous selection of dessert wines from virtually every region of the country, made mostly by the *passito* (dried grape) method. Most Vin Santos and other Italian dessert wines cost from $20 to $60 dollars for a full bottle or the equivalent. Many of these wines are available in half and 500 milliliter bottles because most people don't drink much of them at a time.

1995 *Tenute Marchese Antinori,*
Vin Santo del Chianti Classico　　★ ★ ★ ★ $$$

Gorgeous amber color. Classic Vin Santo nose of nuts, figs, singed orange peel, and intentional oxidation. This is a sweet Vin Santo, and it's beautiful, with generous, sweet fig and orange flavors. The finish is dry with a lovely note of grilled nuts.

1998 *Pellegrino, Passito di Pantelleria*　　★ ★ ★ $$

Huge aromas of white raisins, white chocolate, orange peels, and fresh white grapes leap from the glass. Thick and very sweet, with orange and raisin flavors. The finish has a refreshingly bitter hint of nuttiness.

1994 Umberto Cesari Colle del Re,
Albana di Romagna Passito   ★★ $$
The apricot and earth nose is reminiscent of Sauternes, with a hint of spice and mushroom. Fairly dry, the wine has a dried-apricot flavor and a persistent finish.

1993 Lungarotti Vino Santo,
Vino da Tavola   ★★ $$
Beautiful burnished-orange color. Strong nose of oxidation, orange peel, raisins, flowers, tea, anise, and Sherry-like aromas. Medium bodied and medium sweet, this has perfect balancing acidity, which allows the toasted-hazelnut, citrus, and raisin flavors to linger long and harmoniously before the final finish—a pleasingly bitter nip of toasted nuts.

1993 Meloni, Moscato di Cagliari   ★★ $$
A lovely orange color and ravishing orange-peel, flower, and spice nose promise more than the wine delivers on the palate. Still, there are fresh-grape, orange, and spice flavors. A bit of hot alcohol on the finish.

1997 Soletta Dolce Valle, Sardinia   ★★ $$
Enveloping nose of orange, caramel, anise, pepper, and flowers. Charming orange and mulled-wine flavors with a slight note of bitter almond in the finish. Only moderately sweet and somewhat light bodied.

United States
Dessert wines from the U.S. offer tremendous fruit flavor, but sometimes they suffer from a lack of balancing acidity. Very good Late-Harvest Rieslings, Sémillons, and Gewürztraminers, as well as the occasional Eiswein, can be found that hail from the cooler areas of California, such as the Anderson Valley, Monterey, and the Russian River Valley, and also from the Pacific Northwest and New York State. At the low end of the price range, beginning around $12, U.S. sweet wines can offer compelling value. At the high end, however, the quality often does not match the steep prices asked (a few U.S. versions are pushing $40 for a half bottle). Be selective.

1997 Joseph Phelps Johannisberg Riesling Special Select Late
Harvest, Anderson Valley   ★★★★ $$$$
Flamboyant, honeyed perfume of pears, peaches, citrus, and a strong note of red berry. Tremendously thick and sweet, with peach, strawberry, and spice flavors. This complex, powerful, yet elegant gem delivers a long wave of minerals and palate-cleansing, fruity acidity in the finish.

1997 Clos du Bois Late Harvest Sémillon, Knights Valley
★ ★ ★ ★ $$

Lovely nose: poached pear, mulling spices, mineral, and peach. Very thick and sweet, yet just enough acid gives it surprising balance for a California dessert wine. Lots of botrytis lends apricot and earth flavors. Full and smooth.

1996 Beringer Johannisberg Riesling Special Select Vendange Tardive, California
★ ★ ★ $$

Penetrating tropical and citrus fruit aromas accented by honey and spices. The cloying sweetness of some previous vintages is vanquished here by bracing acidity that accentuates the taste of fruit and provides a well-balanced, palate-cleansing finish. This medium-bodied, moderately sweet dessert wine has always been one of our favorites.

1997 Hunt Country Vidal Blanc Ice Wine, Finger Lakes
★ ★ ★ $$

Aromas and flavors of cinnamon-dusted baked apples. Vibrant, mouth-watering acidity perfectly counterbalances lush sweetness, allowing the fresh grape and apple flavors to linger on the zippy finish.

1995 Chappellet Chenin Blanc Moelleux, Napa Valley
★ ★ $$$

Characteristic Chenin Blanc aromas of apricot, quince, herbs, toffee, and lanolin, with a faint note of varnish. This motor-oil-thick wine has adequate balancing acidity, but the mushroom and overripe apricot flavors make it seem a touch heavy. Still, it's quite attractive in its lushness.

1998 Quady Essensia, California
★ ★ $$

Exuberant, gushing aromas of apricots, fresh grapes, orange peel, bergamot, and honeysuckle. This charming Muscat-based wine is surprisingly full bodied and full flavored for its price. A delicious dessert wine.

vintage chart

Is that great 1985 Bordeaux you've been hoarding ready to drink yet? Is it coming into its own, or have you let it wait too long? This chart answers such questions for the wines most

	1982	1983	1984	1985	1986	1987	1988
BORDEAUX							
Right Bank	★★★★	☆☆☆	☆	★★★★	☆☆☆	☆	★★★
Médoc	★★★★	☆☆☆	☆	★★★★	☆☆☆☆	★★	☆☆☆
Red Graves	★★★★	☆☆	★★	★★★★	☆☆☆☆	★★	☆☆☆
White Graves	☆☆☆	★★★	o	★★★	☆☆☆	★★	★★★
BURGUNDY							
Red	☆☆☆	☆☆	☆	☆☆☆☆	☆☆☆	☆☆	★★★
White	★★	☆☆☆	o	☆☆	★★★	★★	★★
LOIRE							
Chenin Blanc	★★	☆	☆	★★	☆☆☆	☆	★★★
Cabernet Franc	★★★	★★	o	★★★	☆☆	☆	★★★
RHÔNE							
Northern Red	☆☆☆	★★★★	☆	★★★★	★★★	☆☆	☆☆☆☆
Southern Red	☆☆☆	☆☆☆	☆☆	★★★★	★★	★★	☆☆☆☆
ITALY							
Piedmont and North	☆☆☆☆	☆☆	☆	★★★★	★★	☆	☆☆☆☆
Tuscany and Central	★★★	★★	o	★★★★	★★★	☆☆	☆☆☆
SPAIN							
Rioja	☆☆☆☆	☆	o	☆☆☆☆	★★	★★★	★
Ribera del Duero	★★★★	★★★	☆	★★★	o	★★★	★★
GERMANY							
Mosel-Saar-Ruwer	☆	★★★★	☆	★★★	☆☆	☆☆	☆☆☆
Rhine Regions	☆	☆☆☆☆	☆	☆☆☆	☆☆	☆☆	☆☆☆
CALIFORNIA							
Cabernet Sauvignon	☆☆☆	☆☆	★★★★	★★★★	★★★★	★★★★	★★

o = Very bad vintage, a disaster
★ = Poor to average vintage, only the best wines are good quality

★★ = Good to very good vintage
★★★ = Excellent vintage
★★★★ = Outstanding vintage

commonly aged. The quality of each wine is indicated by the number of stars, just as elsewhere in this book (see key, bottom left). The color of the stars (see key, bottom right) tells where the wine is most likely to be in its progress from not ready through well past peak. For example, ★★ indicates a good wine at peak, ☆☆☆, an excellent wine whose time has passed.

1989	1990	1991	1992	1993	1994	1995	1996	1997	1998
☆☆☆☆	☆☆☆☆	O	☆	☆☆	☆☆☆	★★★	★★★★	☆☆	★★★★
☆☆☆☆	☆☆☆☆	☆	★	☆☆	★★★	★★★★	★★★★	☆☆	★★★
☆☆☆☆	☆☆☆☆	★	★	☆☆☆	☆☆☆	★★★	★★★	☆☆☆	★★
★★★★	★★★★	☆	☆	★★	☆☆☆	☆☆☆	☆☆☆	☆☆☆	☆☆☆
★★★	☆☆☆☆	☆☆	☆☆	☆☆☆	★★	☆☆☆☆	★★★	☆☆☆	★★★
★★★	★★★	☆☆	★★★	☆☆	☆☆☆	☆☆☆☆	★★★★	☆☆☆	☆☆☆
☆☆☆☆	★★★★	O	★★	★★★★	☆☆☆	★★★★	★★★★	☆☆☆	★★★
★★★★	★★★★	O	O	☆☆☆☆	★★	☆☆☆☆	★★★★	☆☆☆	NA
☆☆☆☆	★★★★	★★★★	O	★★	☆☆☆	★★★★	☆☆☆	☆☆☆	★★★
☆☆☆☆	☆☆☆☆	☆	☆	★★	★★	☆☆☆☆	☆☆	☆☆☆	★★★★
☆☆☆☆	★★★★	★★★	★★	☆☆☆	☆☆	★★★★	★★★★	★★★★	NA
★★	★★★★	☆☆☆	☆☆	★★★	★★★	☆☆☆☆	★★★	★★★★	NA
☆☆☆	☆☆☆	☆☆☆	★★	★★	★★★★	★★★★	★★★	★★★	NA
★★	★★★	☆☆☆☆	★	★★	★★★★	★★★★	★★★★	★★★	★★★
★★★	☆☆☆☆	☆☆	★★	☆☆☆	★★★★	☆☆☆☆	★★★★	☆☆☆	☆☆☆
☆☆☆	☆☆☆☆	★★	★★	★★★	☆☆☆	☆☆	★★★	☆☆☆	☆☆☆
★★★	☆☆☆☆	★	☆☆☆☆	☆☆☆	☆☆☆☆	★★★	★★★	★★★	★★★

Names you can trust

An E-mail from your spouse: Can you pick up a bottle of wine on the way home? You'd usually enjoy giving this request your full attention, but it's been a long day. You enter the nearest wine shop, and it seems to be filled with regiments of bottles staring mutely at you like so many silent soldiers. How do you find the heroes among them quickly?

There is a shortcut. Luckily, some excellent importers have done a lot of the work involved in choosing for you, and, further good fortune, their wines are widely available across the United States. Each of the following individuals or companies specializes in one or a few wine styles or regions and has selected an extraordinary group of wines to import from top-quality growers and estates. Look for bottles with these importers' names on the label. You are virtually guaranteed a wine of quality and character.

Cape Classics
Looking for guidance in South African wines? You can't go wrong with the excellent estates represented by this firm.

Cellars International
Represents many of Germany's established, elite estates. Quality is high, but prices can be, too.

Robert Chadderdon
Always reliable, but often expensive, importer of high-quality French wines.

Classical Wines
Excellent, subtle wines from many of Spain's and two of Germany's finest producers. Some stunning bargains.

Marc de Grazia
Now augmenting his huge selection of Piedmont and Tuscan wines with a large group from southern Italy. Controversial for the oak-influenced, ultramodern style he prefers.

Robert Kacher

French wines, especially Burgundies, emphasizing clear, concentrated flavors and generous use of new oak.

Leonardo LoCascio Selections

No one has unearthed more intriguing Italian treasures than LoCascio. The wines are true to their regions, and the prices are easy to swallow.

Louis / Dressner Selections

Hand harvesting, natural yeasts, and low yields are among the high-hurdle requirements here. Concentrated, complex French wines at bargain-basement prices.

Kermit Lynch

Lynch has turned up many handcrafted, *terroir*-infused, traditional-style wines from both famous and less-known areas of France. Almost every one is a gem.

Jorge Ordonez

Refreshing, fruity wines from Spain. Excellent values.

Eric Solomon European Cellars

Robust, intense, fruit-filled wines from traditional regions of France, Italy, and Spain. Superb quality at good prices.

Terry Theise

An energetic importer of Champagnes and Austrian and German wines from small, often obscure, but first-rate growers.

P. J. Valckenberg

Top estate wines and great German wine values and from one of Germany's oldest merchant shippers.

Vin Divino

A magnificent collection of Austrian wines in addition to a broad selection of equally outstanding Italian classics.

food & wine american wine awards

This year marks the third annual F&W American Wine Awards, with which we salute a broad range of achievements on the wine scene. Armed with a list of nominees, we brought together a panel of F&W editors, contributing writers, and former award winners to taste and to talk about what and who is now most noteworthy. Each of our selections has helped make this an extraordinary time for wine.

WINERY OF THE YEAR
Beringer Vineyards, Napa Valley
A behemoth with boutique quality.

WINEMAKER OF THE YEAR
Helen Turley, Marcassin Winery, Sonoma
Her own formula: wild yeast and ultraripe grapes.

IMPORTER OF THE YEAR   Vin Divino, Chicago
Elevated the profile of little-known Austrian wines.

RETAILER OF THE YEAR   Grape Vine Market, Austin
Tutorials, an in-house chef, a huge array of wines.

INNOVATOR OF THE YEAR
Bill Hambrecht, W. R. Hambrecht & Co.
Pioneered Internet initial public offerings for wineries.

BEST VALUE WHITE WINE OF THE YEAR
1997 Estancia Pinnacles Chardonnay, Monterey
Consistent quality for 10 bucks.

BEST VALUE RED WINE OF THE YEAR
1997 Rabbit Ridge Zinfandel, Sonoma
Full of fruit flavor and flexible with food.

SPIRIT OF THE YEAR
1992 Knappougue Castle Irish Whiskey
Quintessential unblended whiskey.

WINE LABEL OF THE YEAR
L'Ecosse Cabernet Franc, Napa
An homage to Joan of Arc at the Battle of Orléans.

WINE BOOK OF THE YEAR
Drink: A Social History of America, Andrew Barr
Witty and highly opinionated.

top wine shops

Kudos to these excellent stores—our picks for those across the country that offer the best selections, service, and advice.

alabama

CLASSIC WINE COMPANY
1817-B 29th Ave. S., Birmingham
205-871-9463

OVERTON & VINE
3150 Overton Rd., Birmingham
205-967-1409

alaska

BROWN JUG WAREHOUSE
4140 Old Seward Hwy., Anchorage; 907-563-3286

arizona

RED KANGAROO WINES M
10625 N. Tatum Blvd., Phoenix
602-951-9486
www.redkangaroo.com

SPORTSMAN'S FINE WINE & SPIRITS M
3205 E. Camelback Rd., Phoenix; 602-955-7730

A.J.'S FINE FOODS
23251 N. Pima Rd., Scottsdale
602-563-5056
888-563-5039
www.ajsfinefoods.com

PLAZA LIQUORS
2642 N. Campbell Ave., Tuscon; 520-327-0452

THE RUMRUNNER
3200 E. Speedway Blvd., Tuscon; 520-326-0121

arkansas

COLONIAL WINES & SPIRITS
11601 W. Markham St., Little Rock; 501-223-3120
www.colonialwineand spirits.com

THE GRAPE VINE WINE & SPIRITS
10901 Rodney Parham Rd., Little Rock
501-227-6009

HEIGHTS FINE WINES & SPIRITS
5012 Kavanaugh, Little Rock; 501-664-9463

POPATOP, INC.
1901 S. University Ave., Little Rock; 501-663-3276

california

KERMIT LYNCH WINE MERCHANT M
1605 San Pablo Ave., Berkeley; 510-524-1524

NORTH BERKELEY WINE M
1505 Shattuck Ave., Berkeley
510-848-8910
800-266-6585
e-mail nbw@slip.net

THE WINE STOP M
1300 Burlingame Ave., Burlingame
650-342-5858
800-283-9463

ENOTECA WINE SHOP
1345 Lincoln Ave., Ste. C, Calistoga
707-942-1117
www.neteze.com/enoteca

DUKE OF BOURBON
20908 Roscoe Blvd., Canoga Park
818-341-1234
800-434-6394
www.dukeofbourbon.com

HI-TIME WINE CELLARS O, A
250 Ogle St., Costa Mesa
949-650-8463
800-331-3005
www.hitimewine.com

VALLEY WINE COMPANY M
417 G. St., Davis
530-758-9463

RED CARPET WINE
400 E. Glenoaks Blvd., Glendale; 818-247-5544
800-339-0609
www.redcarpetwine.com

WALLY'S LIQUORS M, O
2107 Westwood Blvd., Los Angeles
310-475-0606
888-992-5597
www.wallywine.com

THE WINE HOUSE M, O
2311 Cotner Ave., Los Angeles
310-479-3731
800-626-9463
www.winehouse.com

BELTRAMO'S WINES & SPIRITS
1540 El Camino Real, Menlo Park
650-325-2806
888-710-9463
www.beltramos.com

DRAEGER'S SUPERMARKET O
1010 University Dr., Menlo Park
650-688-0688
800-642-9463
www.draegers.com

WINE EXCHANGE M, O
2368 N. Orange Mall, Orange; 714-974-1454
800-769-4639
www.winex.com

VIN, VINO, WINE
437 California Ave., Palo Alto; 650-324-4903

CORTI BROTHERS M
5810 Folsom Blvd., Sacramento
916-736-3800
800-509-3663

M = mail order   **O** = for sale on-line   **A** = auctions

**DAVID BERKLEY
FINE WINES &
SPECIALTY FOODS M**
515 Pavilions Ln.,
Sacramento
916-929-4422

**ST. HELENA WINE
MERCHANTS M**
699 St. Helena Hwy.,
St. Helena
707-963-7888
800-729-9463

SAN DIEGO WINE CO.
5282 Eastgate Mall,
San Diego
619-535-1400
888-650-9463
www.sandiegowineco.com

PLUMPJACK WINES
3201 Fillmore St.,
San Francisco
415-346-9870
www.plumpjack.com

THE WINE CLUB
953 Harrison St.,
San Francisco
415-512-9086
800-966-7835

THE WINE HOUSE M
535 Bryant St.,
San Francisco
415-495-8486
www.winehouse-sf.com

THE WINE RACK
6136 Bollinger Rd.,
San Jose; 408-253-3050
e-mail
wineracksj@aol.com

**DRAEGER'S
SUPERMARKET O**
222 E. 4th Ave.
San Mateo
650-685-3700
800-642-9463
www.draegers.com

WINE CASK M, O
813 Anacapa St.,
Santa Barbara
805-966-9463
800-436-9463
www.winecask.com

MISSION WINES O
1114 Mission St.,
South Pasadena
626-403-9463
www.missionwines.com

**PRIMA TRATTORIA &
NEGOZIO DI VINI M, O**
1516 N. Main St.,
Walnut Creek
925-945-1800
800-707-7462
www.primawine.com

coLorado

LIQUOR MART M, O
1750 15th St.,
Boulder
303-449-3374
800-597-4440
www.liquormart.com

**VINTAGE'S WINES
& SPIRITS M**
9 S. Tejon,
Colorado Springs
719-520-5733
e-mail
vintageswine@msn.com

WINES OFF WYNKOOP
1610 16th St., Denver
303-571-1012
e-mail
WOWwines@aol.com

**TONY'S WINES &
SPECIALTY BEERS**
4991 E. Dry Creek Rd.,
Littleton; 303-770-4297

connecticut

**NUTMEG DISCOUNT
LIQUOR**
279 Greenwood Ave.,
Bethel
203-743-4945

LA VINOTHÈQUE
206 Main St.,
Farmington
860-677-9224

**HORSENECK WINE &
LIQUOR**
25 E. Putnam Ave.,
Greenwich
203-869-8944
www.horseneck.com

SPIRITS WINES O
367 Main St
Hartford
860-247-5431

M&R LIQUOR
120 Tolland Turnpike,
Manchester
860-643-9014

deLaware

**THE WINE & SPIRIT
COMPANY OF
GREENVILLE O**
4025 Kennett Pike,
Greenville
302-658-5939
www.greenvillewines.com

**FRANK'S UNION
WINE MART O**
1206 N. Union St.,
Wilmington
302-429-1978
800-283-7265
www.frankswine.com

**KRESTON
LIQUOR MART O**
904 Concord Ave.,
Wilmington
302-652-3792
800-752-8110
www.krestonwine.com

fLorida

THE WINE CLUB M
645 Atlantic Blvd.,
Atlantic Beach
904-246-6450
e-mail markclub@aol.com

VAL'S FINER FOODS
1736 Drew St.,Clearwater
727-446-6926
e-mail redwine9@gte.net

WINE WATCH O
901 Progresso Dr.,
Ft. Lauderdale
954-523-9463
800-329-9463
www.winewatch.com

BROUDY'S
353 Marshlanding Pkwy.,
Jacksonville; 904-273-6119

**RIVERSIDE LIQUORS &
VILLAGE WINE SHOP**
1035 Park St.,
Jacksonville
904-356-4517

**FOREMOST SUNSET
CORNERS**
8701 Sunset Dr., Miami
305-271-8492
e-mail mbwine@aol.com

CROWN WINE &SPIRITS
12555C Biscayne Blvd.,
N. Miami
305-892-9463

ABC FINE WINE & SPIRITS
530 TPC Blvd.,
Ponte Vedra Beach
904-285-5760
800-942-9463
www.abcfinewineandspirits.com

PIC PAC FINE WINES & SPIRITS
6609 Central Ave.,
St. Petersburg
727-347-0743

J.D. FORD, PURVEYOR OF FINE WINE & SPIRITS M, O
1925 S. Osprey Ave.,
Sarasota; 941-362-9463
800-362-9463

BERN'S FINE WINE & SPIRITS M
1002 S. Howard Ave.,
Tampa; 813-250-9463
www.bernssteakhouse.com

VINTAGE WINE CELLARS
3629 Henderson Blvd.,
Tampa; 813-879-2931
e-mail vinwine@gte.net

WINE CLUB
3310 W. Bay to Bay Blvd.,
Tampa; 813-839-5601
e-mail tampawine@aol.com

B-21 FINE WINE & SPIRITS O
43380 U.S. 19 N.,
Tarpon Springs
727-937-5049
888-221-9463
www.B-21.com

Georgia

ANSLEY WINE MERCHANTS
1544 Piedmont Rd.,
Atlanta
404-876-6790

BUCKHEAD FINE WINE
3906 Roswell Rd.,
Atlanta
404-231-8566

PEACHTREE WINE MERCHANTS
3891 Peachtree Rd.,
Atlanta
404-237-7128

TOWER PACKAGE STORE
2161 Piedmont Rd.,
Atlanta; 404-881-0902

TOWER PACKAGE STORE
5877 Buford Hwy.,
Doraville; 770-458-3272

Hawaii

FUJIOKA'S WINE MERCHANT
Market City
Shopping Center
2919 Kapiolani Blvd., #22,
Honolulu; 808-739-9463
www.fujiokawine.com

R. FIELD WINE COMPANY
Foodland Supermarket
1460 S. Beretania St.,
Honolulu; 808-596-9463
800-524-4275
e-mail rfield@aloha.net

VINTAGE WINE CELLAR
1249 Wilder Ave.,
Honolulu; 808-523-9463
e-mail winejk@aol.com

Idaho

THE BOISE CONSUMER CO-OP M
888 W. Fort, Boise
208-342-6652
www.boisecoop.com

Illinois

GOLD STANDARD CHALET M, O
3000 N. Clark St.,
Chicago; 773-935-9400

SAM'S WINES & SPIRITS M, O
1720 N. Marcey St.,
Chicago; 312-664-4394
www.sams-wine.com

MAINSTREET WINES & SPIRITS
5425 S. LaGrange Rd.,
Countryside; 708-354-0355
888-354-0355
www.mainstreetwine.com

KNIGHTSBRIDGE WINE SHOPPE, LTD. M
824 Sunset Ridge Rd.,
Northbrook
847-498-9300

SCHAEFER'S WINES, SPIRITS AND GOURMET FOODS M, O
9965 Gross Point Rd.,
Skokie; 847-673-5711
800-833-9463
www.schaefers.com

CONVITO ITALIANO M
1515 Sheridan Rd.,
Wilmette; 847-251-3654

Indiana

HAMILTON BEVERAGE
2290 E. 116th St., Carmel
317-844-0872

JOHN'S SPIRITS, FINE WINE & DECANTERS
25 N. Pennsylvania,
Indianapolis
317-637-5759

KAHN'S FINE WINES
5369 N. Keystone Ave.,
Indianapolis; 317-251-9463
800-621-8466

Iowa

INGERSOLL WINE & SPIRITS
3500 Ingersoll Ave.,
Des Moines; 515-255-3191

THE WINE EXPERIENCE
7696 Hickman Rd.,
Des Moines; 515-252-8798

J.T.'S FINE WINE & SPIRITS M
5010 E.P. True Pkwy.,
W. Des Moines
515-224-2997

Kansas

JENSEN RETAIL LIQUOR
620 W. 9th St., Lawrence
785-841-2256
e-mail elff@sunflower.com

RIMANN LIQUORS
15117 W. 87th St. Pkwy.,
Lenexa; 913-492-1604
e-mail rimannliquors
@planetkc.com

LUKAS LIQUORS
7541 W. 119th St.,
Overland Park
913-894-1782
800-436-3519
www.lukasliquor.com

M = mail order   **O** = for sale on-line   **A** = auctions

LARRY EVERS WINES & SPIRITS
7728 E. Central Ave., Ste. B
Wichita; 316-685-6868

ROSSITER RETAIL LIQUORS
4808 E. Central Ave.,
Wichita
316-686-6921

kentucky

THE PARTY SOURCE
95 Riviera Dr., Bellevue
606-291-4007

LIQUOR BARN, THE ULTIMATE PARTY SOURCE
3040 Richmond Rd.,
Lexington
606-269-4170

TATES CREEK SPIRIT COMPANY
Tates Creek Center,
Lexington
606-273-4242

LIQUOR OUTLET
1800 S. Hurstbourne
Pkwy., Louisville
502-491-0753

THE PARTY SOURCE
4301 Towne Center Dr.,
Louisville
502-426-4222

Louisiana

BOTTAVINO WORLD WINES
8966 Interline Ave.,
Baton Rouge
225-201-9080

ZEELAND STREET MARKET WINE & DELI
2031 Perkins Rd.,
Baton Rouge
225-387-4546

MARTIN WINE CELLAR
714 Elmeer Ave., Metairie
504-896-7300
800-298-4274
www.martinwine.com

MARTIN WINE CELLAR
3827 Baronne St.,
New Orleans
504-899-7411
800-298-4274
www.martinwine.com

maine

AURORA PROVISIONS
64 Pine St., Portland
207-871-0201
e-mail
auroraprov@aol.com

R.S.V.P. DISCOUNT BEVERAGE & REDEMPTION CENTER
887 Forest Ave.,
Portland; 207-773-8808

maryland

MILLS WINE & SPIRIT MART O
87 Main St., Annapolis
410-263-2888
800-261-9463
www.millswine.com

NORTH CHARLES FINE WINE & SPIRITS
6213-A N. Charles St.,
Baltimore; 410-377-4655
www.northcharles
finewine.com

WELLS DISCOUNT LIQUORS
6310 York Rd.,
Baltimore; 410-435-2700
www.wellswine.com

CALVERT DISCOUNT LIQUOR
10128 York Rd.,
Cockeyville
410-628-2320

STATE LINE LIQUORS, INC.
1610 Elkton Rd., Elkton
410-398-3838
800-446-9463
e-mail
stateline@dpnet.net

JASON'S WINE & SPIRITS
9339 Baltimore Nat. Pike,
Ellicott City; 410-465-2424

BELTWAY FINE WINES
8727 Lochraven Blvd.,
Towson; 410-668-8884

massachusetts

BROOKLINE LIQUOR MART M, O
1354 Commonwealth Ave.,
Allston; 617-734-7700
800-256-9463
www.blmwine.com

BAUER WINE & SPIRITS
330 Newbury St.,
Boston
617-262-0363
www.bauerwines.com

FEDERAL WINE & SPIRITS
29 State St., Boston
617-367-8605
e-mail fedwine@aol.com

MARTIGNETTI'S
1650 Soldiers Field Rd.,
Brighton
617-782-3700
www.martignetti.com

BEST CELLARS
1327 Beacon St., Brookline
617-232-4100
www.bestcellars.net

BUSA WINE & SPIRITS
55 Bedford St.,
Lexington
781-862-1400
e-mail
busabros@juno.com

MARTY'S FINE WINES
675 Washington St.,
Newton; 617-332-1230

TABLE & VINE M, O
122 N. King St.,
Northampton
413-584-7775
800-474-2449
www.tableandvine.com

THE WINE CASK
407 Washington St.,
Somerville; 617-623-8656

michigan

MERCHANT OF VINO
2789 Plymouth Rd.,
Ann Arbor; 734-769-0900

VILLAGE CORNER
601 S. Forest Ave.,
Ann Arbor
734-995-1818
www.villagecorner.com

MERCHANT'S CELLAR COLLECTION M
254 W. Maple St.,
Birmingham
248-433-3000

MERCHANT'S FINE WINE M
22250 Michigan Ave.,
Dearborn; 313-563-8700

ELIE WINE COMPANY
405 S. Main St.,
Royal Oak
248-398-0030
www.eliewine.com

minnesota

**FRANCE 44 WINES &
SPIRITS M, O**
4351 France Ave. S.,
Minneapolis
612-925-3252
800-416-3582
www.france44.com

**HASKELL'S WINE &
SPIRITS M**
81 S. Ninth St.,
Minneapolis
612-333-2434
800-486-2434
www.haskells.com

**HENNEPIN LAKE
LIQUORS**
1200 W. Lake St.,
Minneapolis
612-825-4411

SURDYK'S LIQUOR M
303 E. Hennepin Ave.,
Minneapolis
612-379-3232

**THE CELLARS WINES &
SPIRITS M, O, A**
859 Village Center Dr.,
North Oaks
651-483-1767
888-351-4222
www.thecellars.com

mississippi

**BRIARWOOD MART
LIQUOR & WINE**
4949 Old Canton Rd.,
Jackson
601-956-5108

**WINE & SPIRITS
DISCOUNT CENTER**
1855 Lakeland Dr.,
Ste. A-10, Jackson
601-366-6644
e-mail
wsdc@netdoor.com

**TERRA NOVA WINES &
SPIRITS**
1074 Hwy. 51N,
Madison
601-853-1533

missouri

THE CHEESE PLACE M
7435 Forsyth Blvd.,
Clayton
314-727-8788

**THE WINE
MERCHANT M**
20 S. Hanley St.,
Clayton
314-863-6282
800-770-8466

**BERBIGLIA WINE &
SPIRITS**
1103 E. Bannister Rd.,
Kansas City
816-942-9085
www.berbiglia.com

**GOMER'S MIDTOWN
FINE WINES & SPIRITS**
3838 Broadway,
Kansas City
816-931-4170

MEINER'S SUNFRESH
14 W. 62nd Terr.,
Kansas City
816-523-3700

RED-X FINE WINES
2401 W. Platte Rd.,
Riverside
816-741-2171

**BROWN DERBY
INTERNATIONAL WINE
CENTER M, O**
2023 S. Glenstone Ave.,
Springfield
417-883-4066
www.brownderby.com

montana

THE WINE MERCHANT
2720 2nd Ave. N.,
Billings
406-252-8050
e-mail
vinooryes@aol.com

nebraska

**MEIER'S
CORK 'N BOTTLE**
1244 South St., Lincoln
402-476-1518

N STREET DRIVE-IN
1835 N St., Lincoln
402-477-6077

SPIRIT WORLD
7517 Pacific St., Omaha
402-391-8680

SPIRIT WORLD
11424 Davenport St.,
Omaha; 402-334-7123

THE WINERY M
741 N. 98th St., Omaha
402-391-3535
800-884-9463

nevada

**LEE'S DISCOUNT
LIQUOR**
9110 Las Vegas Blvd. S.,
Las Vegas; 702-269-2400

new
hampshire

THE WINE CELLAR
650 Amherst St.,
Nashua
603-883-4114
members.aol.com/
winecell/winecell.htm

**CERES STREET WINE
MERCHANTS**
65 Ceres St., Portsmouth
603-431-2640
www.cereswine.com

new jersey

BROOKDALE BUY-RITE
1057 Broad St.,
Bloomfield
973-338-7090

**CARLO RUSSO'S WINE
& SPIRIT WORLD O**
102 Linwood Plaza,
Fort Lee; 201-592-1655
800-946-3276
www.wineaccess.com/
wineworld

**SPARROW WINE &
LIQUORS**
126 Washington St.,
Hoboken; 201-659-1500

**CARLO RUSSO'S WINE
& SPIRIT WORLD O**
626 N. Maple Ave.,
Ho-Ho-Kus; 201-444-2033
e-mail
russowine@aol.com
www.wineaccess.com/
wineworld

M = mail order   **O** = for sale on-line   **A** = auctions

273

MOORE BROTHERS WINE COMPANY O
7200 N. Park Dr.,
Pennsauken; 856-317-1177
888-686-6673
www.moorebros.com

THE WINE EMPORIUM
25 Valley St., S. Orange
973-762-9682
e-mail
wine_emporium@att.net

New Mexico

KELLY LIQUORS
2226 A Wyoming Blvd.,
Albuquerque
505-296-7815

KOKOMAN LIQUORS
Hwy. 285, Pojoaque
505-455-2219
e-mail
kokoman@nets.com

KOKOMAN CIRCUS
301 Garfield St., Sante Fe
505-983-7770

New York

SKYVIEW DISCOUNT WINES & LIQUORS
5681 Riverdale Ave.,
Bronx
718-601-8222
www.skyviewkosher.com

MOUNT CARMEL WINES & SPIRITS M
612 E. 187th St., Bronx
718-367-7833

HEIGHTS CHATEAU WINES & SPIRITS
131 Atlantic Ave.,
Brooklyn; 718-330-0963
e-mail
htschateau@aol.com

MICHAEL'S WINES & SPIRITS M
66 Hicks St., Brooklyn
718-875-0590

TOPS WINES & SPIRITS MERCHANTS M
2816 Ave. U., Brooklyn
718-648-7300
e-mail
topswines@aol.com

CRAZY BILLY'S M, O
1887 Deer Park Ave.,
Deer Park; 516-667-8070
www.crazybillys.com

WINE & SPIRIT COMPANY OF FOREST HILLS
108-50 Queens Blvd.,
Forest Hills
718-575-2700

POP'S WINES & SPIRITS M, O
256 Long Beach Rd.,
Island Park; 516-431-0025
www.popswine.com

PREMIER WINES & SPIRITS
3445 Delaware Ave.,
Kenmore
716-873-6688
800-666-6560
www.winedeals.com

YOUNG'S FINE WINES & LIQUORS
505 Plandome Rd.,
Manhasset; 516-627-1234

67 WINE & SPIRITS
179 Columbus Ave.,
New York; 212-724-6767
888-671-6767
www.67wines.com

ACKER MERRALL CONDIT CO. M, A
160 W. 72nd St.,
New York; 212-787-1700
e-mail
ackerbids@aol.com

ASTOR WINES & SPIRITS M
12 Astor Pl., New York
212-674-7500
www.astoruncorked.com

BEST CELLARS M
1291 Lexington Ave.,
New York; 212-426-4200
www.bestcellars.net

CORK & BOTTLE
1158 First Ave.,
New York
212-838-5300

CROSSROADS
55 W. 14th St.,
New York,
212-924-3060

GARNET WINES & LIQUORS M, O
929 Lexington Ave.,
New York
212-772-3211
800-872-8466
www.garnetwine.com

K & D WINES & SPIRITS M, O
1366 Madison Ave.,
New York; 212-289-1818
www.kdwine.com

MORRELL & CO. M, O, A
One Rockefeller Plaza,
New York; 212-688-9370
www.winesbymorrell.com

PARK AVENUE LIQUOR SHOP M, O, A
292 Madison Ave.,
New York; 212-685-2442
www.parkaveliquor.com

SHERRY-LEHMANN M, A
679 Madison Ave.,
New York; 212-838-7500

CENTURY DISCOUNT LIQUOR & WINES M
630 Ridge Road W.,
Rochester; 716-621-4210
800-992-7651

HOUSE OF BACCHUS
1050 E. Ridge Rd.,
Rochester
716-266-6390
e-mail bacchus@eznet.net

ZACHYS WINE & LIQUOR M, A
16 E. Pkwy., Scarsdale
914-723-0241
800-723-0241

POST WINES & SPIRITS
510 Jericho Turnpike,
Syosset; 516-921-1820
800-767-8846

BRIGHTON LIQUOR M
930 Brighton Rd.,
Tonawanda
716-833-2606

THE FRENCH WINE MERCHANT
1504 Old Country Rd.,
Westbury; 516-832-1990
800-946-3496

North Carolina

THE WINE MERCHANT
1256 NW Maynard Rd.,
Cary; 919-469-1330
www.
thewinemerchantinc.com

ARTHUR'S WINE SHOP M, O
4400 Sharon Rd.,
Charlotte; 704-366-8610
e-mail
aurthurswine@msn.com

REID'S M
707 Providence Rd.,
Charlotte; 704-527-2669
800-998-9855
www.reids.com

SOUTHEND BEVERAGE M
1443 South Blvd.,
Charlotte; 704-335-0600

THE WINE VAULT M, O
813 Providence Rd.,
Charlotte; 704-334-9463

CAROLINA WINE COMPANY
6601 Hillsborough St.,
Raleigh; 919-852-0236
888-317-4499
www.carolinawine.com

THE WINE MERCHANT
1214 Ridge Rd., Raleigh
919-828-6929
www.
thewinemerchantinc.com

NORtH Dakota

BERNIE'S WINES & LIQUORS
1557 S. University Dr.,
Fargo; 701-232-3434

HAPPY HARRY'S BOTTLE SHOP M
2051 32nd Ave. S.,
Grand Forks
701-780-0902
www.happy-harrys.com

OHIO

PAPA JOE'S TO GO WINE SHOP
1561 Akron Peninsula Rd.,
Akron; 330-923-7999
www.papajoes.com

WEST POINT MARKET
1711 W. Market St.,
Akron; 330-864-2151
800-838-2156
e-mail gdtaste@west
point-market.com

VILLAGE BOOTLEGGER
8945 Brecksville Rd.,
Brecksville
440-526-5885

CHUCK'S CHEESE AND WINE UNLIMITED
23 Bell St., Chagrin Falls
440-247-7534

THE WINE MERCHANT
3972 Edwards Rd.,
Cincinnati; 513-731-1515

THE ANDERSON GENERAL STORE
7000 Bent Tree Blvd.,
Columbus
614-766-9500

CARNADO WINE & CHEESE M
1735 W. Lane Ave.,
Columbus; 614-486-7474
e-mail
carnwine@aol.com

GENTILE'S, THE WINE SELLERS O
1565 King Ave., Columbus
614-486-3406
www.gentiles.com

GRAPES OF MIRTH
59 W. Spruce St.,
Columbus; 614-221-9463
e-mail
mirthone@aol.com

HILL'S MARKET
7860 Olentangy River Rd.,
Columbus; 614-846-3220

SPAGIO CELLARS
1291 Grandview Ave.,
Columbus; 614-486-1114

DOROTHY LANE MARKET O
6177 Far Hills Ave.,
Dayton
937-434-1294
www.dorothylane.com

JUNGLE JIM'S INTERNATIONAL MARKET
5440 Dixie Hwy.,
Fairfield
513-829-1919
www.junglejims.com

REGENCY WINE STORE
117 Merz Blvd., Ste. 112
Fairlawn; 330-836-3447

MAUMEE WINES
2556 Parkway Plaza,
Maumee
419-893-2525

WESTERN RESERVE WINES M
34101 Chagrin Blvd.,
Moreland Hills
216-831-2116
e-mail wrwines@aol.com

PAT O'BRIEN'S FINE WINES-GOURMET FOODS M
30800 Pinetree Rd.,
Pepper Pike
216-831-8680

HINMAN'S
19300 Detroit Rd.,
Rocky River
440-333-0202

okLaHoma

EDMOND WINE SHOP
1532 South Blvd.,
Edmond
405-341-9122
e-mail
thewineshop@msn.com

BEAU'S WINE BIN & SPIRIT SHOPPE
2810 W. Country Club Dr.,
Oklahoma City
405-842-8866

PARKHILL'S LIQUORS & WINE
5111 S. Lewis Ave., Tulsa
918-742-4187

RANCH ACRES WINE AND SPIRITS
3324-A E. 31st St.,
Tulsa; 918-747-1171

THE WINE RACK
6953 S. Lewis
Lewis Crossing Center,
Tulsa
918-492-1220

OReGON

GREAT WINE BUYS M
1515 NE Broadway,
Portland
503-287-2897
888-717-9786
www.teleport.com/
~winebuys

M = mail order   **O** = for sale on-line   **A** = auctions

LINER & ELSEN WINE MERCHANTS M
202 NW 21st Ave.,
Portland; 503-241-9463
800-903-9463

MT. TABOR FINE WINES M
4316 SE Hawthorne Blvd.,
Portland; 503-235-4444
e-mail
mttabor1@aol.com

PORTLAND WINE MERCHANTS M
1430 SE 35th St.,
Portland
503-234-4399
888-520-8466
www.teleport.com/~drvino

pennsylvania

LIBERTY BELL WINES & SPIRITS SHOPPE
401 Franklin Mills Circle,
Philadelphia
215-281-2080

rhode island

GASBARRO'S
361 Atwells Ave.,
Providence; 401-421-4170

TOWN WINE & SPIRITS
179 Newport Ave.,
Rumford; 401-434-4563

south carolina

HARRIS TEETER GROCERY STORE,
290 East Bay St.,
Charleston; 843-722-6821

THE WINE SHOP
3 Lockwood Dr.,
Charleston
843-577-3881
e-mail
debbiewine@awod.com

FRUGAL MACDOOGAL'S
3630 Festival Dr.,
Fort Mill; 803-548-6634

south dakota

REGAL LIQUORS
2022 S. Minnesota Ave.,
Sioux Falls; 605-335-3918

tennessee

ARTHUR'S WINE & LIQUOR
964 June Rd., Memphis
901-767-9463

BUSTER'S LIQUORS & WINES
191 S. Highland St.,
Memphis
901-458-0929
www.bustersliquors.com

FRUGAL MACDOOGAL'S
701 Division St., Nashville
615-242-3863
e-mail
frugalmact@aol.com

NASHVILLE WINE & SPIRITS
4556 Harding Rd.,
Nashville; 615-292-2676

WEST END DISCOUNT LIQUORS & WINES
2818 West End Ave.,
Nashville; 615-320-1446

texas

THE AUSTIN WINE MERCHANT
512 W. 6th St., Austin
512-499-0522
e-mail bonvin@ibm.net

THE CELLAR M
3520 Bee Caves Rd., Austin
512-328-6464
www.citysearch.com/aus/thecellar

GRAPE VINE MARKET
7938 Great Northern Blvd., Austin
512-323-5900
www.grapevinemarket.com

TWIN LIQUORS
5408 Balcones Dr., Austin
512-323-2775

LA CAVE WAREHOUSE M
1931 Market Center Blvd.,
Ste. 129, Dallas
214-747-WINE
www.lacavewarehouse.com

MARTY'S FOOD & WINE M
3316 Oak Lawn Ave., Dallas
214-526-7796
800-627-8971
www.martysdfw.com

POGO'S BEVERAGES
5360 W. Lovers Ln.,
Ste. 200, Dallas
214-350-8989

RED COLEMAN'S #14
7560 Greenville Ave.,
Dallas
214-363-0201
www.redcoleman.com

SIGEL'S BEVERAGES, L.P.
2960 Anode Ln., Dallas
214-350-1271
www.sigels.com

BOURJALAIS BEVERAGE EMPORIUM
2720 N. Mesa St.,
El Paso
915-542-2658/533-2381
e-mail
bourjalais@aol.com

LOMART FINE FOOD & WINE
6600 N. Mesa, El Paso
915-584-3731

MAJESTIC LIQUOR
1111 Jacksboro Hwy.,
Ft. Worth; 817-335-5252

LUKAS LIQUORS SUPERSTORE M, O
11621 Katy Freeway,
Houston; 281-531-7727
888-545-7727

RICHARD'S LIQUORS & FINE WINES
5630 Richmond Ave.,
Houston
713-783-3344

SPEC'S LIQUOR STORES WAREHOUSE
2410 Smith St.,
Houston
713-526-8787
888-526-8787
www.specsonline.com

WINES OF AMERICA M, O
2055 Westheimer, Ste. 155
Houston
713-524-3397
www.houstonwines.com

JOE SAGLIMBENI FINE WINES
638 W. Rhapsody, Ste. 1,
San Antonio
210-349-5149
www.jsfinewine.com

**SEAZAR'S
FINE WINES & SPIRITS**
6422 N. New Braunfels,
San Antonio
210-822-6094

utah

**STATE LIQUOR STORE
#34**
1901 Sidewinder Dr.,
Park City
435-649-7254

**UTAH STATE
WINE STORE**
255 S. 300 E.,
Salt Lake City
801-533-6444

vermont

**THE CHEESE OUTLET
FRESH MARKET**
400 Pine St.,
Burlington
802-863-3968
800-447-1205
www.cheeseoutlet.com

virginia

ARROWINE M
4508 Lee Hwy.,
Arlington
703-525-0990
www.arrowine.com

TOTAL BEVERAGE
13055 C. Lee Jackson Hwy,.
Chantilly
703-817-1177

TASTINGS M
502 E. Market St.,
Charlottesville
804-293-3663
e-mail
tastings@earthlink.net

WEST SIDE WINE SHOP
4702 Hampton Blvd.,
Norfolk
757-440-7600

CORKS & KEGS
7110 A Patterson Ave.,
Richmond
804-288-0816

TASTE UNLIMITED
638 Hilltop West
Shopping Center,
Virginia Beach
757-425-1858

washington

**DELAURENTI
SPECIALTY FOOD
MARKETS**
1435 First Ave.,
Seattle
206-622-0141

LARRY'S MARKETS
10008 Aurora Ave. N.,
Seattle
206-527-5333

**MCCARTHY &
SCHIERING WINE
MERCHANTS O**
6500 Ravenna Ave. NE,
Seattle
206-524-9500
www.mccarthy
andschiering.com

**PIKE & WESTERN WINE
SHOP M**
1934 Pike Place, Seattle
206-441-1307
www.
pikeandwestern.com

washington, d.c.

ACE BEVERAGE M
3301 New Mexico Ave. NW
202-966-4444

BELL WINE SHOP M
1821 M St. NW
202-223-4727

CALVERT WOODLEY M
4339 Connecticut Ave. NW
202-966-4400
www.calvertwoodley.com

**MACARTHUR
LIQUORS M**
4877 MacArthur Blvd. NW
202-338-1433
www.bassins.com

**MORRIS MILLER
LIQUORS M**
7804 Alaska Ave. NW
202-723-5000

**SCHNEIDER'S OF
CAPITAL HILL**
300 Masachusetts Ave. NE
202-543-9300
800-377-1461
www.cellar.com

**WIDE WORLD OF
WINES M**
2201 Wisconsin Ave. NW
202-333-7500
e-mail estaren@aol.com

west virginia

**THE WINE SHOP AT
CAPITOL MARKET**
800 Smith St.,
Charleston
304-343-9463

WISCONSIN

OTTO'S WINE CASK
4600 W. Brown Deer Rd.,
Brown Deer
414-354-5831

**STEVE'S LIQUOR &
MORE M,O**
8302 Mineral Point Rd.,
Madison
608-833-5995
www.stevesliquor.com

GRAPES & GRAIN
11301 N. Port
Washington Rd.,
Mequon
414-240-0206

**HEIDEN'S WINE &
SPIRITS M**
8510 W. Lisbon Ave.,
Milwaukee
414-462-0440

DISCOUNT LIQUOR INC.
919 N. Barstow St.,
Waukesha
414-547-7525

wyoming

**TOWN & COUNTRY
SUPERMARKET
LIQUORS**
614 S. Greeley Hwy.,
Cheyenne
307-634-3474

M = mail order   **O** = for sale on-line   **A** = auctions

best stores for books on wine

A good source for wine books is hard to find. Each of these stores has a significant selection. Of the 530 Barnes & Nobles in the U.S., the 64 here have the best stocks of books on wine.

california

COOK'S LIBRARY M
8373 W. 3rd St.,
Los Angeles; 323-655-3141

THE GREYSTONE CAMPUS STORE AND MARKETPLACE
2555 Main St., St. Helena
707-967-2309

THE BOOKSMITH M, O
1644 Haight St.,
San Francisco
415-863-8688
800-493-7323
www.booksmith.com

A CLEAN WELL-LIGHTED PLACE FOR BOOKS M, O
601 Van Ness Ave.,
San Francisco
415-441-6670
www.bookstore.com

GREEN APPLE BOOKS M, O, S
506 Clement St.,
San Francisco
415-387-2272
www.greenapplebooks.com

STACEY'S BOOKSTORE M
581 Market St.,
San Francisco
415-421-4687
800-926-6511
www.staceys.com

TREEHORN BOOKS S
625 4th St., Santa Rosa
707-525-1782

PLAZA BOOKS M
40 W. Spain St., Sonoma
707-996-8474
888-309-7051

READERS' BOOKS
127 E. Napa St., Sonoma
707-939-1779

SONOMA BOOKENDS
201 W. Napa St., #15,
Sonoma; 707-938-5926

new york

THE CRAIG CLAIBORNE BOOKSTORE M
433 Albany Post Rd.,
Hyde Park; 914-452-7648
800-677-6266

KITCHEN ARTS & LETTERS M, S
1435 Lexington Ave.,
New York; 212-876-5550

pennsylvania

PRESQUE ISLE WINE CELLARS M
9440 W. Main Rd.,
North East; 814-725-1314
800-488-7492
www.piwine.com

vermont

SMALL BOOKS M, S
207 N. Branch, Bennington
802-442-2778

NORTHSHIRE BOOKSTORE M
4869 Main St.,
Manchester Center
800-722-1807

BARNES & NOBLE STORES

arizona
10500 N. 90th St.,
Scottsdale
602-391-0048

california
4735 Commons Way,
Calabasas; 818-222-0542

552 Contra Costa Blvd.,
Pleasant Hill
925-609-7060

2550 Taylor St.,
San Francisco
415-292-6762

3600 Stevens Creek Blvd.,
San Jose; 408-984-3495

700 4th St., Santa Rosa
707-576-7494

4950 Pacific Ave.,
Stockton; 209-472-1885

1149 S. Main St.,
Walnut Creek
925-947-0373

colorado
2915 Pearl St., Boulder
303-442-1665

9370 Sheridan Blvd.,
Westminster
303-426-7733

connecticut
360 Connecticut Ave.,
Norwalk; 203-866-2213

1076 Post Rd. E., Westport
203-221-7955

delaware
4801 Concord Pike,
Wilmington
302-478-9677

CATALOGS
THE WINE AND FOOD LIBRARY S
1207 W. Madison, Ann Arbor MI, 734-663-4894
KELLGREN'S WINE BOOK CATALOG O
P.O. Box 616, Croton-on-Hudson, NY
914-271-5121; 800-274-4816
www.wine-lovers-page.com/kellgren

fLORIDA

18711 NE Biscayne Blvd.,
Aventura; 305-935-9770

23654 US 19 N.,
Clearwater; 727-669-1688

5377 Tamiami Trail N.,
Naples; 941-598-5200

GEORGIA

2952 Cobb Pkwy., Atlanta
770-953-0966

2900 Peachtree Rd. NE,
Atlanta; 404-261-7747

ILLINOIS

1441 W. Webster Ave.,
Chicago; 773-871-3610

1701 Sherman Ave.,
Evanston; 847-328-0883

590 E. Golf Rd.,
Schaumburg; 847-310-0450

INDIANA

4601 Grape Rd.,
Mishawaka; 219-277-9482

Louisiana

3721 Veterans
Memorial Blvd., Metairie
504-455-4929

maryLand

601 E. Pratt St., Baltimore
410-385-1709

4801 Bethesda Ave.,
Bethesda; 301-986-1761

massachusetts

98 Middlesex Turnpike,
Burlington; 781-273-3871

michigan

3245 Washtenaw Ave.,
Ann Arbor; 734-677-6475

6575 Telegraph Rd.,
Bloomfield Hills
248-540-4209

2800 S. Rochester Rd.,
Rochester Hills
248-853-9855

minnesota

118 E. Broadway,
Bloomington
612-854-1455

3225 W. 69th St., Edina
612-920-0633

801 Nicollet Mall,
Minneapolis; 612-371-4443

15 First St. SW,
Chateau Theatre,
Rochester; 507-288-3848

missouri

420 W. 47th St.
Kansas City; 816-753-1313

new Hampshire

235 Daniel Webster Hwy.,
Nashua; 603-888-0533

new jersey

765 Rt. 17 S., Paramus
201-445-4589

3535 US Rt. 1 S.,
Princeton
609-897-9250

240 Rt. 22 W., Springfield
973-376-8544

1156 Rt. 46 W.,
West Paterson
973-812-0180

new york

1542 Northern Blvd.,
Manhasset; 516-365-6723

600 5th Ave., New York
212-765-0590

33 E. 17th St., New York
212-253-0810

160 E. 54th St., New York
212-750-8033

240 E. 86th St., New York
212-794-1962

1972 Broadway, New York
212-595-6859

495 South Rd.,
Poughkeepsie
914-485-2224

3349 Monroe Ave.,
Rochester; 716-586-6020

NORth caroLina

1925 Hampton Inn Ct.,
Winston-Salem
336-774-0800

OHIO

7800 Montgomery Rd.,
Cincinnati; 513-794-9440

pennsyLvania

150 W. Swedesford Rd.,
Devon; 610-695-6600

1805 Walnut St.,
Philadelphia
215-665-0716

RHODE ISLAND

1441 Bald Hill Rd.,
Warwick; 401-828-7900

south caroLina

3400 Forest Dr.,
Columbia; 803-787-5600

texas

10000 Research Blvd.,
Austin; 512-418-8985

7700 W. Northwest Hwy.,
Dallas; 214-739-1124

2922 S. Shepherd,
Houston; 713-529-2345

1029 W. Bay Area Blvd.,
Webster; 281-554-8224

vermont

102 Dorset St.,
South Burlington
802-864-8001

VIRGINIA

1035 Emmet St.,
Charlottesville
804-984-0461

1851 Fountain Dr., Reston
703-437-9490

washington

600 Pine St., Seattle
206-264-0156

2700 NE University
Village, Seattle
206-517-4107

washington,D.C.

3040 M St. NW
202-965-9880

WISCONSIN

7433 Mineral Point Rd.,
Madison; 608-827-0809

M = mail order   **O** = on-line sales   **S** = secondhand books

279

50 Hottest Wine Web Sites

Whether you want to learn about wine, shop for wine, talk about wine, or search for wine, the Web is a great place to start. Don't forget to add www. before each address.

News and Reviews

grapevineweekly.com
Dynamic on-line magazine gives the latest wine news.

wine-lovers-page.com
Wine lovers of the world unite! Read reviews and share views.

wineonthe web.com
Multimedia, talking site packed with information.

wineratings.com
Searchable database of wine reviews.

wine-school.com
Electronic courses on tasting, serving, cellaring.

winetoday.com
Wine news from *The New York Times*.

Lots of Links

4wine.com
Points you to general info on the world's wines.

drinkwine.com
Wine and winery information direct from top winemakers.

hotwine.com
Hip layout links you to wine producers, peddlers—and poets.

winecellar.com
Links to sites dealing with buying and storing wine.

vine2wine.com
Constantly updated guide to over 2,000 wine sites.

wine.com
Links to wine merchants, auctions, products galore.

wines.com
Features for wine lovers; resources for wine pros.

Buy On-Line

avalonwine.com
Wines from the Pacific Northwest.

auctionvine.com
Bid on fine and rare wines on-line; a practice auction gets you ready.

evineyard.com
Vast selection with a tell-me-more option for every wine.

finestwine.com
Purveyors of fine, rare, and impossibly expensive wines.

tinamou.com
The place for dessert wines and Port.

virtualvineyard.com
Buy wine, food, or gifts—or e-mail your questions to the Cork Dork.

winex.com
A user-friendly catalog of wine and spirits.

wineplace.com
Everything you need to make your own wine.

winebid.com
Fine wines and spirits on the block, with an on-line library of past auction results.

World Wine Regions

bordeaux.com
Whimsically designed primer to Bordeaux wines.

germanwines.de
The official site of the German Wine Institute.

ivp.pt
Learn about Portugal's most famous wine from the Port Wine Institute.

liwines.com
Official Web site of the Long Island Wine Council.

napawine.com
A network of Napa winery sites.

madeirawine.com
Madeira—her story, her wines.

nywine.com
Uncork New York with the New York Wine & Grape Foundation.

nzwine.com
A virtual tour of New Zealand's wines.

terroir.com
The wines of France, from making to partaking.

washingtonwine.org
Monthly updates on Washington State wines.

wine.it
Discover wine culture and lifestyle the Italian way.

wines-france.com
Clever, funny, and unpretentious.

winetitles.com.au
A comprehensive guide to Aussie wines.

WINES FROM UNEXPECTED PLACES

hr/wine
Welcome to the wines of Croatia.

indagegroup.com/index.htm
Somewhat surreal site promoting India's wines.

WINE CLUBS

ambrosiawine.com
Six wine clubs for various tastes and budgets.

connseries.com
Connoisseur's Series delivers hard-to-find, ultrapremium wines.

secretcellars.com
Monthly deliveries from California's small wineries.

twgga.com
The Texas Wine and Grape Growers Association.

vivanewmexico.com/wines.html
Visit the oldest wine-growing region in the U.S.

SPECIAL INTEREST

kov.org
Amiably goofy official site for the Brotherhood of the Knights of the Vine.

smartwine.com
Market news for the wine investor.

winebrats.org
Irreverent site aimed at wine lovers in their 20s and 30s.

wine.gurus.com
Official site of the Society of Wine Educators.

wineinfonet.com
Lists sites of wine associations across the country.

wineinstitute.org
California wineries band together to influence public policy.

BYTES OF THE BUBBLY

champagnes.com
Straightforward introduction to the what, where, and how of Champagne.

4champagne.com
A bevy of links to Champagne-related sights.

CONTACT US! Send your comments and personal ratings of the wines in this guide and of your other favorite wines to:

www.foodandwine.com

And join FOOD & WINE Magazine on-line year-round for even more wine information, tips, and surveys.

most exciting wine tours

Bike through Napa, cruise down the Rhine in Germany or the Rhône in France, take a turn-of-the-century train through California's wine country or a 1955 limo through Australia's. If you've a love of travel to go along with your love of wine, here's the spot to start looking for tours that let you learn about wine right where it's made.

WORLDWIDE

AVALON WINE TOURS
P.O. Box 3004,
Newport Beach,
CA 92659
949-673-7376
www.
avalon-tours.com

BUTTERFIELD & ROBINSON
70 Bond St.,
Toronto, Ontario
M5B 1X3
Canada
416-864-1354
800-678-1147
www.butterfield.com

MJK TOURS
133 S.W. 2nd. Ave.,
Suite 220,
Portland, OR 97204
503-224-8001
800-659-9723
e-mail
Travel@MJKTours.com

VBT BICYCLING VACATIONS
P.O. Box 711,
Bristol, VT 05443
802-453-4811
800-245-3868
www.vbt.com

X.O. TRAVEL CONSULTANTS, LTD.
38 W. 32nd St.,
Suite 1009,
New York, NY 10001
212-947-5530
800-262-9682
e-mail xotravel@
compuserve.com

FRANCE

FRANCE IN YOUR GLASS
814-35th Ave.,
Seattle, WA 98122
800-578-0903
www.inyourglass.com

FUGUES EN FRANCE
11 Square Jean Cocteau
F-91250 St-Germain-
Les-Corbeil
France
011-33-1-60-75-88-33
www.
wineonline.co.uk

GASCONY TOURS
5 Ledgewood Way, #6,
Peabody, MA 01960
508-535-5738
800-852-2625
e-mail juliahoyt@aol.com

THE SAVOUR OF FRANCE
244 Madison Ave.,
Suite 715,
New York, NY 10016
800-827-4635
www.
savourfrance.com

ITALY

AMELIA TOURS
28 E. Old Country Rd.,
Hicksville, NY 11801
516-433-0696
800-742-4591
e-mail
ameliatours@att.net

BELLAVISTA TOURS
7 Marshall St.,
Boston, MA 02108
617-723-0802

COLLETTE TOURS
162 Middle St.,
Pawtucket, RI 02860
800-248-8991
www.collettetours.com

DONNA FRANCA TOURS
470 Commonwealth Ave.,
Boston, MA 02215
617-375-9400
800-225-6290
e-mail
dtours2156@aol.com

THE PARKER COMPANY
152 Lynn Way,
Lynn, MA 01902
800-280-2811
www.
theparkercompany.com

SPAIN & PORTUGAL

ALTA TOURS
870 Market St.,
Suite 784,
San Francisco, CA 94102
415-777-1307
800-338-4191
www.altatours.com

FREEGATE TOURISM, INC.
585 Stewart Ave.,
Suite 310,
Garden City, NY 11530
888-373-3428
www.
freegatetours.com

SARANJAN TOURS
12865 NE 85th St., #102,
Kirkland, WA 98033
425-869-8636
800-858-9594
www.saranjan.com

germany & austria

ELEGANT CRUISES & TOURS, INC.
24 Vanderventer Ave.,
Port Washington,
NY 11050
800-683-6767
e-mail
elegantcruises@att.net

GERMAN WINE ACADEMY
P.O. Box 1660
D-55006 Mainz
Germany
011-49-61-31-28-29-0
fax
011-49-61-31-28-29-50

HERZERL TOURS
127 W. 26th St.,
New York, NY 10001
212-366-4245
800-684-8488
www.herzerltours.com

KD RIVER CRUISES OF EUROPE
2500 Westchester Ave.,
Suite 113,
Purchase, NY 10577
914-696-3600
800-346-6525
www.rivercuises.com

RIVERS OF EUROPE
11802 Washington Blvd.,
#121,
Los Angeles, CA 90066
310-397-3899
800-999-0226

UNIONTOURS
245 Fifth Ave., Suite 1101,
New York, NY 10016
212-683-9500
e-mail travel@union tours.com

california

NAPA VALLEY WINE TRAIN
1275 McKinstry St.,
Napa, CA 94559
800-427-4124
e-mail
reservations@wine train.com

WINE DESTINATIONS
895 Jackson St.,
Suite 330,
Napa, CA 94559
707-224-8500
800-630-9463
www. winedestinations.com

south africa

AFRICAN MARIMBA
4000 Yonge St.,
Unit #516,
Toronto, Ontario
M4N 2N9 Canada
416-487-4117

CLASSIC ENCOUNTERS
50 E. 42nd St., Suite 2500,
New York, NY 10017
212-972-0031
e-mail
gowildsa@aol.com

australia & new zealand

ABSOLUTE AUSTRALIA
180 Varick St.,
New York, NY 10014
212-627-8258
888-285-6094
www. absoluteaustralia.com

THE BEST OF NEW ZEALAND
2817 Wilshire Blvd.,
Santa Monica, CA 90403
310-988-5880
800-528-6129
email info@bestofnz.net

NEWMANS SOUTH PACIFIC VACATIONS
6033 W. Century Blvd.,
Suite 1270,
Los Angeles, CA 90045
310-348-8282
800-421-3326
www.newmans.com

WINE TOURS AUSTRALIA
P.O. Box 7443,
St Kilda Rd.,
Melbourne, Victoria
Australia 3004
011-61-0-500-899-877
fax
011-61-0-500-899-878
www.wine-tours.com.au

terms used in this guide

ACID   A basic component of all grapes and wines. The main wine acids are the sharp malic acid, found in unripe fruit, and the softer tartaric, which is unique to grapes. Acid gives wine its liveliness, making it refreshing, and contributes to its longevity.

AFTERTASTE   See finish.

ANAEROBIC FERMENTATION   Fermentation that takes place without air. Cut off from oxygen, grape cells begin to digest their own stored carbohydrates in order to generate energy, creating alcohol and carbon dioxide as by-products. See also carbonic maceration.

AROMA   Term used for the fragrance of a young wine.

ASTRINGENT   The mouth-puckering effect caused by a combination of high acidity and high tannin.

BALANCE   A happy interplay among acidity, tannin, alcohol, residual sugar, and the flavors of a wine. If one characteristic, or more, dominates, the wine is said to be unbalanced.

BARREL   An oval-shaped wooden vessel used for fermentation, maturation, and storage of wine. It can hold anywhere from 50 liters to 600 liters or more. Barrels allow oxygen to slowly penetrate into the wine, making it more mellow and harmonious. New barrels impart flavors as well.

BARRIQUE   A traditional Bordeaux barrel holding 225 liters or 300 bottles of wine. The phrase small oak barrels usually refers to ones of this size.

BIG   Describes a full-bodied wine high in alcohol.

BLOCKBUSTER   A wine that gives the impression of tremendous weight and power, usually due to high tannin and alcohol content and concentrated flavors.

BODEGA   Spanish term for winery.

BODY   The weight or thickness of a wine from light to full. Think of skim milk as light bodied, whole milk as medium, and heavy cream as full-bodied.

BOTRYTIS CINEREA   Scientific name for a fungus that attacks grapes in warm, humid conditions, causing shriveling. When it enhances the wine made from the grapes, it is noble rot. When unwanted, it is simple gray rot.

BOUQUET   The complex aromas of a mature wine. Not used for young wines.

CARBONIC MACERATION   A specialized form of anaerobic fermentation employing carbon dioxide to blanket whole grapes. The resulting wines are mellow, fruity, and low in tannin. Commonly used in Beaujolais.

CASK   A wooden vessel of any size, generally barrel shaped.

CLONE   Vines that have been propagated asexually from a single parent. Clones are propagated from parents selected for particular qualities desired by the grower or winemaker.

COMMUNE   Synonym for village.

CONCENTRATION   Intensity of flavor, partially a result of the actual amount of solid flavoring matter in the wine.

COOPERATIVE   An organization in which a single winery facility buys grapes from its member farmers and then vinifies and bottles the resulting wines under its own name. The members share in the profits. Co-ops set standards of quality, some exceptionally high.

CROSSING   A grape variety produced by the sexual mating of two vinifera vines.

CRU   (1) Literally, growth. (2) A vineyard site recognized under the Appellation d'Origine Contrôlée system of France, as in Premier Cru and Grand Cru. (3) Ranking of the châteaux of the Haut-Médoc according to the classification of 1855, in descending order from Premier Cru to Cinquieme Cru (first to fifth). (4) Also in common usage to mean any single-vineyard site, even those outside France.

CUVÉE   A particular bottling or lot of wine, usually a blend.

DRY   Describes the absence of sugar. Not to be confused with the absence of fruit flavor. Fruity wines can be, and usually are, dry.

EARTHY   Having a taste of the soil in which the grapes were grown. Often a positive term; sometimes negative if the flavors are overwhelming or rough.

ELEGANT   Delicate and subtle, with a good balance of the various characteristics of the wine—flavor, acidity, sweetness, tannin, and alcohol. An elegant wine is the opposite of a blockbuster.

EXTRACT   The solid minerals and trace elements that create flavor and palate impact along with the water, alcohol, acid, and sugar. High extract buffers acidity and is a sign of good quality in wine.

FERMENTATION   The conversion of sugar into alcohol by the action of yeasts.

FINISH   The flavors that remain in the mouth after swallowing a wine. A good indicator of quality. The longer the finish lasts, the better the wine.

FLOR   The yeast that forms on the surface of Fino and Manzanilla Sherries (see page 234) while they're in the barrel. Flor produces acetaldehyde, digests glycerine and volatile acidity, and protects against oxidation, giving Finos and Manzanillas their distinctive personalities.

FOCUSED   Description of a wine with crystal-clear flavors.

GARIGUE   Used to describe the aromas of wild herbs and baked earth that pervade the air in the countryside of southern France, particularly Provence.

HECTARE   A measure of land area equaling 10,000 square meters or approximately 2.47 acres.

HECTOLITER   A measure of liquid capacity equivalent to 100 liters or about 26.42 gallons.

HYBRID   A grape variety produced by the sexual mating of a vinifera with a nonvinifera vine.

JAMMY   A cooked or preserved-fruit scent or flavor in a wine; reminiscent of jam.

LATE-RIPENING GRAPE   A grape variety that ripens later in the season than most. Late-ripening grapes have more exposure than early-ripening varieties to often deleterious autumn weather conditions.

LEES   The solid residue of dead yeasts and grape pulp, seeds, and skins left after fermentation. White wines may be left on the lees to develop nutty, toasty flavors. Lees protect against oxidation, keeping both whites and reds fresh during the period before bottling.

MACERATION   Keeping the skins of red grapes in contact with the must or wine. In general, the longer the maceration time, the more tannin, color, and flavor are extracted and go into the finished wine.

MALOLACTIC FERMENTATION   The conversion of harsh malic acid into milder lactic acid by the action of malolactic bacteria. Usually takes place naturally immediately following the fermentation into alcohol. Malolactic fermentation mellows the wine and sometimes contributes buttery flavors. It can be encouraged or blocked depending upon the style of wine desired by the winemaker.

MOUSSE   The French term for fizziness in sparkling wines. Finer bubbles are more desirable and indicative of a high quality wine.

NÉGOCIANT   Strictly speaking, merchants who purchase lots of finished, but unbottled, wines from growers too small to commercialize their own wines or simply uninterested in doing so. They blend and bottle the wines under their own names. In practice, many *négociants* purchase grapes, must (juice), or wines in various states of maturity and vinify or finish the wines themselves. Some *négociants* even own land and grow some of their own grapes.

NEW WORLD (1) Winemaking countries outside Europe. (2) A winemaking philosophy relying on technology to produce bold-flavored, fruit-driven wines.

NOSE The aroma or bouquet of a wine.

OAK The wood most commonly used for barrels and vats because of its tight grain, which allows slow, controlled penetration of oxygen. Oxygen mellows the rough, new wine before bottling. New-oak barrels impart tannin and flavors, especially of vanilla, spice, toast, smoke, and coffee; whereas old oak is like a used teabag—without much effect on taste or tannin content. The percentage of new oak is determined by the number of barrels of wine in the final blend that have been aged in new barrels versus previously used barrels. New oak is very much in fashion today.

OLD WORLD (1) European winemaking countries. (2) A style that is subtle and complex, characteristic of many fine European wines.

OXIDATION Occurs when oxygen combines with must (juice) or wine. Properly controlled, it is essential in the making of many styles of wine, smoothing and mellowing them.

POWERFUL High in tannin, acid, alcohol, and/or extract. A wine that makes a forceful impression.

RESIDUAL SUGAR Sugar from the grapes still in the wine after fermentation. The fermentation may stop naturally or be intentionally halted by the winemaker to produce a wine with some sweetness. Even dry wines contain some residual sugar.

ROASTED A cooked character of the fruit flavors sometimes imparted by grapes grown in very hot climates.

RUSTIC A bit rough and lacking in sophistication. Can be an appealing quality, but sometimes applied pejoratively.

SHARP Unpleasantly bitter or tart. Wines excessively high in acidity.

SPRITZ A slight bubbliness or fizziness due to dissolved carbon dioxide.

STAINLESS STEEL Material used for temperature-controlled fermentation tanks because of its heat-conducting abilities. Also produces refreshing, fruity wines by preventing interaction with oxygen, which can lead to oxidation.

STEELY A slightly metallic flavor, typical in some wines, such as Puligny-Montrachet.

SUR LIE The technique of leaving a wine in contact with its fermentation lees for a period of time before bottling, as in the case of Muscadet.

SWEET Having significant residual sugar. Not to be confused with fruity. Fruity wines may be completely dry.

TANNIN   An essential component of red wine that, even when not excessive, makes the mouth feel dry and puckery. It's derived from grape skins and is also found in tea. Tannin acts as a preservative, allowing a wine to age.

TEXTURE   The way a wine feels in the mouth.

TRADITIONAL METHOD   The time-honored method of sparkling-wine production: The wine undergoes its secondary fermentation in the same bottle in which it is ultimately sold. As of 1994, replaced the term *méthode champenoise* for all sparkling wines produced in the European Union, except those from Champagne.

VATTING TIME   Total length of time a red wine stays in contact with its skins. Can include prefermention soaking, fermentation, and postfermentation maceration.

VIGNERON   French term for winemaker.

VINIFERA   Or more accurately *Vitis vinifera*. The large family of vines of which all wine-grape vines are members.

VINIFICATION   Winemaking.

VITICULTURE   Grape growing.

WEINGUT   German word for winery.

YEAST   One of many organisms responsible for the production of alcohol through the process of fermentation. The main wine yeast is *Saccharomyces cerevisiae*.

YIELD   The quantity of wine produced from a fixed amount of land, usually expressed in Europe as hectoliters per hectare, and in the New World as tons per acre. Normal yields for quality wines range from 40 to 80 hectoliters per hectare or 3 to 6 tons per acre. In theory, the lower the yield, the better the wine.

ZONE   A defined area, be it a whole region or smaller, such as a village or a specific vineyard. The grapes and wine must be produced within the area to use its name on the label.